D0989480

Praise for *Autism in Heels*

"I am blown away. Never has a book on autism captured the female perspective with so much accuracy, grit, and flair. The perspective of the girl who models herself after typical girls but never quite fits in, and feels fraudulent, is a common but never before clearly articulated phenomenon for women with autism. Jennifer's stories will resonate with women on the spectrum and women everywhere trying to find their identities and find their way navigating their life journeys. I literally could not put this book down and would recommend it to all women, those on and off the spectrum, and the men who want to better understand them.

—Wendy Ross, MD, CNN Hero, Autism Society of America Person of the Year, founder of Autism Inclusion Resources

"Witty, frank, and full of insight, Jennifer O'Toole's *Autism in Heels* is a major addition to a growing body of literature on the distinctive experience of women on the autism spectrum, long overlooked by researchers and clinicians. After helping to pioneer the genre with her groundbreaking *Sisterhood of the Spectrum*, O'Toole takes us deep into her often harrowing process of becoming self-aware in a world built for nonautistics, guiding us through her search for meaning and identity in a voice that is disarmingly candid, appealingly warm, and often hilariously funny. O'Toole is a natural storyteller. *Autism in Heels* is a great book."

—Steve Silberman, author of *NeuroTribes: The Legacy of Autism and the Future of Neurodiversity*, winner of the Samuel Johnson Prize for Nonfiction

"I have always considered Jennifer an Aspie mentor in terms of her insights and wisdom on life as experienced by a woman who has autism. She is a natural talent who, in *Autism in Heels*, has indeed written a love letter to all women. Her memoir will change our perception of autism and how those with autism will perceive themselves."

—Tony Attwood, PhD, bestselling author, international speaker

"Funny, moving, compelling, deep . . . *Autism in Heels* is an absolute must-read not only for women on the spectrum, or people who love them, but anyone who likes a good conversation with an utterly brilliant mind."

—Maia Szalavitz bestselling author and award-winning journalist covering neuroscience and addiction for *Time*, *Scientific American*, and more

"Jennifer O'Toole allows us to witness the workings of her beautiful, brilliant mind, to share in her vulnerability, and to be thoroughly entertained by her storytelling. Through both her content and style, we get a glimpse of the intense empathy and passion that is so often misunderstood about autism, and in particular, about the unique experience of women on the spectrum. Ultimately this is a book for everyone."

—Jed Baker, PhD, bestselling author, international speaker

"*Autism in Heels* is a compelling must-read that proves autism doesn't have a set appearance. Witty and full of real-life experience, O'Toole's writing will appeal to all readers. She inspires hope, individuality, and certainty for those of us on the spectrum that we are not limited by our uniqueness. We really can do anything we set our minds to."

—Rachel Barcellona, autism self-advocate, Miss Southeast International, Unicorn Children's Foundation ambassador

"*Autism in Heels* hit me to the core. Exposing the pain of perfectionism, anorexia, bullying, abuse, and loneliness, Jennifer outlines the sheer need for this memoir in exposing the vulnerability that many girls face from being gifted, talented, and on the autism spectrum. This is an incredible, necessary book that will change lives for the better."

—Barb Cook, editor and author of *Spectrum Women*, founder and editor in chief at *Spectrum Women Magazine*

"Told like no other, this book leaves all of us, autistic or not, better human beings for having known Jennifer O'Toole."

—Sharon Lee Cummings, copublisher/editor at large of *Zoom Autism Magazine*, Autism Society of Virginia board member

"I was immediately captivated by Jennifer's intimate storytelling. *Autism in Heels* is a story of honesty and empowerment and is a must read for women with and without autism."

—Michelle Dean, assistant professor of special education at California State University, Channel Islands; technical consultant for the Netflix/Sony show *Atypical*

"*Autism in Heels* is a fascinating glimpse into the mind of an autistic woman. It's a must-read for anyone without autism to learn a new side of tolerance and inclusion. And for my fellow autistic women, you'll hopefully find parts of her life that parallel your own, as I did, and know you are not alone."

—Carly Fulgham, Autism Society of California board member, Art of Autism board member

"Honest, raw, intimate. Jennifer O'Toole's description of the female autistic life experience will resonate with many generatons of autistic women to come.

—Christa Holmans, autistic author and advocate, Neurodivergent Rebel Blog

"Jennifer O'Toole spares nothing of her experiences and methodically dissects the internal and external realities of what it's really like to be an Aspie female. I urgently recommend this book to clinicians, parents, and self-identified, self-curious humans. Reading it will increase your knowledge, your sensitivity, your worldview, and your love."

—Carol Moog, PhD, clinical psychologist, and coauthor of *The Autism Playbook for Teens*

"An essential read that I cannot wait to share. Writing with a radiating kind of aliveness and breathless honesty, O'Toole tackles all the tough issues—trauma, eating disorders, self-harm, depression, self-doubt—alongside the grace, hope, and joy of a life lived full of meaning and self-discovery."

—Shana Nichols, PhD, clinical psychologist specializing in female ASD, lead author of *Girls Growing Up on the Autism Spectrum*

"Thanks to Jennifer O'Toole, we have established a sturdy, hard-won narrative tradition that has the power to change hearts and minds."

—Valerie Paradiz, PhD, Autism Speaks board member; Director, National Autism Leadership Institute

"Jennifer O'Toole systematically examines issues faced by this group and illustrates with examples from her own journey. . . . Although Jennifer accentuates the positives, she does not sugarcoat vulnerabilities, dangers, and despair that women on the spectrum are likely to face. Her powerfully punching wit and insight are of a beauty and efficacy that only a spectrum mind could imagine."

—Lars Perner, PhD, Autism Society of America executive board member

"This slice of life on the spectrum illustrates just how diverse our lives can be, and how different our inner realities may be from what observers assume."

—John Elder Robison, bestselling author, advisor to the US Department of Health and Human Services, World Health Organization autism advisor, Institute for Autism Research cochair

"Brave, warm, and fiercely honest, Jennifer has broken the autism mold open with her riveting story. From anxiety and eating disorders to relationships and self-doubt, *Autism in Heels* will provide invaluable relief for girls and women around the world who have too long struggled to fit in. A jewel of a book!"

—Susan Stifleman, PhD, bestselling author, *Huffington Post* columnist, *The Today Show* contributor

"In this chipper memoir–cum–inspirational guide . . . O'Toole's compassion and enthusiasm are infectious."

—*Publisher's Weekly*

AUTISM
in Heels

AUTISM *in* Heels

The Untold Story of a Female Life on the Spectrum

JENNIFER COOK O'TOOLE

Foreword by Navah Paskowitz-Asner

Skyhorse Publishing

Skyhorse Publishing books may be purchased in bulk at special discounts for sales promotion, corporate gifts, fund-raising, or educational purposes. Special editions can also be created to specifications. For details, contact the Special Sales Department, Skyhorse Publishing, 307 West 36th Street, 11th Floor, New York, NY 10018 or info@skyhorsepublishing.com.

Visit our website at www.skyhorsepublishing.com.

10 9 8 7 6 5 4 3 2 1

Library of Congress Cataloging-in-Publication Data is available on file.

Cover design by Rain Saukas
Cover photo credit: iStock Photo

Print ISBN: 978-1-5107-3284-1
Ebook ISBN: 978-1-5107-3285-8

Printed in the United States of America

For my mother

And
from the
chaos
of her soul
there flowed
Beauty.

— Louise Alexandra Erskine

It doesn't interest me what you do for a living. I want to know what you ache for—and if you dare to dream of meeting your heart's longing. It doesn't interest me how old you are. I want to know if you will risk looking like a fool—for love—for your dreams—for the adventure of being alive.

— *Oriah Mountain Dreamer*

CONTENTS

FOREWORD

I am incredibly honored to write this foreword to *Autism in Heels.*

I am a mom of a blended family of six kids, including three autistic boys, each with such staggering variations of that wonderful wild spectrum. When we met at the Autism Society of America's National Conference in 2017, it was clear that, as mothers, Jennifer Cook O'Toole and I were a lot alike, both inspired and motivated through struggles, separations, and reinventions.

What I didn't realize, until reading *Autism in Heels,* was how very much or how very deeply Jennifer's own story of self-discovery would resonate with me as a woman in my own right.

I, too, took a while to truly understand who I was and how I fit into the world. I didn't meet adult expectations and had been told since as far back as I can remember by my Stanford-educated physician father that I was slow or stupid. I struggled to process verbal interactions. I had crippling social anxiety. I couldn't look anyone in the eye or speak to anyone but my immediate family until I was a teenager. Because of my unusual upbringing, I was forced to adapt. I would have become a casualty if I hadn't.

I went through incredible childhood trauma (as shown in the documentary *Surfwise*) struggling with my sense of self. Paralyzed by self-hatred from being told on a daily basis by my family of eight brothers that "I was just a girl" and that "guys hate fat chicks." We lived the surfing lifestyle, and for me, the lone girl, my value as a human was all about how I looked in a two-piece bikini. I became a model, and this shallow qualification became even more important manifesting in a lifelong cycle of anorexia and bulimia. I didn't start my path of healing until my children were born.

Now we know that autistic girls and women are more vulnerable to abuse as well as eating disorders. They are often misunderstood and misdiagnosed by adults. I am currently going through the formal diagnosis process myself. I can only hope that with new research and heightened visibility of autism in girls, others will not experience the same struggles I have endured throughout my life.

My passion to start The Ed Asner Family Center with my husband, Matt, and my father-in-law, Ed Asner, was fueled by the complete lack of mental health support for the families that desperately need it. My goal was simple: create a space where, within the same facility, a single mom could join a support group or have a one-on-one session with a marriage and family therapist while her special needs child took an art, dance, media, or vocational training course. Ours is a mission of inclusive strength and authentic community built one heart at a time. It's what we do. It's also what Jennifer has done in *Autism in Heels.*

Jennifer, thank you for writing this book, thank you for befriending me, and thank you for giving a voice to so many girls—of all ages, sizes, and shoe preferences—who are struggling with feeling lost, different, or misunderstood. Thanks to *Autism in Heels,* we need never be alone again.

—Navah Paskowitz-Asner
Cofounder, The Ed Asner Family Center
May 2018

PREFACE

On Language

I am a woman on the human spectrum who also happens to be autistic. I have autism. I am a person living with autism. I'm an autistic person. And an autistic woman.

All of these things are true.

Some people care very much about what specific language choices are used to describe themselves in relation to their autism. There is a lot of good discussion and thinking out there in all sorts of directions, and my goodness. If remembering to arrange words in a particular order really matters to someone else, then I most certainly am going to do my utmost to respect that preference! Really, how petty would it be to do anything less?

Personally, though, I don't really mind one way or the other. Call me whatever you want, as long as it's nice.

Since this is the story of *my* experiences, *Autism in Heels* reflects my preference . . . for a lack of preference. Whatever flowed best when I typed is what stayed. I will always do my best to honor others, and I hope that my choice will be treated with equal regard.

Asperger Syndrome or Autism Spectrum Disorder? Which Is Which?

The short answer is "yes." Or "either." (Although I do not *at all* favor the "disorder" in ASD and would much prefer it stand for "dynamic.") All of which leads me to the longer answer and why you'll notice both terms throughout this book.

I was diagnosed with Asperger Syndrome (AS) in 2011. Yes, AS was always considered part of the autism spectrum. In reality, though, AS was an entirely distinct medical diagnosis indicating that an individual had an average to above-average IQ and had experienced no significant early speech delay. Indeed, many who might not have thought of themselves (or of their children) in terms of autism *did* find their way to Asperger diagnoses and, in doing so, tapped into a vast, kind of "geektastic" support network where the very word *Aspie* (an affectionate term coined by author, self-advocate, and now personal friend Dr. Liane Holliday Willey) served to build a sense of positivity, familiarity, and community.

For sure, that group included me and my children. As a layperson, I never would have reckoned my bright, chatterbox daughter or her equally quick brothers with my idea of "autistic." I wouldn't have sought psychiatric and/or psychological insight to support their "autism." Or mine. There is, after all, a reason that I named my book series "Asperkids," not "autism kids." *Asperger Syndrome* was the term I was given, and therefore it was the term I had. And tweaked.

As with anything, though, the meaning of a word isn't just its definition, but also includes its connotations. I remember the first time I read the back cover description my UK-based publisher used for a book I'd written about purposeful play. The activities, it said, "exploited the interests and talents of children with Asperger Syndrome." Technically, *to exploit* means to make full use of and derive benefit from (a resource). That's the definition. And it's positive sounding. Or, at worst, neutral. In the United States, *to exploit* something or someone implies that there are unethical or even abusive motives in play. Connotation alone changes the entire takeaway.

Used as we did—and as some people and parts of the world still do—the words *Asperger Syndrome* were innocuous. Absolutely good and absolutely moral. They were tools of social subversion, winding around ignorance and stigma, creating pathways toward self-empowerment all around the world. However, because AS was made distinct by its relative strengths (cognitive capabilities, normal speech arrival), while autism was defined by its relative challenges, many clinicians, diagnosticians, and researchers came to use AS as a somewhat hierarchical term. Furthermore, by emphasizing the more "normal" appearance of someone with AS, the very real if more-masked struggles frequently remained unsupported *or* blamed on bad behavior. Soon, those connotations filtered into vernacular use among appearance-conscious parents and insecure individuals who used it to mean "not autistic like *them*." You might even say that the words *Asperger Syndrome* were *exploited* in ways that disempowered us all. If we were a house divided against ourselves, none of us would be left standing.

In 2013, the American Psychiatric Association eliminated AS as an independent diagnosis and amended the criteria for autism spectrum disorder (ASD) to absorb the "Aspie" profile, removing IQ and early speech from the equation entirely. Instead, the new standards, as laid out in the fifth edition of the *Diagnostic and Statistical Manual of Mental Disorders (DSM-V)*, highlight specific patterns of sensory processing and social interaction, common areas of uniquely autistic experiences.

The transition has not been entirely smooth or without unresolved issues, but—five years on, I believe it has been for the greater good. Defined, now, by commonality instead of difference, we more accurately embody autism. It is now our charge to explain that regardless of how obvious our autism is to others, it is equally present to the person living it. It is our job to correct those who reject some for being too "high-functioning" or forget those who are more visibly challenged. It is our privilege to speak aloud for those who can't and to have compassion for those who can. To the research community, educators, scientists, psychologists, and—most important—to regular folks like you and me . . . the best answer isn't that we're Aspie or that we're autistic.

The best answer is . . . we aren't any one word.

We are the spectrum.

ACKNOWLEDGMENTS

Autism in Heels is an endeavor that has been four years, many hands, many minds, and many voices in the making . . . including the ones holding it right now.

To every single reader, *thank you* for granting me a moment in your heart. I cannot thank you enough.

Thank you to John Elder Robison for suggesting I write this book in the first place, to Temple Grandin for insisting I do it well, and to Steve Silberman for his animated, enthusiastic belief in me both personally and practically, and most especially for recommending me to his agent . . .

. . . who became mine, and so very much more. Beth Vesel, you have been the champion of this adventure. Cheerleader, therapist, confidante, visionary. You saw and believed. You insisted and persevered. What's more, you made sure I did, too. Any and all good that comes to this world from *Autism in Heels* has your fingerprints all over it. Thank you, my friend.

Heart-shaped thanks to Tony Lyons, president and founder of Skyhorse Publishing, for caring so much about this story and for welcoming me so warmly to the family. And giant hugs to my resilient editor, Lindsey Breuer-Barnes, for laughing along with me . . . despite my defiant use of ellipses.

Navah Paskowitz-Asner, I can't stop breaking into happy dances over your foreword. A woman can have no more beautiful features, I think, than a spirit emboldened by truth and vision made fierce by love. And you *are*, indeed, a beautiful woman. Thank you, from the bottom of my heart, for adding your name and voice to mine.

If ever anyone in the history of the world made "something beautiful out of something broken," it is Helen and Mark Goldstein and Rebecca Mullen. The daughters you raised were extraordinary human beings . . . because you are. I love you.

Maura, Sean, and Gavin, your love is everything to me. Everything. Thank you for having faith in me. Thank you for being proud of me. Thank you for laughing and crying with me. You are, quite simply, my favorite people in the whole, wide, world.

With one addition. Thank you, Mom. For once, I am speechless. You know my heart. And I know yours. And we will always be in it together.

INTRODUCTION: THIRTY-FOUR YEARS

For thirty-four years, I didn't know I was autistic. I just knew Me.

Me. The little redheaded girl who had learned to substitute attention for affection. Who had written to Santa asking for a friend for Christmas, without much of a result.

Who became a college cheerleader and sorority social chair because they were markers of social confidence. Who, even with a 4.0 at Brown University, still believed she was nothing but a beautiful facade.

I starved myself into the hospital. I accepted intense, damaging love that left bruises on my body and scars in my heart.

For thirty-four years, I didn't know I was autistic. But I'd always sensed that I was different. I'd always felt the frantic need to find my footing. And in hindsight, that may be exactly why I've always known that I had a thing for shoes.

Shiny, light-catching, patent leather tap shoes, tied with bows of soft-glow satin. My grandmother's 1940s peep-toe pumps, carefully wrapped in tissue paper, tucked in her closet. Clear-vinyl-and-gold-lamé heels, Mom's homage to the 1980s, that, at least to a child's eye, looked a lot like Cinderella's glass slippers. Daddy's clunky Oxfords, solid, freshly shined, and always smelling just a little bit of shoe polish. These were my playthings and my objects of study. Bits of material culture that carried the clues I needed to understand other people. A reference point for associations. An exercise in categorization. A treasure trove for a devoted sociologist in a pixie cut and Strawberry Shortcake nightgown. Each shoe had its own identity to lend. And I wanted to try on every one.

Hour upon hour sailed by while I delighted in the sounds and scents, structure and shine of buckles and boxes. I stood before the bathroom mirror, watching myself teeter, slide, and tap around, taking in the sculptures beneath my feet. Each new pair gave a new way of relating to myself. A new kind of character study. I could change shoes and change the way I stood. The way gravity pulled. The way my hips moved or my knees bent. With one switch, the brush-brush swish of slippery soles on carpet became a mesmerizing click-click rhythm of stilettos on tile. With one switch, I could inhabit another body. Could uncover other people's disguises . . . and find bits of myself.

For thirty-four years, I played dress-up, and I guess I've never stopped ever-more-confidently playing with aspects of my own identity. Evolving characters and suiting moods in whimsical, malleable ways that respect the girl I have been . . . broadcast the woman I am . . . or highlight bits of both. In a world that prefers to constrict women rather than encourage us to expand, I've discovered that dress-up is the perfect quick-change way to have it all. To say, "Actually yes. I am this AND that. Although I may change my mind tomorrow." And while I'm very much still a private work in progress, my progress happens on international stages. Like the UK and Denmark, where I've given keynote addresses to royalty. About autism . . . and shoes.

I've been called names my whole life long. They've been among the identities I saw in the mirror and wondered at the fit. Then came a new name: *autistic*. And that one has changed everything about everything.

In the few years since, I've been lauded publicly until I blush: "Humanitarian. Role model of hope. Heroine for girls everywhere." Just as publicly, I've been cut to the bone as a "high-achieving, popular, pretty, spoiled, tactless, rich girl blessed with every opportunity." There's a stiletto's-width fine line between "who, me?" and "why not me?" That much I've learned through trial and error.

When I'm asked, "How does all of this feel?" I know I have to have an answer that is at once both sincere and prepared. No gratitude clumsily balanced by some shy list of accomplishments. I'm a person for whom social nuance is absent. That's key. That's autism. Yet publicly and privately, I'm still expected to navigate the minefields deftly—called out when I don't. It's ironic, really. A bit like chiding a blind person who trips over your foot . . . while she's competing in the Special Olympics . . . where you are part of the cheering crowd. Not quite fair.

Because, just like everyone else, I'm just doing my best. And no label is one size fits all. Not woman. Not female. Not autism.

Regardless of how articulate or poised any one of us is, how introverted or bombastic, how sharp or soft, we are all made up of intimate, vulnerable, never-spoken-aloud slippery bits. We are all works in progress. All living lives in progress. All finding our footing.

This is the story of just one woman. A woman who has had extraordinary global adventures and enough from-the-inside truth to fill a library. It is my story of a not-your-average, sometimes-beautiful, always real, glitterously female life. Of my own autism diagnosis and the transformation it ignited. Of girls, women, autism, and the new-old tale of all three. It's a love song to thousands of yet-unidentified spectrum girls and women, championed by some, yet still overlooked by many "experts," still misunderstood by much of society, still, too often, alone and disconnected. It's a nonfiction parable in the making, inviting you to know me . . . and, through me, to know the Someone Else you came here to understand in the first place.

For thirty-four years, I didn't know I was autistic. And for the rest of my life, I'll know I'm not alone. None of us are. We are simply different. Together.

CHAPTER 1

Backwards in Heels: My Story in Reverse

"I barely made it here today," I admitted to my therapist, voice low and wavering. "You see, I'd thought it was me. But I'm not it. The link, I mean."

Her forehead crinkled. "To their Asperger's, Jennifer? Is that what you mean? You thought you might be the connection to your children's diagnoses?" I nodded, wiping away a rogue tear. "Okay, then. Tell me," she pressed.

I opened my secret blue notebook and, words pouring out of me, began explaining all that it held: months of research, unspoken personal details, disconnected stories.

Tears spilt until my eyes fell away from the psychologist. I didn't really need to reference the pages anyway. This was my life story I was telling. I knew it by heartache.

And then there was silence. Somewhere in the office, a murmur. "Jennifer? Jennifer, why does it matter to you? The diagnosis?"

Suddenly, the room was back—or maybe I was back in the room. My body shook. My eyes burned. Someone closed a door in the hall.

"Because," I replied, "it would mean that I'm not a total failure at being human."

She smiled gently. "You're not a failure, Jennifer. And yes, I'm quite certain you do have Asperger's."

Background Check

In so many ways, the last year had been rough. My best friend—my sister, really—had been diagnosed with aggressive, stage IV breast cancer.

She was thirty-one at the time and fighting for her life. My daughter had been a Make-A-Wish kid after seven years in and out of hospitals. I'd given birth to my third child, and shortly thereafter, my two eldest children—Maura, seven, and Sean, four—had been diagnosed with Asperger Syndrome. To top it all off, just that day, their dad had unceremoniously told me that he had been diagnosed with Asperger's, too. He'd come home from his psychologist appointment and said that, actually, he and the therapist hadn't been talking about the kids for a while.

"I had to fill out a whole bunch of questionnaires," he'd said, popping open a can of Diet Coke. I'd sat in silence for a moment, then stepped closer. Nonchalantly, he'd pried a piece of Nicorette from its bubble pack. There it was. Teeth clenched, vein thrumming at his jaw. The giveaway. The message: keep your distance. You are too much for me. Or at least, that's what I read.

It was a sensation I knew well. From friends. Boyfriends. When my dad would light up or my mom would roll her eyes impatiently, telling me to get to the point. Something about me, though I couldn't name it or change it, was always too much.

Maybe it was understandable. This discombobulation. After all, no matter what follows, the very word *diagnosis* is scary. No one diagnoses happiness. You don't go to a doctor to joyously find out whether you will be diagnosed with pregnancy. On the contrary, diagnosis goes hand in hand with life's deepest hurts. Diagnosis is what I heard before the words *terminal lung cancer* and my dad's name were mentioned in the same sentence.

Which was why, I imagine, that despite the endless debating about autism, one constant loomed. A unanimously agreed-upon expectation. Every website, clinical article, celebrity parent tell-all made room to say: people are expected to grieve an autism or Asperger's diagnosis. It's the norm. It was morally obligatory. Diagnosis. Autism. Put each of those two loaded words together, and combustion follows. And good people—healthy, loving, normal people—are devastated.

Who in her right mind would feel any differently? Who in her right mind, indeed?

The Missing Link: Family Connections

Information has always been my life preserver when feelings get too deep. My dad was the same way. Facts. Theories. Give my brain something to grasp hold of, and I will not drown. No matter what. Which is why I reacted to my children's diagnoses like a scholar. If I was going to be able to empower and embolden them, I'd simply learn everything I could about Asperger's. Autism. ADD and ADHD and a plethora of other acronyms that ran together like a perverse alphabet soup.

I pored through the most respected books—close readings, the likes of which I hadn't done since graduate school. Family anecdotes, professional journals, to-do lists, and teacher strategies. I attacked them all with fierce analysis, neon highlighter between my teeth and pencil in hand, scribbling in margins and filling every square inch of that blue journal.

All for the kids.

It wasn't long before, neck deep in all of this spectrum self-education, I'd begun to recognize someone else in the stories and bullet points.

If my daughter and son were what Asperger's looked like, then surely, my father, who'd passed away only a few years before, had been their genetic twin.

Joe Cook was a brilliant, beloved man. An international commercial litigator who'd represented an entire country but often couldn't remember the names of the couples who'd been in his bridge group for fifteen years. He was awkward and anxious in social settings; I still remember how he'd managed, during a dinner event, to walk into the ladies' room of a favorite restaurant. Twice. And, harder to swallow, on the weekends I'd come home to visit from college or graduate school, he'd likely light a cigarette, pour a glass of J&B Scotch, say some hellos, make a few (famously bad) jokes, and head out to spend a night or two on his boat. The thing is—I never doubted that he loved my mother or me. Never. What I *did* question was . . . why wasn't I enough to keep his interest? Or, confusingly, why was I too much? But if I reframed him—reconsidered him in terms of autism—suddenly my absent-minded-professor daddy seemed a whole lot more . . . human. Not distant or selfish, but vulnerable. Forgivable. Knowable. And every bit as lovable.

Even relatable. I remembered when, a night ten years before, my father had looked up at the inky sky and whispered, "Jenny, I think you understand me better than anyone in the world." Now, an awakening tickled the back of my mind. Slowly, gingerly, a kernel of hope began to germinate. Maybe there was a reason I'd "seen" him differently. Maybe, I dared to wonder, there was grace enough for two of us. Maybe autism hadn't skipped a generation. In fact, maybe it would explain every disconnect I'd felt for the last thirty years.

Cracking the Diagnostic Code

It was time for research, and I dove right in. Or at least I tried to. Almost immediately, I ran headfirst into a dead end. Asperger Syndrome and general autism checklists were easy to come by, though most were very clinical, not any kind of "here's what that looks like in real life" scenario. But I'd already worked through the techno-jargon-meets-actual-people conundrum for my children. By this point, I was pretty much bilingual. Besides. I lived with three "Asperkids," was married to a man with Asperger's, and had most probably had been raised by a dad on the spectrum, too. I didn't need a portrait of an Aspie for my own benefit. I could go into a room and pick out who was who by instinct as much as anything else.

But instinct does not a diagnosis secure.

This lawyer's daughter knew that, in order to go into a psychologist's or psychiatrist's office and articulately lay out a theory, she needed a precedent. So—where were the girls? Where were the women? Where could I find an equally-bright-but-happens-to-love-lipstick-and-heels version of Asperger's? Someone to check myself against, and then, perhaps, point to and say, "Recognize anyone?" The trouble was that no matter how hard I looked, I couldn't find her—I couldn't find a me. I was looking to hold a candle to myself, only to be met with long darkness—no one who embodied my way of moving through the world with my precise, aslant rhythm.

In the early days of autism research—the foundational days, really—teams of all-male scientists, like Dr. Hans Asperger, observed all-male patients, mostly children. Eventually, those clinicians' notes became the basis of the autism profile. Logically, more boys fit criteria that came from studying and describing boys. No wonder I couldn't find my reflection. How was a catalog of autism spectrum characteristics based on little boys in prewar Vienna going to help me? In twenty-first-century suburban America. In a minivan. And bra. With a predisposition toward glitter.

And hardly anyone to talk to. My world, at that point, was light-years away from European scholarly inquisition. Like many mothers of small children, I had only one chance to socialize with other adults (read: have any conversation *at all* with someone taller than three feet), and that was with whomever I managed to meet at children's activities. Kindermusik. Library story time. Gymboree. These were the match-making centers for highly educated, slightly stir-crazy women who had left the world of paid employment and were now hungry for friends—people who could conjure up memories of life before nursing bras and were only too happy to cohost family cookouts where partners could bond over burgers and dogs.

After-Noah's-Art-class lunch at Dean & Deluca could make or break a gal's social prospects in a way rivaled only by middle school cafeterias. And though I was usually the one to suggest lunch (the best way to be included, I'd learned), I never actually got to join in. Week after week found me driving past the outdoor eateries, teary-eyed, watching the other mommies laugh and gossip while their little ones napped in strollers or happily chomped on Cheerios. My kids didn't rest. They didn't sleep or sit contentedly with a toy. They were . . . intense. And constant. So *I* was constantly wound up on hypervigilant meltdown-prevention duty. I'd try, on occasion, to connect—to explain why I was uptight . . . but people get turned off by things they fear will contaminate their world.

They stop listening when you let the smile out of your voice for too long.

These little ones were mine, and I loved them *big*—I would (and will) *do anything* they need of me. At the same time, though I hated myself for feeling it, I was tired of living beyond the realm of easy. Decade after decade, relegated to watching the life I wanted play out. Too close to look away. Too far to be remembered. This was the perpetual "almost" that I wanted to understand . . . *if* I could understand autism. And me. And if I could keep it together long enough to get to "someday."

Life, as I knew it, took place in a full-twenty-four-hour pressure cooker with hardly any sleep and barely any division between day or night. (And no. There was no such thing as sex.) Consciousness was driven almost entirely by caffeine, bookended by drop-off and pick-up lines, empty of the seemingly mythical "baby nap" other parents enjoyed, riddled with sixteen anxiety-filled "but what if" questions an hour, peppered by cross-town trips to and from play therapy and occupational therapy appointments (with enough waiting room activities packed along to entertain whichever unlucky siblings came in tow), soundtracked by endlessly looping DVDs and parroted full-length scripts, and every ninety minutes, all of this was supposed to stop so that I could deliver an emotionally regulating "sensory diet" to each of my three children.

The protocol was exacting and precise: first, I would perform a specific choreography of surgical brushstrokes on little legs and backs and arms and hands. Then I moved to joint compressions on all their knees and shoulders, hips and elbows, wrists and fingers. Step three required age-appropriate vestibular (movement) activities—say, laying the toddler down onto a beach towel and dragging him behind me all around the kitchen (while singing) and spinning the preschooler in a desk chair and pushing the kindergartener back and forth on an Ikea swing that had been drilled into our ceiling. Last, I had to convince them to do "heavy work"—pulling giant beanbags up and down the staircase, jumping on the trampoline in the living room, doing donkey kicks or plank poses or crab walks or pulling on exercise bands. All of this. With three not-always-interested, not-always-cooperative, not-always-happy-with-one-another children. Every ninety minutes. Changed up for variety. Recorded and reviewed at weekly therapy appointments.

And if anxiety levels didn't come down or they continued to completely refuse some basic sensory experiences (like noisy movie theaters, finger painting, or joining other children on the playground equipment) while still talking too loudly or spinning or jumping off the furniture . . . the inevitable question from the therapist would be "Mom"—because that's your identity to everyone . . . just "Mom"—"have you been keeping up with the sensory diets?"

No. I was never able to. I wonder if anyone truly could. In hindsight, the whole thing sounds ludicrous and impractical. But when it's you there, when a disappointed "expert" looks your way and shakes her head, no excuse is good enough to explain why you haven't come through for your own children. Sometimes, in a small, cracked voice, I'd begin to say, "I'm trying but they run different directions and I'm so tired and lonely." But I'd catch myself. I'd try harder. Always harder. Sleep even less. Drink more coffee. Love more fiercely. And privately pray that there was some sense to make of it all.

Praise the Lord and pass the ammunition.

Mine was going to have to be a one-woman proving ground. If I was going to be able to add to the autism conversation, to translate male to female, to say about any one common spectrum trait, "yes, that's true—and also," then I'd first need to know *why* the boys did what they did. What behaviors might we, gals, employ that looked different enough to avoid professional notice but might actually be serving the same purpose?

Big question. And I was going to find the answer. Of that, I was certain. For all of my other insecurities, when faced with intellectual puzzles, my confidence never wavered. Since early childhood, I've, inexplicably, been able to see information differently from other people. Be they words on a page or two musical phrases in an entire score, patterns have simply emerged to me that somehow seem invisible to everyone else. So, as long as facts, not folks, were what had to be solved, the system was simple: I'd begin with what I knew, gather as much information as possible, then sit back and watch. Like pictures hidden within Magic Eye paintings, the answers show themselves. They always did. They always do.

True to plan, I began with what I knew: all human beings share the same fundamental needs. Of course, there are the basics like food and shelter and safety. But there's so, so much more. Communication. Spirituality. A sense of belonging. Of purposeful work. Every culture in every age in every land has had different ways of addressing the specifics.

So what universal needs were those Viennese boys meeting? That's what I was going to have to figure out in order to explain, coherently, why the Aspie profile glowed in the dark for me.

Dr. Asperger's patients, apparently, loved train timetables. Maps of their routes, too. The modern parent questionnaires I'd had to fill out for my own children's diagnoses asked whether they played with wheels on toy cars—which many girls don't even have! Those dang train timetables weren't the key. This was going about it backwards. Clearly, they had been one way of satisfying an obviously acute, probably common need. Like saying that only going to weekly Mass or attending Shabbat services or morning prayers at mosque was evidence of a spiritual life, instead of the other way around: that every human has spiritual needs, and all of these (and more) are valid ways of satisfying those needs. My task, then, was to forget the details and extrapolate. Close my eyes and imagine. Get rid of positive or negative connotations. Put aside the intellectual, go for the emotional—what would feel good about watching wheels or knowing which engine would be where, when?

I had it instantly. Intuitively. The beauty of order. The reliability of fact. People are changeable. Unpredictable. Facts, though, are sturdy. A display of pleasure without anxiety. That was the reason for the beloved train schedules and mapmaking. It was also the reason why, as a child, I'd memorized every genealogical and historical fact associated with *Little House on the Prairie* author Laura Ingalls Wilder. Why I'd pored over nonfiction books like *The Extraordinary Origins of Everything* to know the history and understand the purpose of everything I saw—from tampons to nursery rhymes. Why I'd collected scores of "British Royals" postcards into a big, black photo album and arranged them into a millennium's worth of family trees. It was the same reason why I'd chosen to write my honors thesis on Barbie and the particulars of twentieth-century women's fashion. In the highest-brow of academic ways, I'd naturally fulfilled the same need for security and predictability as the boys. Restyled, with a modern-girl makeover.

All right, but what about the famous tendency to line things up? "Does child line up toys like trucks or trains?" had been a question on my kids' evaluation forms. One had. The other two . . . well, they'd sort of *displayed* things. *I* certainly hadn't lined up trucks or trains. I didn't even *have* any trucks or trains—which, as I thought about it, were examples of toys that *do* sort of line up even in typical play. Train cars attach and make long chains in Thomas the Tank Engine *and* in real life. Cars and vehicles in a row? Look on the street. Traffic *does* assemble in lanes. All kinds of kids organized trading cards in binders full of see-through plastic sleeves. LEGO sets were designed to be built and displayed. At eighteen months, my youngest squealed with delight at his carefully arranged row of football helmets, not so different from adult collections of sports memorabilia sitting on shelves for all to admire. Did these kids get upset if someone knocked over their arrays? Yes. But who *wouldn't* be bothered if someone else didn't recognize how much effort had been put into something and simply disassembled it or treated it carelessly?

Which left me with three takeaways.

First. Checklists are supposed to be succinct descriptions of what is. But in the case of autism, most sounded more like one-dimensional prescriptions for how autistic people were *supposed* to behave. If it swims like a duck, walks like a duck, follows Mama Duck, it's probably a duck. Unless it's the Ugly Duckling—a.k.a. the swan who's failing at being who/how others say he ought, instead of being a natural at being himself. And let's face it, he's probably going to have much better explanations for what he was doing all along than would a duck who had watched him struggle with his lack of duckiness.

Professionals stand behind the "authority" of autism spectrum checklists, ticking off items by rote with cool, evaluative distance. Personally, though, I think that most textbooks, bullet points, and assessment tools are flat, unimaginative, and completely devoid of perspective. Where were the fleshed-out versions that had benefited from first-person analysis and perspective? Only living people who have, well, quacked the quack or honked the honk can truly add texture or depth, scope or dimension, insight or accuracy to lists of regurgitated clichés.

When I looked at lists of "autistic" behaviors and characteristics, it seemed strikingly obvious (and oddly unmentioned) that in many, many ways the *actions* in question were not, actually, that unusual—neither were the associated interests or emotions. However, the *intensity* of the experiences and responses *was distinct*—which was worth noting and unpacking. Human spectrum first. Same end. Different means. In the *intensity of the drive* toward "display-focused" play, *of the stress* over other kinds of interaction, and *of the distress* in any change in the order created, I could *see* some of the uniquenesses of an autistic mind, like literal thinking, cognitive rigidity, and difficulty, with spontaneous social interaction.

Meaning that if I was going to be able to discern whether any of the Asperger/autism "criteria" fit *me*, I would have to be deliberate, intentional, and analytical along every step of the way.

What was more, I'd have to confront the second takeaway: autism assessment screening tools were (and sadly still are) rife with some of the most egregious, systematic gender bias employed by twenty-first-century science (not to mention some hangers-on from the twentieth, as well). Male-focused examples of autistic behavior belie tests compiled by professionals with little to no understanding of how similar experiences of autism actually present themselves in girls and women. Since those tests themselves are skewed, so, too, are the score keys used in evaluating them, and the results they provide—meaning bad data for researchers, the perpetuation of invisible-but-intrinsic prejudices among the general public, educators, mental health providers, and, worst, the trusting parents asked to evaluate their sons *and* daughters in ways that almost certainly end up shortchanging the girls *and* their families.

So, I was going to have to peer behind every diagnostic criterion and gender-biased bullet point, identify the "human-spectrum" psychological "itch" it scratched, and *then* consider how, as a girl or an adult woman, I may have sought to accomplish the same thing. This was not going to be a quick process.

Or was it? This was common sense. No, no train sets or toy trucks in *my* past. But . . . I *had* sat for hours and hours every Christmastime, arranging and rearranging my mother's nativity set. What's more, she had eventually begun taking the three-foot-tall light-up version down from the attic a full day *before* she'd intended to put it on display out front. There were probably fifteen pieces in total, and my mom knew how much I adored those little plastic lambs, the shepherd with a real metal staff, the collapsible manger, the purple-robed wise man, and Mary with her blue veil and the camel. All Saturday and Sunday, I would populate our living room with giant, plastic Bible people, creating and recreating (rather tacky) Bethlehem tableaux . . . sometimes secretly inserting myself as Jesus's little-known sister. It was calming. Satisfying. Very Zen. And almost intimate. As I got a little older, I *had been* very particular about the way my Smurf houses sat. And I *did* line my Barbies up for wedding album photo shoots rather than make up stories with them. Logically, my parents had chalked my "quirkiness" up to my being very bright *and* an only child. I was used to playing on my own (whether by others' choice, by my uncertainty with other kids, or the circumstance of not having any siblings in the house), I was used to *my* things staying where and how *I* put them.

Now, I began to wonder whether that explanation had been totally off the mark.

Day in. Day out. In stolen moments, I built a composite portrait—a Chick-List Checklist—both from what I read and from what I watched in my children. Reinhabiting them in my imagination. Experiencing the same visceral reactions. Scanning my memories for unique-but-alike matches.

Then it was over. All of my research, for nothing. In one moment—that morning—my husband had cornered the intergenerational genetic link. I'd had a lifetime of not quite fitting in—and had almost solved it all. Now, the possibility of forgiveness and relief and understanding had been snatched away just before I could grab hold. All I was left with was serious shame. And blame. And invisibility. Again.

I wasn't crying in my driveway, hopeless because I was sad for my children. I wasn't afraid for their dad. I was crying for myself. I was jealous of them all.

I didn't even fit in with the people who didn't quite fit in. I'd get over it, I knew. I'd champion my kids and just keep moving . . . after this. This one, private breakdown. After allowing myself this mourning session in a minivan, grieving answers that were almost mine, but now belonged to the people I was dedicated to loving.

Just as I'd felt hope slip from my grasp—I was given the greatest gift no one expects to want: the words "You do have Asperger's."

Everything else stopped. And for me, real life began.

In so many ways, I was . . . am . . . unexpected. And I've learned that things get really messy when something—or someone—who is familiar turns out to be more or less or just different than we'd expected.

Even average, common, dead-center-of-the-bell-curve familiar doesn't mean entirely known. Think about it. How many times have people been sure about something only to discover how wildly wrong they've been? Like knowing that the Earth was flat? Or that educating girls would send all the blood to their brains and away from their reproductive organs? Or that the Y2K apocalypse was going to send us back to the Stone Age?

My final takeaway: being on the autism spectrum is just another a variation on the theme of being human. Autism appears in every culture, on every continent, in every class, race, sexual orientation, and gender profile, and, like any other human condition, varies in complexity and intensity from person to person and day to day. Identification, of course, doesn't make one autistic, any more than calling out "It's a girl!" at a birth turns the child female. Nor is the word itself a marker of inferiority. "Autistic" is a neurological, not pathological, profile—a constellation of highly attuned cognitive and sensory skills that happens to come packaged along with some equally exquisitely particular challenges.

In 2015, for the first time ever, "neurodiversity" was added to the dictionary, beginning an unzipping of what and who we are as people—self-actualization in reverse. Discovery and awareness made clear, only after years and years of wasted time. Of misunderstandings, hurt, isolation, victimization, shame, and trauma.

Until quite recently, women around the world were dying in terrific numbers from heart disease because they were looking for "traditional, expected" symptoms of heart attack, like shooting pains or sudden weakness. These are, most definitely, symptoms of heart attack—in men. Women (and their doctors), by and large, were dismissing sudden-onset lethargy, indigestion, even nonspecific, general malaise because they didn't experience numbness down their arms or shortness of breath. In other words, they fatally ignored normal female histology simply because everyone expected female bodies with the same medical condition to present exactly as male patients did.

Let me be clear. I don't believe that doctors were intentionally being irresponsible or unprofessional. They did the best with what they knew—but what they knew was decidedly (and disturbingly) incomplete.

As the American Heart Association's "Red Dress" campaign set about educating society about women's symptoms, it gained celebrity attention and increased public awareness. Soon, medical professionals were integrating the female expression of heart disease into their understanding of overall presentation. In other words, symptoms that "look like a female heart attack" finally caught eyes and minds and attention as additional manifestations of "a heart attack," regardless of the patient's gender.

Autism is pretty much the same. Or it should be. Like heart disease or any other human condition, no clinical or "vernacular" idea of "what autism/Asperger's 'looks like'" can be complete if it is "skewed" to include one gender more readily and frequently overlook or mislabel the other. To be accurate, representations of the spectrum must include all phenotypic expressions of our neurological hardwiring. Except . . . often, they don't.

Frankly, autism needs more pink. Maybe some lipstick. Throw in some piercings or sensible pantsuits. I don't really care how any particular woman does her own version of female, so long as we get to be part of the club. After all, we've earned our membership. Years ago, a reporter asked Ginger Rogers if she found it hard keeping up with Fred Astaire. With a coy smile, she answered him simply. "Not really. After all, I did everything he did. Only backwards and in high heels."

Amen, Ginger. Welcome to autism in heels.

What Ifs

Normal, I think, is something so usual that we no longer notice it. Regular. Common. Average. It's life's expected stuff—test grades, height, intelligence, behavior. Math and science folks illustrate all of those on line graphs called bell curves. You've seen them before. They're common, too. Which makes sense, because basically, the whole point of a bell curve is to make very clear what is normal . . . and what's not. Average shows up as the peak, or crest, right in the middle of what becomes a bell-shaped arch. About two-thirds of everything (or everyone) being counted are darn near that center mark. Under the dome. One deviation out, you'll still include 95 percent of whatever or whomever you're measuring. Just beyond the "bell" are about 3ish percent of folks, who are, indeed, noticeably "not" center. And then there are the outliers—those remaining few furthest from the norm, who barely squeeze under the rim. From my red hair to school smarts—and later, to my intensity, drive, and lifetime full of almost-never-ending crises—this has always been my domain. I just never truly understood why.

Sometime during second grade, I came upon an official-looking paper from school: "IQ Test Score: Jennifer Cook." Of course, I hadn't the slightest idea what it meant. On the other hand, I knew that tests and scores were important. Even out of context, I remembered that number for five years—until I was twelve and taking some college courses on Saturdays. One of them happened to be psychology, and there, in the textbook section called "IQ: Atypicalities," I saw my first bell curve. What's more, I saw that, according to this chart, I was out in the hinterlands. One-tenth of one percentile. Literally, as far as I could get from the average range without falling off the page.

There it was. Hard-core, down-on-paper confirmation. I was not typical. That much I knew. But something in the following paragraphs didn't sit right with me. Something about the words was wrong.

Which is why my little forehead crinkled in concentration over the next sentences of the psychology textbook. Atypical was a description of fact. Got it. Less of me, more of Them. But then something went wrong. The author began to use "typical" and "normal" interchangeably. I sat back and pursed my lips, thinking hard. No. That was inaccurate. Typical was about statistics. How many of something. Normal was a lot more relative. And a lot more . . . judgmental. Compare me to people in general, and no. I wasn't not typical . . . but . . . I shook my head and shut the book with a thud. No. This guy was wrong. Typical and normal were not synonyms, and I knew it firsthand. While I would never be typical compared with 99.9 percent of folks, for me and the rest of the 0.1 percent on the edges, I was and always will be normal. *My* normal. *Our* normal.

In that tiny distinction was the kernel of a life-changing epiphany. Even one-tenth of a percent is more than one person. Which meant there were other people like me. And I wasn't alone.

Bell(e) Curve

That year, a certain animated beauty threw normal for a very *real* curve. Belle, of *Beauty and the Beast*, felt so utterly familiar. Ariel, of *The Little Mermaid*, will always be my redheaded soul sister. But, I *got* Belle. Enchanted by books, feisty, a bit of a daddy's girl. Unlike everyone else in so many indescribable ways—socially, emotionally, intellectually. I recognized this story, all right. She was musical and bright, believed in the underdog, was curious and unafraid of being authentic. She was also friendless and naive. Behind her back, as behind mine, folks gossiped, with false sympathy, about the "odd" girl who was so very *not* one of the "rest of us."

Except . . . there was a catch to Belle's story. Something, at that point, I'd never conceived of, much less experienced. Belle's "peculiar" brand of zeal and intellect and compassion—the things I recognized in myself—didn't ruin her life. They turned out to be exactly what made her the heroine. In fact, Belle longed to push every limit possible—something I understood perfectly. Like me, Belle yearned for something bigger, some kind of purpose in the "great wide somewhere."

She, too, had a belief in some nameless calling, a certainty of hidden logic amidst hurtful chaos, confidence in a resilient heart meant to survive the heartache. Belle means "beautiful." So, what if Belle's Curve could be a different kind of bell curve? What if it could be beautiful? Perhaps, even full of possibilities and adventures that couldn't be found anywhere else. And what if I could live my life there?

Maybe I didn't have to teeter off of some line graph, too alone and too far away from typical to be safe. Instead, I could keep searching for ways to be my version of normal. Tease out what that really meant. Try to find other girls like me. And maybe, just maybe, I'd be able to build an authentic, curious, passionate life on the beautifully atypical Belle Curve. Maybe we all could.

For those of us who spend so much of our lives feeling just outside that magical place of easy friendships and happy Happy Hours, we girls are outside the outsiders, still knocking on the door. In other words, while those of us with autism may all be skirting the edges of various bell curves, we gals ought to be dancing . . . on the Belle Curve.

It shouldn't take half a lifetime—plus research and investigative work by the individual herself—to declare, "Congratulations! You're not broken. You're a different kind of normal. Now. Let us tell you all about some things that might be challenging and how to navigate them. Not to mention all the wonderful talents that you have that you probably never considered to be lovable, wonderful gifts. And, oh, by the way—there are *loads* of people out there just like you. So, welcome to the club!"

After I was finally diagnosed, my daughter's psychiatrist (for whom I have always had great regard) began a session by asking if she might first speak to "Mommy" alone. Nervously, I closed the office door and waited. What she said was completely unexpected. It was also powerful and powerfully courageous.

"Jennifer, I don't know whether I ever said so, but I didn't see your daughter's Asperger's at first. The boys? Absolutely. But not her," she admitted calmly and then leaned in. "But, you made the case, point by point, and asked me to stick around without judgment for a month or so. You were tired and had been through a wringer of psychologists and specialists and I'll be honest, I thought you'd be wrong about her. Jennifer, you weren't. Every observation was spot on, and four years later, not only do I have no doubt about her Asperger's, you taught me what some of the world's best medical schools couldn't." She smiled and sighed. "Be sure. By sharing your own journey, thousands upon thousands of girls will be blessed. You will be doubted, for certain, just as I doubted you at first. What I don't doubt, Jennifer, is that you will do anything to save hearts from suffering. So go out and teach the world, just as you've taught me."

The reverse-self-discovery process of receiving an adult diagnosis is bizarre. It's a strange thing to read a profile, a list of traits and characteristics, and most powerfully, explanations of how they will play out in real life—only to find that you're actually looking in a rearview mirror and seeing the infinite moments and memories on the road behind. As if, all along the way, from childhood through this very moment, you've been navigating life at the whim of an unseen Autism Conductor. You've been making turns and choosing highways, feeling in control when, instead, you've been on autopilot the whole time. Sure, the specific scenery along the way differs from person to person, like variations on a theme of music. But by and large, you've taken the neurologically prescribed route as surely as if you'd been using a DNA GPS, reliably exhibiting "spectrummy" patterns and preferences the whole way.

It took thirty-four years to reframe my life. To find the relief of identification. That's such a long time, when lived twenty-four hours a day, three hundred and sixty-five days a year. I made it to thirty-five, not without scratches or bruises. But still, I made it. Some of us simply can't hold out that long. Nor should anyone have to. Every one of us deserves more than a life repaired in retrospect. We deserve full lives. On the human spectrum. Right now.

I am, most definitely, still learning how to hear my own voice. But I *have* learned how to tell my own truth. Along this mottled journey, I have fallen—many times. And every time, I've gotten back up on my feet. Not always gracefully and not always quickly. But I *have* gotten up. And I am proud of the scars I bear because they are proof that I am stronger than whatever or whoever has wounded me. Today, I choose to keep dancing. To turn my stumbles into part of the routine. Because I'm making this up as I go along.

I will do my best to unzip time for you. To share my yesterdays and illuminate someone else's tomorrows, hopeful that I may be brave *and* broken, and that this world has room for an imperfect, atypical heroine.

Just me. Another ginger. Dancing backwards in heels.

CHAPTER 2

Camouflage: Hiding in Plain Sight

The number *4* is yellow. The vowels *A*, *O*, and *U* are girls. *I* and *E*, however, are boys. So you would think that Wednesday, with both of its *e*'s, would be a boy. But it's not. For some reason, the day is a shy and somewhat messy British girl with drab, gray clothes and droopy knee socks. Friday, on the other hand, is a beguiling, hypnotic-eyed beauty whose name trails off to the right in curled, purple cursive. All words are *really* like that—neither wispy whispers nor squiggled shapes. They exist in front of the eyes even when there is no page there. They have their own personalities and stories. Listen. Try to catch them from the air, pull them toward one another as you might do on a touch screen. Give them a moment and watch the height of letters appear like notes on a conductor's score, emerging like sculpture from the marble.

I realize all of that may sound incredibly strange. Or confusing. Or crazy. Or all three. I *do* realize that. But I didn't always, because to *me*, none of it *is* strange. To *me*, it's fact—a firm description of the world as I've always experienced it, as clear as the nose on my face, as unchanging as the ocean being blue and the sun being yellow. It's what *my* senses say just *is*. To *me*, knowing that *3* and *5* are boys and that the number *7* is sharp and tastes metallic isn't strange at all. Nor is it odd that distinguishing between spoken words or names with similar letter patterns is hard. For example, I consistently send email meant for Lindsey, my editor, to Leslie, my publicist, and vice versa. Both women's names begin with a tall *L* followed by a "male" vowel and finish up with an *e*. Even if I'm *hearing* them, I'm really *seeing* them—which is why, if I'm going to have a shot at getting it right, I have to close my eyes briefly, concentrate hard on the name I want to see, then stare at the *To:* box, all before I type. And none of that is remotely peculiar . . . to *me.*

From my perspective, what's strange, or even sad, is that others *don't* see or taste or hear those things. Neurotypicality seems such a foreign, depleted reality. A place I've come to understand intellectually but still can't quite believe.

A World You Don't See: Synesthesia

Picture what it would be to grow up in a world where most people *don't* see color. Not the yellow-green of new grass or the rich, warm tones of pine forests, not the blood red of rubies or the deep pinks of blood oranges. They don't see it. But you do. Your eyes look, your brain knows, your mouth speaks—and the words sound like nonsense to everyone who listens.

Imagine the confusion of being small and innocently describing the world you know, only to watch as heads shake, brows raise, and eyes roll. Adults dismiss you. Kids inch away. Imagine the loneliness of not being understood. The hurt of being disregarded. Imagine what seeds of lifetime self-doubt are planted—what permanent paradigms are being created: maybe, somehow, you really *are* imagining it all . . . or worse, maybe you *are* crazy.

When you can do all of that, you have a sense of what it is to inhabit an invalidated mind. Your truth is denied, disregarded, and disdained, and by proxy, so are you. This is what it was like for me as a child, realizing that my own mother had no idea what I was talking about. Discovering early that being honest meant that *I* didn't make sense. That I couldn't trust what my own eyes saw or ears heard. That no one else talked about colored numbers or girl letters. Four years old, and already I felt strange, and stupid, and even a little bit scared. So I pretended I was like everyone else and said nothing more.

Nothing, that is, until, as an adult, I happened upon a book called *Wednesday Is Indigo Blue.* The author described how, to him, there was an overlap between the way he conceived of days of the week and color. The experience is called *synesthesia*, a rare neurological circumstance in which information from one sense automatically triggers the brain to engage a second sense. Those with synesthesia, he wrote, might taste music or associate personality, color, or even gender to letters, numbers, or the calendar. They might even see sounds as well as hear them.

Flabbergasted, I shut the book, looked up in astonishment, and announced to Barnes & Noble that "It really *is* a thing! Eight really *is* green!" Needless to say, more than a few people edged their reading a little further away. But I could not have cared less.

According to an article on the American Psychological Association's (APA) website, "Everyday Fantasia: The World of Synesthesia," the phenomenon derives its name from the Greek, meaning "to perceive together," and occurs in several, sometimes overlapping, varieties. Some of those with synesthesia hear, smell, taste, or feel pain in color. Others taste shapes, and still others perceive written digits, letters, and words in color.

Then there are synesthetes who also possess what researchers call "conceptual synesthesia": they see abstract concepts, such as units of time or mathematical operations, as shapes projected in the space around them (which accounted perfectly for the virtual touch screen of ideas I see). And many synesthetes—a group that clearly included me—experience in multiple, sometimes overlapping varieties.

The APA article concluded with one final are-you-*kidding*-because-apparently-they've-been-watching-me-for-decades: "The condition is not well known," it read, "in part because many synesthetes fear ridicule for their unusual ability. Often, people with synesthesia describe having been driven to silence after being derided in childhood for describing sensory connections that they had not yet realized were atypical."

It was stunning, breathtaking déjà vu all over again . . . this was me. That was my life. Only a year or so after I had *finally* found validation in a thing called "autism," I was finding further legitimacy in recognizing something totally different—"synesthesia."

Except . . . that wasn't quite right, either. In reading through the most recent research I could find, I quickly discovered that in happening upon it and identifying instantly as a synesthete, I had independently—and unknowingly—affirmed my own autism identification. Because, scientists had begun to confirm, autism and synesthesia were related—particularly among women.

In 2013, Professor Simon Baron-Cohen of Cambridge University was able to show a significant link between autism and synesthesia. His researchers tested 251 adults. Some participants were on the autism spectrum; some were not. Upon review, results indicated that synesthesia is nearly three times as common in adults with autism spectrum disorder than in the general population—and, according to the American Psychological Association, it is between three and six times more common in women. Put those numbers all together, and the significance of synesthesia to the female experience of autism cannot be denied.

Carol Povey, director of the UK's National Autistic Society, for whom I hold great personal and professional affection, reacted to Baron-Cohen's findings with curiosity and respect. People on the spectrum often "find [aspects] of everyday life confusing," she empathized. "Research like this . . . helps us to improve our understanding of autism . . . and about the ways people with autism experience the world."

In hindsight, Dr. Baron-Cohen acknowledged, the links between autism and synesthesia make a lot of sense.

As infants, everything we know, we know through sense. It's intrinsic to survival. A newborn turns her head at the scent of her mother's breast. Thrives on human touch. Startles drastically at a loud noise or unexpected movement. And all along the way, as soon as six weeks into our new little lives, those baby brains are cleaning house, "pruning" away at some nerve connections and making way for other, more complex links. That process, called *apoptosis*, gradually reduces the amount of sensory information that we take in. Too much of a good thing is, after all, too much. The wealth of input we relied upon as newborns can get in the way of other, "higher-order" thinking processes, like language, logic, and so on.

Therein lies the kicker. Neurologically, both autism and synesthesia involve overconnectivity of neurons in the brain. In both conditions, the "pruning away" doesn't occur at the usual rate. Because our brains retain some of those connections beyond infancy, those of us with autism *and* those of us with synesthesia find ourselves flooded with sensory information that neurotypical people can literally no longer access. But we can. We do. We're not imagining things. Our brains literally *do* perceive some things in ways most people cannot. And sometimes, yes, our brains literally *cannot* perceive other things in ways most people can.

Staying calm, focusing, seeing the "bigger picture" (both literally and metaphorically) rather than getting caught in the proverbial weeds is tough to do while the world bombards your senses. It's a bit like having the worst headache in the middle of Christmas mall crowds while wearing an itchy wool sweater under strobe lights—while being asked to do calculus, ask your great aunt about her bunions, and rationally invest in the best 401(k) option. It just isn't going to happen. When sounds are louder and textures rougher and crowds feel more pressing, senses overload. Patience shortens. Emotions run high.

Which is a whole lot of explanation. The thing is, though, that I needed *all* of it—needed *all* of that *stuff*—just to validate myself *to myself*, much less to anyone else. To authorize me to even consider my own reality as legitimate. Once again, I'd discovered there *was* a word—a word for a part of me I'd tried to hide. And if there was an actual word, there had to be actual meaning to it. As before, I wasn't crazy. Or a liar. Or overdramatic. I was legitimately, accurately different. Yet once again, it took hearing myself in someone else's story for me to drop my guard. It took being able to cite published studies for me to tell anyone my story. It took knowing strangers would not instantly dismiss me or reject me. It took external validation before I would believe in the Me that had always been true.

Yet. Without the legitimacy of a profile to fit or a name to be called, my reality, my just-as-authentic-as-anyone-else's neurology, sounded like nonsense. *Even to me*. I'd learned to wear masks. To adopt other people's versions of truth and reject my own. And through that wide-open door came all harms that have ever been done to me by others or by myself.

Sketch the Portraits: The Masks We Wear

Across the board, studies report that autistic girls and women are more socially motivated than autistic boys or men. But my experience and the conclusion of prominent psychological studies is that "intraspectrum" social disparities aren't unique to autism. It takes a village to raise a child, not so much to take down a woolly mammoth. We may (finally) live in a world where anyone can do the child-rearing or mammoth hunting, but the sociological effect of millennia remains. Generally speaking, women have long relied upon community and interdependence. Our survival, and the survival of our children, required the strength of numbers. Is it any wonder, then, that our interactions would still be governed by such nuance and subtlety?

At the end of each annual well visit, pediatricians in the United States hand parents a strange-looking line graph. These clinical growth charts, printed in both pink and blue versions, plot the child's stature, weight, and body mass index as compared to other girls or boys of the same age. Girls evaluated against other girls. Boys against other boys. So, for example, at fifteen years old, a boy who is five feet nine is taller than 75 percent of his male peers. A girl of the same age reaches the seventy-fifth percentile at five feet six. We might, of course, call either child "tall." It's a gender-neutral descriptor. But the moniker's accuracy depends on likening girls to girls and boys to boys. If we compare across the sexes, the gender-neutral designation "tall" no longer makes sense. At five feet six, the same height as that *tall* girl, a boy is only in the thirty-fifth percentile for stature. He's not only *not* tall, he's not even average.

The same "true-true-unrelated" system *must* hold true for assessing autism. But often, it hasn't.

In 2012, Francesca Happ, a cognitive neuroscientist at King's College London, observed fifteen thousand boy-girl twins. Her research team measured the occurrence of "autistic traits" within that group, compared them against formal autism diagnoses, and came away with important, though sadly not surprising, results. When the boys and girls showed similar levels of autism characteristics, girls had to display either more significant intellectual disabilities than the boys, more behavioral problems than the boys, or more of both, in order to be diagnosed. In other words, objectively speaking, girls had to be "worse off" than boys to be identified as autistic even when they showed the same amount of overall "autistic-ness."

Kevin Pelfry, a leading autism researcher at Yale University's acclaimed Child Study Center and the father of a daughter on the spectrum, thinks he knows why. His team has discovered that the way in which the brains of girls with autism analyze social information is reduced, relative to neurotypical girls. To any autistic woman, this is not a big shock. Or even a little shock.

The *really* important finding is that the brains of girls with autism are *also* operating differently from the brains of *boys* with autism. Scans showed that each autistic girl's brain behaved more like that of a typical boy of the same age, which, compared to typical girls, has reduced activity in regions normally associated with socializing. The brain-activity measures of autistic girls would not be considered "autistic" in a boy. Instead, the brain of a girl with autism may be more like the brain of a typical boy than that of a boy with autism.

All of which is good to know but should *not* be misused to diminish or question the female experience of autism. *Autistic*, like *tall*, is a gender-neutral descriptor. The same hallmarks of autism—a specific set of qualities, challenges, and traits—are present regardless of sex. You'll find them in men, women, transgender people, and people who don't identify with any gender at all. But the assessment and impact of those traits has to be considered relative to what is typical for each biological sex.

Real life isn't studies or brain scans. Real life is playgrounds and lunchrooms, office parties and social cliques. Our self-images aren't established in an MRI machine. They're formed in relationship to and interaction with other girls and women. So, if our social competency is, by and large, akin to typical males, we most definitely *are* handicapped—a deficit that often begets exclusion, ridicule, depression, self-loathing, anxiety . . . and a lifetime of pretend.

Among autistic woman and girls (whether identified or not), there is, in fact, a social phenomenon known as "camouflaging." Simply put, it's a masquerade in which we work, both consciously and subconsciously, to "pass" as neurotypical. Or at least not autistic. Or autisticish. It's impersonating someone else's world. And it's a full-time job, with a declining success rate as we mature.

I've heard it said that when a woman declares, "I have nothing to wear today," she really means, "I don't have clothes that match who I am today." So, no, I certainly don't think playing with aspects of identity is unique to those of us whose neurology is different. I just know that being left out is awful. Being rejected is hell. And, that for some of us, camouflaging is about a lot more than just fitting in. For some of us, to paraphrase the musical *Rent*, being part of an "us" instead of a "them" is the stuff of dreams and miracles.

So we learn to parrot phrases and piece together personas. Many of us (yours truly included) fall in love with the theater as a way to try on movement, character motivation, voice modulation, even humor. Scripts tell us exactly what to say, and the stage directions literally *tell us* how people will react, so we know what to expect there—and in the world. We copy bits of pop culture and bits of the playground. We copy popular peers and read scores of biographies and psychology and sociology books, building theses out of therapy. We study YouTube tutorials. Mimic gestures. Master accents. We are walking metaphors. We're doing *this*. But we really mean *that*.

How good are we? Of course that depends on the person, the moment, the time. Here's what I can say. I grew up on theater. Danced for twenty years, acted in commercials. Starred in every school musical and, once I felt how powerfully a good persona could affect *everything* else in my life, bedecked myself in any outward marker of social success I could—an Ivy League diploma, sorority letters, a cheerleader's pompom.

Now let's talk speech. Mimicry is an autistic specialty. In spectrum kids, echolalia is not uncommon. Essentially, it's a calming verbal practice of repeating words, sounds, and phrases. In some, the behavior is quite obvious. In others, it is more subtle—looping song lyrics, TV or movie scripts, or . . . accents. We are ninja-level dialectic chameleons. For example, I studied Spanish for eleven years, and though neither of my parents knew Spanish, native speakers have always thought that I must've been raised on the language—specifically, I'm told, with distinctly Argentinian flair. And, though I was raised in the Northeastern US and have lived in the South since I was twenty-one, I can just as easily convince Brits that I'm a London native as Irish folk that I'm County Cork, born and raised.

Sure. Playacting can be great fun (just look at the number of people who cosplay!). It can be a survival skill for the stranger in the strange land. But in no case is wearing a neurotypical mask a game. Plainly put, it's a lose-lose situation for everyone.

If we don't camouflage well, we tend to find ourselves ridiculed, shamed, ostracized, or abused. If we *do* camouflage well, we can disguise ourselves right out of identification, not to mention out of the compassion, resources, and insight diagnosis can bring. Instead, our misunderstandings are misread. Our intentions mistaken. We are vulnerable to the presumptions we've allowed others to make about us about our abilities to discern friend from foe and predator from lover, about how much direction we really do need, or self-awareness we really do have.

As we grow into adolescence and womanhood, social rules get more complicated. Stakes get higher. Our gaffes get bigger and more dangerous. We make friends and fall in love, but we aren't particularly good at recognizing conflict in those relationships before they implode. As kids, maybe we were ignored at school. Now we're ghosted by someone we've been intimate with, clueless, until then, that there had ever been a problem. We may have burned bridges that impact the lives of our family members. Or have totally misread professional situations—like, perhaps, going into a biannual review prepared to ask for a raise, only to discover we're being let go. She says from personal experience.

These are the "failures" that feel relentless. Inescapable. Like cheap shots to the gut when your guard is down. We are pulling the carpet out from under ourselves, tripping into invisible pitfalls we've helped to dig. These are the "failures" we so often try to remedy by taking control of *something*—perfectionism, compulsions, addictions. Punishing our bodies. Punishing our own hearts.

Even if a woman has been identified, the day-to-day life of family, career, school, and community require a fluency that isn't our natural state. Paying bills on time and meeting deadlines and keeping appointments straight and remembering to send in my kid's field trip money while smiling casually enough to blend in with the other moms at the bus stop is harder for me than I can explain. Generally, I can't do it all. So, I try to do what shows, first. Make a good impression, even if I don't have the stamina or system in place to sustain myself. Or stay on track. Or know to ask for help. I'm embarrassed not to have my game together as others do. As it seems I should. As people expect that I will, even though they know I am autistic. Even though *I* know it.

So I just keep dancing as fast as I can. And when the mask finally feels too loose, when it really begins to slip, when I have no more energy or don't know how to reconcile who I am with who I'm meant to be—I run. And burrow. And hide. Like Milli Vanilli running offstage when the music began to skip. The exposure is too bright to bear. Bestselling author.

Genius. Award-winning parent. It's a lot to live up to when I can't even push "play" on my voicemail right now. The light is blinking, nagging at me, chastising me for avoiding such a basic chore. But as I look around the chaos of half-put-up Christmas decorations, hear the clanking of my daughter's fork against her ceramic mug as she stabs at frozen coffee . . . as I preside over a dog treat dispute, field room-mom emails, reschedule therapy appointments, request medication refills, submit a magazine article . . . and write a book. I know that I am too tired, too emotionally strained, and too nervous to keep the mask on—to respond rather than react or, as I must, think out every word before I text or type . . . I am too sensitized to even listen to the expectation or transferred emotion of a human voice on that danged machine. I literally *cannot* do it.

Sure, my autism diagnosis makes it clear why those things are true. Autistic neurology classically involves challenges to executive functioning skills, like difficulty with switching tasks and working memory, with scattered attention and social anxiety. But . . . explain all that to whoever called and left a voicemail. Or emailed (there are 3,446 unread messages in my inboxes at this moment). They won't care. May not even believe me. Not *every* time I step in it, anyway.

My IQ means I'm smart. My Wikipedia entry means I'm known. Neither means I am no longer *actually* autistic, which, in very many ways, is still what the world asks. Studies show, over and again, that in any group, *social* intelligence is actually five times more important to success than individual IQ. Well, my IQ is in the top 0.1 percent, globally, meaning that it's *higher*, on average, than 99.9 out of every hundred people. However. My ability to read the emotions of people *right in front of me* (never mind via email, phone, or text) is in the thirtieth percentile, *fewer* than seventy out of those same one hundred people. It's a tremendous, invisible skill gap. A disparity that is, and always will be, my greatest vulnerability. In this life, even as "one of the most prominent figures in the autism world," it's keep the label, keep the mask; I'm just trying to keep up. My head knows it's unfair. Illogical. Like asking a chair to be a table and being annoyed when it isn't very good at *being* a table. And yet . . . in my deepest heart of hearts . . . I still feel embarrassed. Still feel judged. Still judge myself.

There are few things as tragic as when we tacitly agree to the notion that our unchangeable truth is somehow invalid. Less than. Broken.

Wrong. That pretending is necessary for professional opportunity or personal acceptance. I've done it a million times in ways large and small, and I can tell you this: trying to hide in plain sight is frustrating, disorienting, isolating—an exhausting game of (only possible) short-term gains in exchange for very-certain long-term exclusion. When we agree to play, we not only hide and cast doubt upon our experiences. We've willingly participated in the invalidation of ourselves.

And when you have invalidated yourself, there is no limit to what you will allow others to do.

Tell the Stories: Behind the Mask

Which is why it's so important to explain what's going on behind the mask. To make you see what we see.

People on the spectrum can be particularly literal in our interpretation of language (which makes for all sorts of bumbling). Case in point, my encounter with the word *period*.

Information about the mysterious subject of "getting your period" had reached me in bits and pieces, some of it more reliable than the rest. What I *had* been able to nail down was "menstruation" had to do with sex, though I wasn't entirely sure how they were connected or what the mechanics were. So, really, I had the words *woman*, *egg*, *toilet*, and *period*. Well, chickens laid eggs. And eggs were sort of roundish, kind of the shape of a period (at the end of a sentence, of course). Clearly, then, it had to follow that when a woman got her period, it meant that she went to the bathroom, sat on the toilet, and kind of peed out a little pearl-shaped egg. A period.

Can you even imagine the look on my mother's face when I asked to see the period egg the next time she got hers? I still cringe for us both.

Which is all to say that literal interpretation—saying what we mean, expecting others to mean what they say, and having an absolute love-it-or-hate-it relationship with sarcasm—is a very real (and sometimes very embarrassing) part of the way we communicate and understand. Sometimes. But certainly not always. Not for all of us, in all circumstances.

Many of us also communicate through metaphor—through popular culture references or even lyrics to a song. It helps us assign an emotional, experiential vocabulary, an allegorical dictionary to access within our own internal dialogues when trying to process someone else's behavior and in trying to explicate ourselves to the neurotypical world.

In fact, the most frequent critique I've received to any of my writing is that I "use too much figurative language for autistic people." Which makes no sense. *I* am autistic. The way I speak is the way I think. And clearly, I think the way I understand. Perhaps the way I process or describe the world is not literal enough for *some* people. But here I find myself, again, slipping easily into the position of defending my right to call my own experience valid. Instead, I'll repeat the simple fact that "autistic people" are not a monolith. We are a diverse group with diverse daily experiences . . . just like everyone else in the world.

The point to be made here is an essential one: experience precedes identification. Invalidated realities are not the fault of those who live them. They are the frontiers for those who don't. Or at least, they should be.

Yes. I can morph and mask. I can camouflage. Can dress almost any part. But underneath, I am always Me, a woman who both leaves a little of herself with and takes a little of herself from every character she's ever played. Authentic and learned. I am Jenny. Whatever others think "Jenny"—or people like her—is "supposed" to be, I *am her.* And I am real.

I connect dots that typical minds don't see. I really *do* "catch words" and ideas in front of me as if they were on a giant touch screen. That really *is* how I think. It's how I can detect patterns within vast quantities of information, sometimes seeing arrangement, form, or relationship between experiences or facts that I encounter decades apart. It's also why I rely heavily on analogies. I'm really just connecting more dots—experiences, people, points in time—through stories. It's how I make Me make sense to others. And how I make *We*, those of us behind the masks, make sense to the world.

Actually, I just did it a moment ago. Here. In sharing my synesthesia story (really an analogous complement to my autism diagnosis), I invited you into a metaphor of sorts. I asked you to imagine yourself, seeing color in a colorblind world, and then to imagine the feelings of "otherness" you would experience. You stepped into a situation that is not your own. But it *is* mine, in parallel. And you had a way to relate to it. What could have continued to sound fantastic and feel downright weird now had the space and landmarks to become foreign, yet understandable. That's what analogies, metaphors, and stories do for me. They animate dry fact. Give life to bullet points. They behave like a translator does for words or a function does for numbers. Put in the unrelatable. The Other. Switch on the story. Out comes relevance. Humanity.

We see and are seen.

Which is an accomplishment. Communication, in the best of circumstances, isn't easy. It takes effort, purpose, and not a small amount of creativity, especially if whatever you're trying to explain *isn't* an experience many people share. It takes just as much to tease apart a reality that is a given to most, but for you is just a hinted-at, unclear set of expectations. Being an autism translator is a full-time job. Largely, that's because without even being aware of it, we are all operating based on assumptions. Everyone. Constantly. How you interpret my phrasing. How I read your body language. No person is a tabula rasa—a blank slate. Meaning that no matter how well you think you understand someone else—or yourself—any time you feel confused, there's a good chance that assumptions and misunderstandings are to blame.

In a lot of ways, we each live in our own little worlds—and we like those little worlds. But if we're going to connect with others in the *real* world, the trick is to stop arguing about whose "miniverse" is right and whose is wrong. Instead, we have to readjust our focus and learn to experience life together—as "and" instead of "but."

Which is harder than it seems. Every day, we hear old tapes playing in new situations instead of listening to what's actually being said. We overrely on past experiences and limited frames of reference to interpret entirely new events and people. We filter others' words and actions and then recalibrate them within our own minds to jibe with what's more familiar, logical, or understandable.

The result is a hodgepodge of distorted understanding. Of ourselves, of people we know casually, and of the people we love deeply. On most days, in many ways, we are very busy loving, despising, dismissing, and reacting to "facts" and folks that are, at least in part, fictional. And I believe that just isn't good enough.

Finding just the right way to convey a feeling can save a life. Having just the right explanation can save a soul. Words matter. Which is why I put so danged much energy into them. Into languages and translations and etymology and writing and speaking well. They're the best tool I have for making the world a safer place to be human.

In Spanish, the word *miga* refers to the white, squishy, doughy part of the inside of a roll or bagel or loaf of bread. One *palabra* says it all. Perfectly, concisely. One Spanish word for a whole bunch of English that doesn't even really specifically say the same thing and leads me to say, "You know what I mean?" even after all the effort. High school genetics gave me the same kind of beautifully elegant word: *phenotype*. (And yes, that was me using an analogy again.) In case you're foggy, there's genotype, the actual DNA sequences, and then there's phenotype, the way those genes are expressed, or show up. Phenotype is "how it looks in real life," like green eyes or red hair—or autism.

There is a time and a place for the evaluation of intricate data. There are professionals who are trained to discuss the genomes. I speak in stories and pictures. I speak phenotype because real-life experiences make the science make sense. And because, after all, we *are* talking about people. Not data.

See and Be Seen

Strangely enough, a lot of that talking happens in bathrooms. At least for me.

As far as I can tell, for most women, bathrooms are the settings for some of our lives' most significant, most human moments. They are great leveling fields. Confessionals where we share secrets, toilet paper, and maybe lipstick, building a sense of tribe among complete strangers.

When a truth gets too big to hold, it must be shared. From Phoenix to Copenhagen, from Birmingham, Alabama, to Birmingham, England, the "belle" curve silhouette is, at once, a revelation and the start of a revolution. And the truth of the ladies' room is that we, ladies, need room to find one another.

During every talk I give, I take care to mention the disparity in male to female identification. To mention my insistence that the animated superhero kids on the cover of my first book include a girl. To tick off at least some of that ever-expanding Chick-List Checklist. No matter the hosting continent, economy, or culture, for many in the audience, it's the first time they've ever considered the profile or seen the silhouette of a woman on the edges of the "belle" curve. It's the first time someone has spotted the patterns, sketched a framework of bullet points, and brought them to life—with stories from *her* own life.

Lift the mask. Use the metaphors. We see and are seen.

Nuns. Lesbians with blue hair. Dignified elderly women. Tweens in sassy T-shirts. Behind nervous giggles, through tears, in whispers—mothers knock on the stall door, girls hesitate behind me as I fix my eyeliner, professionals try to make conversation over paper towel dispensers.

"Excuse me, Jennifer," they begin. "May I ask you a quick question?"

It's the same question that I asked myself in 2011: What about me? Could this be my answer, too?

One by one, they approach with whispers braver than any loud-mouthed declaration. They come to me, a stranger, and speak aloud words that they've never said to anyone—maybe not even to themselves. Breathless voices catching, they explain how, in my stories, they've caught unexpected glimpses of themselves. And, between the noisy hand dryers and toilet flushes, they gift me with the most vulnerable, sentient, existential moments of their lives.

It's a story of such proportion that even my own daughter thought it *must* be hyperbole. Then, at age thirteen, she traveled to New York with me. After the keynote, I began to walk her to the ladies' room and, as we got closer, asked her to give me some space. "They'll come, Maura," I promised. She looked back over her shoulder. "Mom," she whispered, her eyes gone wide, "they already are. They really actually *are* following you to the bathroom." Much to her surprise, I hadn't exaggerated. Though I *did* give it a second thought. Maybe they *were* following. Or maybe they were joining. Either way, the conversations came, just as they always do.

"I came here today," the women say, "for [insert 'my clients' or 'my patients' or 'students' or the name of a loved one]. But when I heard you speak . . . I realized, so many things made so much sense . . . because, you were talking about me. And suddenly, *everything* makes *so* much sense. I'm sure I'm the only one bothering you like this. It's just that I never, ever knew *what* was different about me . . . and now I do. I think I'm on the spectrum, too."

Labelish, Much?

We're taught that "labels," as a rule, are limiting. That they lead to stereotyping and discrimination. Certainly, that can be true if the label is *used* by someone with limited understanding. It's been my experience, though, that labels can also be a powerful way of communicating a lot of information in effective, emotionally resonant ways.

Long before my first baby could read, she knew her logos. Mommy would always stop to answer the siren call of that little green coffee mermaid. As her brothers came along, they, too, learned the power of the logo—the hypnotic beckoning of the big red bull's-eye or the promise of new entertainment when a little bitty apple was spotted. Let's face it. Marketing execs the world over pay big bucks to ensure that from our beginnings, we understand the superpower of branding. And they're good at what they do.

It all begins with a label, or "logo," from the ancient Greek *logos*, meaning "word." Like our modern iteration, beyond the literal, *logos* carried philosophical weight, connoting "opinion" or "expectation." *Logos* alluded to reputation in the same way that, today, we have one expectation for a gift arriving in a little blue box, and a very different one for dining experiences held underneath the golden arches. Logos. Labels. Associated expectations. Branding is powerful stuff. Few among us would ever admit to being "label hos" (yes, it's an actual entry in *Urban Dictionary*). We all know that an *LV* on a handbag does not make its owner more fabulous. But we still buy a whole lot of stuff hoping that a little bit of the cachet will rub off.

Like it or not, we are all consumers and bearers of label mania.

Never mind materialism. Our very *names* are labels that connote all sorts of socioeconomic, ethnic, and demographic information about those who gave them. The word *noun* comes from the Latin *nomen*, meaning "name." Which makes perfect sense. The function of a noun *is* to name a person, place, feeling, or idea in a standardized way. In that sense, *all* nouns (and even the adjectives describing them) are language logos, stylized by font or tone of voice, and transmitting expectation, nuance, value.

Whether communicated by an image or a word . . . the mark, the "brand" that is left behind, the point that is made is emotional. Maybe that's why major advertisers prefer simpler logos; the most successful use only an image (Starbucks, Nike) *or* only copy (J.Crew, Prada). We may "see" a label as a picture or text or "hear" it, as we do when we read or listen. Either way, the end product is an impression . . . a feeling: scared or uncomfortable, empowered or valued.

Labels and logos are handy because they work. Divvying a crazy, chaotic world into bite-sized, known quantities, they are sort of a comfortable, emotional shorthand. Familiarity. It's why parents love chain restaurants. We don't have to wonder if our kids will dig the fries at this burger joint. It's McDonald's, and everyone knows the fries are exactly the same, no matter where in the world you order. We know what we're getting.

Or do we? How reliable is that shorthand—that "known quantity"—if the underlying information is bad? Labels and logos cause major heartburn (and heartache) when the "known quantity" is, apparently, not as well known as some might think. The problem isn't that labels or logos are bad. The problem is that in the mouths of uninformed users—many who profess to be experts—they can be very inaccurate.

We're *all* still learning. Even about things we think we know well. To believe anything else is hubris.

More often than not, *Asperger Syndrome* and *autism* are unwanted labels that come with matching sets of equally uncomfortable visuals. Doors shut. Conversations stall. Sympathy is offered. Never was there a "You've just been diagnosed—are you going to Disney World?" celebration (which is why I actually created a "Congratulations!" package for newly diagnosed folks). A realistic picture of autistic people does *not* include *Rain Man*. It *does* include Nobel Prize winners, beauty queens, poets, and even a Ghostbuster.

If that insight is surprising, notice the disconnect between perception and fact and consider how much more there is to learn. If it's not surprising, consider how much more there is to learn, as well. Nothing new happens in the world because everyone looks around and says, "Yup. It's all good. We've got this figured out. Everything's the way it should be." The world only changes—grows—stretches and changes and evolves and gets beautifully, magically better when someone thinks differently and does differently, too. History is full—*full*—of wonderfully amazing people who fit a spectrum profile . . . they're the same folks who fill history textbooks and "who's who" lists . . . because they include some of the world's most memorable minds. And a whole lot of nonsavant, folks next door, too.

When wielded with proper care, a label can be an incredibly helpful descriptor appropriate to a particular situation—an element of identity, not an entire identity. Think of Clark Kent. Bruce Wayne. Diana Prince. You could also call them Superman, Batman, and Wonder Woman. Each alter ego describes some important aspect of the hero, but none reveals the complete character.

Words *are* powerful. They can inspire love and hope. And yes, they can also spread hate and cruelty. I know what it is to be called a slut and a whore and a bitch with no moral character by people who were meant to love me. I can still feel the sting and shame and desperation. So yes, I understand—very intimately—the impact words can have. And. There's a reason *bitch* and *queer* and *autistic* can be repossessed and transformed from insults into agents of empowerment and solidarity. Labels, in of themselves, don't cause the damage. People do.

I could be called *female*, *adult*, *parent*, *pet lover* . . . any word is true and may help others to understand me, depending upon the circumstances, yet none is a complete descriptor. There's also *history buff*, *dancer*, *writer*, *seafood lover*. The descriptor most relevant to the situation is the one that is most helpful. *Writer* isn't going to help me when I look for a restroom—*female* does. That's why I ask for the "ladies' room" not the "writers' room."

At the most basic level, a label is a communication tool that helps us effectively ask for and get what we need. When I was seven years old, I flunked the school's eye exam. Apparently, I was pretty darned nearsighted. So, how, my mother asked me, had I never noticed a problem? I'm sure I *would* have at some point, but I could easily see the paper in front of me—I just presumed that the limits of my sight were the same as everyone else's. My body was my normal; it still is. Without comparison, I had no idea other kids could see farther and more clearly.

There was a time when moms said, "Boys don't make passes at girls who wear glasses!" Should I have been denied the tools (glasses and then contact lenses) that made the world more manageable? Would "four eyes" (which I was never actually called) have been reason to let me try and muddle through, wondering why more and more of life's tasks seemed ill fit for me? Of course not. Give the kid glasses, tell others to close their mouths, and be sure to use whatever you need to be your best. Heck, without those lenses, I would never be able to see the letters in front of me now—so thank goodness for diagnosis and resources. They have helped me maximize my abilities, and never have I felt ashamed for having less-than-typical retinas.

I have heard partners, parents, and professionals complain that an individual is "academically brilliant but socially very immature, and awfully particular about everything." They may see us, as children *or* adults, struggling and hurting. They want guidance. But when answers to their inquiries include the possible label *autism* . . . conversations often end. Fast.

Ego is a powerful thing. This summer, a mother approached me at the Autism Society of America's national conference. She explained that her son was on the spectrum, that she'd come to hear me speak once before, and that apparently I'd really made her angry at the time. Anger frightens me in a deep way, so I'll admit, I got a bit nervous and started looking for ways to politely exit the conversation. The woman, however, went on without seeming to notice. "Yep, I talked to you at the book signing afterwards. I had questions about my son and everything you said really helped." At which point I was utterly confused, so I just nodded and neutrally half-smiled. I had no idea where this was headed.

"You'd discussed a little bit about girls having trouble, too, so I also mentioned a couple of things that were going on with my daughter. You listened and asked a few questions and then said I really ought to look into getting her *tested*!" I was, at this point, truly uncomfortable. Even a little bit scared. But, as is my habit, I said nothing. Did nothing. I just stood there, embarrassed and shaky, and let her continue, "I thought to myself, 'Who the *hell* does this damned woman thinks she is?'"

She scoffed indignantly at me and shook her head. I readied myself for the worst to come. "Well, guess what? About a year later, she was diagnosed with Asperger's, too. You were right!" Knock me down with a feather, but the woman was actually *laughing*. I, on the other hand, was shell-shocked by the intensity of disdain she had apparently felt for me when I'd clearly been trying to help. I really do hate that feeling.

After an awkward "I'm so glad; thanks for sharing," I made my way out of the hall, wondering just one thing: why had it been okay for her son to have autism but not her daughter? Was it just a matter of "Oh no, not both of them," or was the issue that, as a woman, the girl was more an extension of herself? Was it something else altogether? I guess I'll never really know the answer. What I *do* know, however, is that if I had a dollar for every time the parent of someone I know personally has come to me—repeatedly!—concerned about their child (aged two to twenty-two), only for them to shrink back, almost offended after the fact, I'd be rich. After it had happened a time or two, I got *really* careful about my script, being certain to practice active listening, suggesting, if appropriate, that it might be helpful to review an online spectrum checklist, provide a link, and offer to talk afterwards, if needed.

Which *literally* got me "reported" to the school administration for "diagnosing children on the playground" *and* instructed not to use the words *Asperger's* or *autism* on campus again.

My kids don't go there anymore.

I understand that people often ask questions to which they don't really want truthful answers. But, come *on*. My area of expertise is autism. You're coming to me because, obviously, you have some thought or feeling that the label might fit. Don't be mad at me when I (very gently) agree *only* that it's worth looking into! I am *not* a psychologist or a psychiatrist, which means that I cannot actually make a diagnosis of any sort. However, I do know what I'm talking about. In *every* case where I've referred *anyone* for a formal evaluation—*every single one*—my intuition has been confirmed. Strangely, only parents have ever reacted negatively . . . parents who have come to *me*, not the other way around. The adults who ask for themselves cry, too, just not in grief. They cry as I did. Out of gratitude and hope.

What this all boils down to is that with better public understanding of what autism really is (and isn't), the label can finally be helpful rather than daunting. Just try to assemble some Ikea furniture if the directions are all in Swedish. When you can't figure out what's what, or what to do with it, your new bed is never going to evolve beyond a pile of *djonk*. Yes. Labels can be used to do harm. They also have an immense power to heal. We don't withhold medicine because it can be misused. Neither can we avoid potential good by shirking our responsibility to challenge stigmas and correct misinformation. If we don't, words that we can use to change lives for the better will, instead, be allowed to remain a source of self-loathing and desperation. Fear and shame are the undoing of kindness and the antithesis of empathy. And we are left to pay for the shortcomings of others.

Far from a curse, an autism diagnosis offers the gift of a label signifying authentic self-awareness, acceptance, and true empowerment. If only each person could hear what I do, as many times as I do, in as many ways and in as many places as I do—she would know what I know: that she never was the only one. She may have been unrecognized. Invalidated. She may have worn thin an ill-fitting mask, without a community, a vocabulary, or a path. Yet even in that loneliness, she was one of so many.

What's it like to be us? Too much. We *feel* too much. *React* too much. *Say* too much. *Need* too much. So says the world. I say: the world is wrong. There is an exquisite trade-off for a life so differently led: complex imagination, limitless curiosity, profound compassion, and restless independent thought. They are the core of everything I am. They will be responsible for whatever legacy I leave behind.

Having now appeared live before hundreds of thousands of people worldwide, I can say that I have never met a girl born before the mid-1990s who was ever even considered for an Asperger Syndrome diagnosis. If they were nonverbal or showed lower cognitive abilities, *female* and *autism* might be spoken together, otherwise, no. Girls had to be *more* obviously affected in *more* ways to be noticed, which is likely why experts believed that, on average, girls with autism had more severe symptoms and more significant intellectual disabilities. Those days are not long gone.

Bright, verbose, articulate, sensitive, intense girls and women—some introverted, some stage divas, some trendsetters, some followers, and some leaders—can be just as "autistic" as the guys and still not be seen by "experts." Or by ourselves.

For those of us born before the midnineties, the most common route to identification is the one I took—the mother of spectrum kids, recognizing myself and my history in my children's present day. At age sixty, fifty, forty, thirty, so many have suffered for so long without the one, accurate identifier that could change everything. And we are asking, now . . . is it finally our turn to make sense?

Without question, there is growing awareness of that underexplored place where women, girls, and autism intersect, and that is great news. At Harvard University, Yale's Child Research Center, UCLA, the University of Washington, the Cleveland Clinic, Cambridge University, King's College London, University College London, Deakin University in Australia, the University of Lausanne in Switzerland, and other major learning centers, important research on the topic has been and is currently being conducted. The result will be a plethora of important advantages for my daughter's generation and those who come afterward. But. Accurate research presupposes the analysis of a quantitatively, as *well* as a qualitatively, significant subject pool. Which creates a certain chick-and-egg quandary. More sensitive, accurate, and gender-appropriate diagnostic tools are necessary to overcome camouflaging and clinical bias and establish a larger, more diverse and representative population eligible for study. By the same token, a larger, more diverse, and representative population has to be identified in order to sensitize and improve gender-appropriate diagnostic tools. But what about *now*? How can that gap be filled in *now*? How can the tide of delayed identification be stemmed *now*, while science plays catch-up?

The answer, I believe, is to listen to those of us who have found our way to identification. Lift the mask. Spot the patterns. Sketch an ever-improving portrait. Then tell our stories around the world.

I have become a Teller *and* Keeper of Stories. A guardian, not an owner. Witness to the disorientation, anger, exhalation, hope, relief . . . sounding board for the frustration and unanswered questions. Why don't professionals know more? Why don't they understand more? Why are so many sisters of spectrum brothers dismissed—their struggles equally real, yet routinely overlooked? Why, after enormous investments of time, money, and energy in "expert" guidance, do so many women and girls still walk away, characters questioned, unhelped, without even compassion or recognition?

Autism. Synesthesia. In both cases, I had to recognize myself in *someone else's* story for me to drop my guard—had to have external validation before I could consider believing my own mind. Right now, there are thousands of women still camouflaged, even from themselves. And while I can't answer all of their questions, I *can* lift the mask.

Point out the patterns. Sketch them into portraits and, right here, be the someone else in the stories . . . so that we can all see and be seen.

Nothing—not even a green number *8*—is as real or as unbelievable as that.

First the portraits. Then the stories.

The "Chick-List Checklist" A Portrait of Women, Girls, and Our Unique Autism Style

- Women and girls are more apt to find less detectable ways to limit or avoid eye contact. We may look at the space between a speaker's eyes in order to reassure them of our attention, while simultaneously reducing our sensory input by avoiding a direct gaze and thus be able to listen to what's being said. If I really focus on looking at someone in a personal conversation, I lose my train of thought almost immediately. So I brought my theatrical training into everyday life. When listening, I will make brief eye contact, accompany it with a nod or smile, then look off into the middle distance as if considering what I'm hearing. If I'm speaking, I may angle my head so that I can cast my gaze slowly but sharply down and to the left, then ahead again, then slowly upward to the right—very practiced theatrical techniques that are both attractive *and* communicate, "I am thinking about what you're saying *or*, extemporaneously, about what I'm saying." In either case, because it's done with a certain amount of "art," until or unless it's pointed out, most people don't notice anything unusual about my eye contact.
- Unlike our male counterparts, it's the level of intensity and almost-professorial knowledge about our special interest, rather than the interests themselves, that set us apart from neurotypical peers.

- Frequent passions (a.k.a. special interests) include genealogy and timelines, Disney, mythologies, folklore, cosplay, history and historical fiction, time travel, literature and literary figures, language, animals, anime, fashion, music, and theater.
- Special interests provide two primary functions: they give our brains a pleasurable topic on which to ruminate and perseverate, and they act as a social buffer, transportation to a distant time, place, species, or social scenario where interpersonal rules, hierarchies, and customs can be "studied and mastered."
- People on the spectrum are much more likely to experience synesthesia. Girls are three times more likely to be synesthetes.
- Gender identity varies with great obviousness among spectrum females. More commonly expected is some level of androgyny in clothing preference and a fluid sexual self-concept. But just as many of us greatly enjoy a rich, distinctly "womanly" sensuality and/or strongly identify with a more classic-Hollywood female aesthetic. And most of us fall in the thousands of spaces in between. As always, there are as many ways to embrace and embody "female" as there are people living the experience.
- Lining up our collections—of books, figurines, dolls, collectibles—is one of the ways we "play," at *all* ages. The enjoyment comes more from setting precise "tableaux"—miniatures, fairy gardens, replicas, even Barbie weddings—rather than engaging in spontaneous, interactive activities.
- Scripting from favorite TV shows, books, plays, and movies is one of the ways we mask social anxiety best. We copy the dialogue perfectly though often miss the innuendos beneath.
- Girls often hyperfocus on one, all-encompassing "best friendship" (and later, romantic relationship), which

evolves into an all-or-nothing self-concept. Girls desperately want friendship and easily direct an inordinate amount of energy and emotion toward someone perceived as "theirs."

- We can have a very difficult time navigating the complexities and nuances of female friendships, which, in comparison to male friendships, rely more acutely on storytelling (though our nonlinear thinking linear and easy distractibility tend to stall conversations instead of furthering them) and emotional and conversational reciprocity (though we can't shift perspectives, unwittingly tend to dominate "air time," and neglect to ask open-ended questions).
- Oversharing or sharing with the wrong people in the wrong circumstances is a common downfall.
- We tend not to act *out* as often as we act *in*. We focus the majority of our anger and frustration at ourselves. If we get in trouble, it's much more likely for sounding like a "know-it-all" or for trouble regulating our moods.
- We are frequent victims of abuse, though we may not understand it as such, and tend to feel overwhelming compassion or sympathy for those who hurt us.
- Girls on the spectrum are often word- or linguistically based thinkers with a keen interest in word and phrase origins, foreign language, and regional accents—which we have an uncanny ability to imitate.
- We frequently have a strong connection to poetry and song lyrics and can detect incredibly subtle patterns within both.
- It is not uncommon to see us collecting and rescuing animals.
- Spectrum girls are more likely to gather and memorize as much information as we can on social rules, social psychology, and sexual expectations. It's our way of compensating for what others pick up naturally.

- We tend to be socially naive, blind to others' motives, and have a tough time clearly distinguishing between levels of a social hierarchy.
- It's not *always* making friends that's difficult. Often, it's our tendency to be unaware of strain in the relationship and/or the sustained effort attention required to maintain relationships that are our downfall.
- Our friendships can be broken down into eras where close ties end abruptly, though the cause of the "breakups" may elude us as we break hearts and provoke tempers without even realizing it.
- We find it difficult to understand manipulation, disloyalty, vindictive or cruel behavior, and social retaliation (because we cannot see strategy or perspective).
- Throughout our lives, we often gravitate toward people who are older and/or younger than us, rather than direct peers. The relationships we prefer have clear roles and rules and less need to spontaneously negotiate dialogue, compromise, and group dynamics. In a situation where we are older, we understand that we are in the teacher/leader/big-sister role, so it's all right to be more didactic. That we're actually *expected* to take the wheel, so to speak. On the other hand, if we're the younger, we can settle into an apprentice role—watching, learning, and following along.
- Girls on the spectrum may feel more intensely connected to fictional or historical characters than to real people.
- Biographies (books, documentaries, films) are a favorite way to study people and from their strategies, choices, accomplishments, and relationships develop a larger personal emotional vocabulary and learn "how to be."
- Hyperlexia—very early, very fast, self-taught, highly skilled reading—is common among spectrum girls.
- Girls on the spectrum are often particularly sensitive to artistic, pattern-based mathematical realities, extending

their concrete knowledge adeptly into musical cadence and visual art.

- Many girls find it very tough to clearly distinguish between levels of social hierarchy.
- We tend to be socially naive, blind to others' motives, have trouble distinguishing acquaintances from close friends, or define what constitutes an actual friendship (we haven't had enough experience).
- For many girls, "show-womanship" skills far exceed comfort with spontaneous or one-on-one social interaction. Intuitive use of this sidestep around social anxiety can lead to excellence in teaching, narrative presentation, litigation, and performance.
- Perfectionism is the all-hallowed deity (and nemesis) of the majority of spectrum girls.
- Challenges with impulsivity, problem-solving, emotional balance, and compulsions make us vulnerable to substance use/abuse (alcohol/prescription and nonprescription drugs) as well as process addictions (eating disorders, self-harm, skin picking, acting out sexually, shopping, gambling), despite our awareness of the negative impact on our lives.
- Eating disorders, like binge eating, anorexia nervosa, and bulimia, are indicators of perfectionist tendencies, a need for artificial control, extreme rigidity, and adherence to routine. They are exponentially more present among girls and women and should be considered serious "red flags."
- Females are more likely than males to try to manage anxiety, depression, trauma, and low self-esteem through self-harming behaviors, such as cutting and skin picking.
- Everything we do, we do intensely and often spend a great deal of time analyzing our own thinking processes (metacognition) as well as larger, complex ideas.

CHAPTER 3

Life with the Volume Turned Up: Intense Minds, Intense . . . Everything

I believe that kitchens are for dance parties (and brownies). That there is no such thing as too much glitter or too many "I love yous." I believe that being brave means feeling afraid and doing it anyway. That life is an endless feast of adventure and possibility and wonder. That thoughts really can be felt across distance and time. That improvisation is the stage of genius. I believe in children. And magic. In connection. In wild brilliance and fierce love. I believe in go big or go home. In doing. In singing loudly and crying hard and speaking your heart in spotlights. I believe that curiosity is essential to living. That you're never too old. And that the whole point of this crazy life is to give the gift of these words: "I see you. I hear you. I believe you. And you are wonderful."

In 2016, *Scientific American* ran an article about autism in women and girls. The piece contained a significant section about me and included this description: "On the outside, she looked pretty much the opposite of autistic." Of course, I *am* autistic. So I can't really look the opposite of what I *am*. But Maia Szalavitz, the author (who has since become a friend), was smart in her choice of expression. The entire reason her words—in an internationally esteemed publication—made immediate sense is that the caricature of a disconnected, disinterested, distant introvert is *that* pervasive. It's also *that* wrong.

I'm autistic. I'm also a Gryffindor. An *Anne of Green Gables* kindred spirit. A Myers-Briggs ENFP—extrovert, intuitive, feeling, perceiving. The "imaginative motivator" whose personality profile reads as follows:

> Warmly enthusiastic and imaginative, you easily find meaning and significance in situations and events, and see connections that others don't. You are interested in almost everything and bring a zest to life that draws people to you. You are insightful and keenly perceptive about people. . . . You experience a wide range of feelings and intense emotions. . . . You express your deepest values with passionate intensity.*

My mother has read that summary. So have my closest friends and my kids. They all agree with my eleven-year-old's summary: "Yep, sounds just like Mommy." Just maybe not the personality associated with "autistic." But that's my point. There's no such thing as an *autistic* personality. According to Myers-Briggs, there are sixteen different personality types. I say there are infinite types. Certainly, there are infinite types of people who also happen to be autistic. Why we do what we do always makes sense, if not to those who observe from a distance. Behavior assessment paperwork that parents, individuals, spouses, and teachers are asked to complete as part of an autism screening literally lists scores of behaviors and asks how often they are "a problem." Blatant criticism masked as neutral—or maybe even compassionate—inquiry.

Counselors and psychologists often remind their clients that "comparison is the thief of joy." I couldn't agree more. Yet those assessments reveal a hypocritical truth: even among the mental health community, we are judged in comparison—"hypersensitive," "overreactive," "too much." We are evaluated by pathology. Which raises the question: who is any one person to decide that another—let alone a whole group of others—is "hyper" anything or "overly" anything or "too" anything? If, instead, those who evaluate us could live just a single day *as* one

---

* Myers-Briggs Type Indicator ® Interpretive Report Copyright 1988, 1998, 2005 by Peter B. Myers and Katharine D. Myers. https://chatsworthconsulting.com/assessments/MBTISampleReport.pdf]

of us, all that is deemed "problematic" would, instead, be understood as perfectly logical responses to the uniquely intense way in which we experience thought and sensation (and emotion, but that's the next chapter). Yes, it can be challenging. It can be overwhelming. It can be a circumstance where support is appreciated. And. It can also be a radiating, beautiful kind of "alive" that typical minds never know.

Splat! People

In 1851, Dr. Samuel Cartwright, a physician from Louisiana, observed a behavior particular to African Americans, yet absent completely among whites. African Americans tended to run away from slave plantations. Caucasians, on the other hand, did not. Cartwright held that contented submission was part of the psychological portrait of the "Negro race." Deviance from that accepted persona was, therefore, unnatural to the mental makeup of the group, with the extreme behavior clearly endemic to a diseased or disordered mind.

Drapetomania, or "runaway madness," continued to appear in medical publications as late as 1915. Which, is, at best, shockingly preposterous pseudoscience . . . and, at worst, irresponsibly dehumanizing prejudice. This is, after all, the twenty-first century. We are evolved. Sophisticated. Unbiased. Modern science doesn't imagine illnesses to account for its own prejudice or lack of understanding. We don't extrapolate stereotypes and proclaim them absolutisms. Not anymore. Right?

Wrong.

This is the point where I'm compelled to sneak in, tap our oh-so-enlightened world on its collective shoulder, and say, "Hey, remember the one about pride going before the fall? Well, 'splat!' people." Hindsight is twenty-twenty. It also happens to be seriously haughty. New century. New group. Same old song and dance.

Getting a grip on big things can be overwhelming. Big ideas. Big feelings. Big quantities. For all of our genius and imagination—and there is so very much of both—there is no shame in feeling small as a child does on the edge of a vast ocean. We are right to be humbled before the scope and majesty of this universe. To be intrigued and inspired and more than a little daunted when considering the dimensions of space, the meaning of life, or the complexities of the human genome. It's just that feeling "daunted" or "overwhelmed" is uncomfortable and unsatisfying. And we don't like uncomfortable.

We're a curious species—always looking under rocks and inside other people's medicine cabinets. We're also very fond of being in control. Which is why when we find ourselves facing those "too big to swallow" mysteries, we make them smaller. We compartmentalize and sort. We make rules and rulings. It's how we make sense of the world—and it's not evil. It's just too binary. Fifty years ago, we classified our species into male and female. Either/or. Today, countries all around the world have law in place to protect the civil rights of a spectrum of gender identities. Fifty years ago, we classified our species by color. There was no "other" box to check. Today, we know that race is a concept that is, at its simplest, part biology and part sociology.

When I first read about Dr. Cartwright, I literally spit out the soda I'd been drinking. It was so ridiculous in so many ways, but the one that really struck me was his total lack of perspective. Was this guy more arrogant or ignorant? I wondered. Did his arrogance keep him ignorant? This "scientist" lived in a time and place where he witnessed, firsthand, the dehumanizing conditions in which enslaved people existed. The poverty. The broken families. The abuse. How could he *not* understand the logic of wanting to escape that hell on Earth? The answer, of course, was simple. Cartwright and his contemporaries considered African Americans as a diminished version of human. Different and apart. Apples and oranges. It would not have made sense to him to even wonder what he might feel or do in their place. Looking through his lens, from the outside in, their behavior would never be understood for what it was—rational, relatable, and very, very human.

If neurology, like race or gender, is, indeed, a spectrum of experience, neither good nor bad (as many believe is the case), then our reactions to the world we inhabit are as valid and logical as everyone else's. They seem less so only because we are, for most practical purposes, *also* understood as a diminished version of human.

Cartwright drew his limited, inaccurate conclusions on the nature of African Americans from the outside. He couldn't square what he saw with what he believed, because real African American people are not caricatures whose realities are dictated by prescription, myth, or stereotype. Neither are real autistic people. The experience of life from within any group has to be described by members of that group.

Mankind is saturated, in countless ways, with color and variety and scope. Our genes prove it. Sort us, and there is still more diversity within, not among, those smaller groups. Culling data is fine as an initial method of research, but it can't be the paradigm or the endpoint. Our brains tend naturally to superimpose familiar experiences onto foreign ones. Meaning we assume a lot. We project a lot. And we misunderstand a lot. In trying to simplify, we often *over*simplify and diminish the respect that natural complexity deserves.

Championing the Human Spectrum: Intellectual Intensity

When I was about six years old, I asked my mother, "Who am I?"

"What do you mean, who *are* you?" she replied. "You're Jenny."

Yeah, thanks. That much I had. As usual, what I meant didn't, apparently, match up with what I was actually saying. My chest tightened; my small brow furrowed in frustration. "No, Mom. What I mean is, who is *me*?" I pressed, straining to explain. "If I can say '*my* brain,' then my brain isn't me, it's something that *belongs* to me. And that'd be the same for '*my* spirit' and '*my*self.' You see? So, who is the *me* behind the '*my*'? You see?"

She didn't see.

Instead, she shook her head and turned around. "Jenny, aren't you exhausted from analyzing everything, all the time? I'm exhausted just from listening!"

Which, to me, made no sense at all. How did one *not* think all the time—about everything? How did anyone *not* want to learn everything about everything? How could anyone *not* wonder about big questions like this? What was more, how could something be so clear in my mind—yet utterly confuse everyone else around me? My mind, then *and* now, always felt transparent—every thought obvious—clearly visible to everyone.

By this point, my mom had (gladly, I'm sure) moved on to something else. But six-year-old me was stuck in my head, and in my heart. My ideas . . . feelings . . . fears . . . questions . . . were simple. I was a child. She an adult. Clearly, then, if I understood a question and its ramifications, *she* did. She'd told me I was exhausting her, only . . . I didn't know how to not be exhausting. I *was* only six, after all. Which meant that, in *my* mind, the only really "obvious" fact was that I wasn't worth answering. That understanding me was a bother. Connecting with me was unnecessary. A nuisance. Draining. Which meant that I, too, was unnecessary and a nuisance and draining.

My mom didn't really understand me. She often doesn't. And that can, alternatively, make her feel overwhelmed, proud, afraid, or embarrassed. But I can assure you, she never believed I was unnecessary or unlovable. Not ever. The thing is—*I* believed those things. I believed that *she* believed them. And I would have given anything on Earth to know how to be the super-smart, precocious redhead who made my mommy smile . . . yet didn't wear out my welcome before I even realized it.

More than thirty years later, I look back on us both with compassion and even some degree of regret. A six-year-old lunchtime existentialist is charming in theory, but exhausting in daily life. Even now as an adult, I know there are few people with whom I can sync up intellectually and emotionally. Everyone else prefers small doses . . . so I've learned to quickly tuck up the deep stuff, bring in the small talk, and smile.

Most of us, spectrum girls and women, don't even know we are part of a group, let alone that there is help navigating the waters. Desperate for inclusion, we are a perpetual dash of "just a bit too much" and often don't discover the people, skills, or supports that could help us (and the world) to enjoy our beautiful version of normal. Which is why we're all here, now. To get inaccurate generalizations out of the way of successfully identifying, supporting, and loving people who *are* on the spectrum but *don't* fit the stereotype.

It's really no wonder that so very many of us are, at some point, misdiagnosed with mood disorders or manic-depressive disorder, now called bipolar disorder. That includes me. I was twenty-five, receiving inpatient treatment for anorexia. The psychiatrist in charge of the unit had called me in to his office to ask a strange question: how fast did my thoughts go? At the time, I didn't realize that this man was poking around to see whether, despite my not fitting most of the criteria, he could make a bipolar diagnosis stick and declare it the cause of my anorexia (ironic, now that we know eating disorders are actually a clear red flag for autism).

Did I have racing thoughts?, he repeated. If my thoughts were cars on a highway, were they like race cars? Of course, at first I wondered why he was asking if I thought about racing. But after a moment, I caught his direction—and answered him like only a person on the spectrum can: honestly, and a bit incredulously. How, I asked, could I know how fast my thoughts traveled? There was no speedometer to use as reference. I couldn't see other people's thoughts, either, so how was I supposed to compare?

The deafening silence and narrowed eyes with which I was met made it clear that I'd annoyed him, although I didn't understand why. I was being utterly sincere—emphatic because I wanted to get the answers right. But typical minds don't perseverate like mine does, so, odds are he thought I was being rude and contentious. In hindsight, then, it was probably a good thing that I didn't say *all* of what I was thinking . . . which was this: if my thoughts—all of which were coherent and logical—were going so fast that, as he'd said, he couldn't keep up . . . maybe I wasn't mentally ill at all. Maybe I was just smarter than him. (And you know what? I still happen to think that was really the case.)

Really, it all made as little sense as the ridiculous pain scale faces in hospitals. At zero, there is a smiling emoji. From one to nine, things go badly for the guy, and by ten, his eyes are clamped shut, tears flying everywhere. This tool is *supposed* to help explain how much physical or emotional pain we might be experiencing. Instead, when I was in the hospital for emergency spinal surgery, the subjectivity sent my brain into absolute overdrive. How did I know what they understood to be "the worst pain ever"? Did it mesh with my perceptions, or were we totally off? How could a doctor or nurse get any kind of clear information about me if I was languishing between numbers, utterly perplexed as to what to say?

The amount of metacognition going on in an autistic mind could light up Manhattan. Just saying.

Friendships. Fashion. Facebook. For all that we *do* intuit that neurotypical people don't, there are many others we have to intellectualize—observing, analyzing patterns, gleaning information from everything and everyone we can. Our minds can be our greatest adaptive asset. Then again, without realizing we've begun down a slippery slope, spending hours planning conversations that should take moments, losing track of what we were saying or why we were saying it. We impulsively underthink some things . . . while chronically overthinking others.

SONG OF MYSELF

My mother wanted to name me "Jenny" but didn't know that was allowed. Allowed by whom, I'm not even sure. Still, you do have to consider the fact that she believed some omnipotent, nebulous Children's Naming Authority existed—and that she *did* abide by said imaginary agency and its imaginary rules. It tells a lot about her. Mom didn't question. Didn't rock the boat. Other than one messy incident of secret hair dyeing with food coloring in her basement, Jane was a good girl. She had to be. A product of Catholic schools, she grew up commanded by nuns *not* of the kindly-Maria-von-Trapp-*Sound-of-Music* Order and a mother whose intelligence, anxiety, and perfectionism are awfully, painfully familiar to me.

Mom was, she says, a very average student. Unfortunately, neither the sisters nor my grandmother cared much for average. Truly, even I can remember my grandmother folding the trash before she'd put it in the can. Neat garbage. Seriously. Now *that's* pressure (on herself *and* everyone else). In a neighborhood where the other girls happened to be straight-A students, schools where perfect obedience was doctrine, and a home where she was called "stupid, stupid, stupid" (because, I'm told, her mother wanted the best for her and couldn't understand what was so hard about schoolwork), my mom's goals were logical: marry a smart husband and have a smart child. Preferably a girl child (my grandmother didn't really like boys).

Enter me. For Jane, it would be by-proxy approval. For everyone involved, it would mean ease and success.

What people saw mattered much more than what was. And impressing the teacher—even if my mother was the one doing it—was paramount. Until third grade, my mother typed my school reports. I'm sure, on some level, my mom was vicariously enjoying my "star student status." A lot of parents would—and there's everything right about being proud of your child. I have zero doubt that she was trying to be helpful . . . but the message I got was that she didn't believe I could do anything right. Appearance trumped authenticity. It's what *she* was taught. And what I was learning.

Which, ironically, was precisely why I told my mom to stop typing when she was only halfway through my blue whale report. Note, I didn't ask. I told. Told. I was eight. It was lunchtime. And it wasn't a matter of ethics. For whatever reason, on that day, in that moment, something clicked—and suddenly, I knew I would do a better job of writing the report. Not of typing, but of actually composing the words. Results were paramount, or so I'd been taught. And I knew I could do better.

In that kitchen on that afternoon, a very complicated power shift took place. For the first time, a new reality dawned: not only could my mind outpace the other kids . . . I could outthink my own mother. Not socially. Not in perspective or in maturity. No way. But factually. Analytically. Academically. I knew it. What was more, so did she. For me, it was an everything-before-now and here-on-out shift. A palpable, ground-moving-under-your-feet kind of turning. My mom looked at me and saw something she couldn't recognize in what a third grader "should" be. I looked at her, the center of my world, and realized she was mortal. That what I'd always felt, I now knew: I was—really, truly was—different.

I can only liken it to Clark Kent lifting the truck off his adoptive, human dad. This was the dawning reality for my mother and the innocent confirmation of power that surged in me. In most of my life, I was so very lonely. Misunderstood. Vulnerable. Desperate. I felt that way at home, at school, really everywhere. In that role reversal awakening, I had discovered a way to flash wild at the world when it attacked. I had power. Big, legitimized, life-changing stuff. Heady. Strange. And eye-opening. Since then, my mother has said—sometimes matter-of-factly, sometimes wearily—that my brain wheels faster, harder, and louder than anyone she's ever met. That there is no way to keep up. That I operate on a different level.

Well, she was *kind* of right. Turns out my brain *isn't* typical.

Just not in any way she'd have expected.

THE NAME GAME

I don't really know how much most people think about their own names. Or, for that matter, about most things. Let's face it. My mind isn't a particularly good measuring stick for "typical." And I think about *everything* a lot. Always have. My mind never, ever stops. Nor does it travel linearly. I'm a bit more of a meander with a lot of zigzags. I'll get you there, but I will also take you on a rather scenic route. (Which you may have already noticed in what is not exactly a conventional chronologically organized memoir.)

Remember that my mom had wanted to name me "Jenny" but thought she wasn't "allowed" to? That's because she thought you had to name the child by the formal version, and then use nicknames if you wanted. I was, therefore, named "Jennifer"—which I'm fine with, except for two problems. First, it only has "boy" vowels: *i* and *e*. So that's disappointing. Second, it has too many versions. Jennifer. Jenny. Jen. I can never figure out what people ought to call me, which is, I guess, kind of ridiculous, being that it's my own name. After all, if there were only one subject in the world I'd feel justified in having some authority over, you'd think this would be it. But it isn't. To me, each variation is a different persona. An utterly different person. "Jen" is a pair of boyfriend jeans, cut far too straight for my hips. "Jennifer" is a little black dress and fabulous shoes. Smart. Sassy. Classic and chic. And "Jenny" hides behind them both, a changeling. She is lace-cuffed white anklets and copper pigtails. Then suddenly she is cat-eye sunglasses and polka dots. She is whom I name myself—but a name that feels too intimate in the mouths of strangers. You cannot tell, but always, always, my mind is in overdrive, analyzing intentions, playing a game of chess. "What's your name?" I don't know. I'm not really sure whom you're expecting.

A month or so after I wrote the paragraph above, I happened upon the phrase "diffuse sense of self," and suddenly the existentialist first grader and nameless adult fused into one person. Me. My sense of self is, I realized, often a lack of it. (Though it does strike me as funny that Walt Whitman's *Song of Myself* is my favorite poem of all time. Huh. There really *are* no such things as coincidences.)

Imagine an aromatherapy diffuser. Add a few drops of highly concentrated essential oil, and poof! Out comes a superfine mist that wafts and dissipates like the scent of a ghost. The human concept of "self" is akin to the oil. Naturally strong. It's established early in life and grows richer with time and experience. Those with a "diffuse" sense of self, however, don't have the same sort of psychological anchor. Instead of highly concentrated potency, our identity is more like the diffused vapor, morphing and floating into crevices.

Clinical psychologist Dr. Kristalyn Salters-Pedneault writes, "Like a chameleon . . . [those with a diffuse sense of self] change who they are depending on their circumstances and what they think others want from them." Understand that she isn't describing the kinds of small adjustments we learn to make in order to fit specific social situations. No, this is a more fundamental sense of transience whereby, very frequently, even full consciousness feels like a delicate place between waking and sleep. Honestly, I wouldn't be entirely shocked to find that surreality *is*, in fact, reality, and none of us were ever here in the first place.

I do think it's worth clarifying, by the way, that we're not talking of a diffuse *personality*, because that is most certainly *not* me. "You are a walking October," my daughter says of me and my birth month. Colorwise, she's sure right. But because she knows me so well, I know that she's not just referring to my hair. She's alluding to my favorite literary heroine (and fellow ginger), Anne of Green Gables, who famously said, "I'm so glad I live in a world where there are Octobers!" I am, too! In October, everything is wild and alight with flame, passionate sunsets, and leaves that beckon us to dive in and play. Yes, that is very much my personality. And personality is not something in which I'm lacking. Not by a long shot (cue: jazz hands). But personality is not self.

A "diffuse sense of self" is, not surprisingly, associated with several mental health diagnoses, including autism. Interestingly, the experience is also frequently recorded among survivors of abuse. Which means, essentially, in any Venn diagram you draw, women on the autism spectrum are right in the middle of everything. Or, perhaps many of those abuse survivors also happen to be autistic. You see, spectrum women have our own movement where sexual, physical, psychological, and emotional abuse are the rule rather than the exception. A #WeToo enclave within the #MeToo masses. Particulars vary. Even in an absence of major incidents, the residue of "little *t* traumas" accumulates: bullying, educational and professional uncertainty, emotional manipulation, discrepancies between what we perceive or express and what others see or express, and gaslighting (being convinced that mistreatment is the invention of one's own mind) make it difficult to imagine—much less establish—healthy interpersonal boundaries or a sense of where "I begin and you end." If others' reactions are our main source of determining who and how we are, and if, as Dr. Salters-Pedneault asserts, those reactions have been unpredictable and/or scary, we are literally without a framework within which to develop a strong sense of identity.

The real irony of all this talk about muted sense of self is that the very word *autism* comes from the Greek root *autos*, meaning "self" (as in "*auto*graph" and "*auto*mobile"). We *are* self-referenced, certainly. It is so hard to understand others' experiences of the world that being able to distinguish *our* wants, desires, and thoughts from anyone else's is almost impossible. Our minds feel transparent. Not because we have so *much* sense of self. But because we have so little.

THE WONDER BREAD CRISIS

Crossing guards aren't meant to wear footie pajamas. At least not on duty. These are the things you learn with time. At least, you do if you're me. Or you hope to. It just doesn't happen overnight.

Hollywood has always had a love affair with precocious children. Little kids who sound like little adults are novelties. Even adorable. Yup. Precocious is cute—on screen, anyway. Real life? Well, that's a different tale altogether.

Over the course of my childhood, my parents were approached by three different talent scouts. Not interested in getting such a little thing into "the Biz," they (wisely) declined the first two. But when I was about six, the story changed.

We'd been at an Easter bonnet contest in the town park, just around the corner from my house. I don't remember much about the day myself, but my mom sure does. During the "judging" portion, which was really just a chance for parents to take pictures of their kids in giant, silly hats, the little girl next to me had started to cry. She was about three, and unsure what was going on. I've always had a propensity for getting along best with people older or younger than myself (notice the chick-list checklist—it's there!), and I guess I've always been a natural teacher. So, I took her hand, explained what was going on, how she looked very pretty, and assured her that all the people were watching her because she'd done such a great job making her special bonnet. There are still photos of the next moments in the family album. In one, she's turned toward me, wiping her eyes. And in the next, she's looking up at the "big girl" with a giant grin. Helping frightened people to feel less alone has always kind of been my thing.

I kept hold of her hand after the ribbons and certificates were awarded. By the time my own mom had weaved her way through the crowd, I was in the middle of a very lively conversation with the girl's family.

Then again, adults are more gracious than children, as a rule. So, instead of an actual *dialogue*, it may have been more of a "grown-up asks question or makes comment and very chatty redheaded kid who likes adults because they think she's cute and not weird fluently uses big words and gestures from dancing school and charms said grown-up by being a little professor with stage presence." Not really give and take. More like give and go . . . on and on.

Anyway, it turned out that the mother was a talent agent. As soon as my mom arrived, she was handed a business card, implored to please consider bringing me in to the office . . . she could get me auditions for commercial work right away and so on and so forth. My parents did a little research, and lo and behold, the lady was legit. And, unlike the previous times my parents had been approached, now I was old enough to have an opinion. Of *course* I wanted to be on TV! Of *course* I wanted to feel that approval. I knew how to impress adults. Even delight them . . . most adults anyway.

Trouble was, I couldn't really "read the room." So, whereas *some* people really loved The Jenny Show, it never occurred to me that what worked in one situation wouldn't work in all. That which is cute can also come off as pompous. And because the idea never entered my mind, I didn't watch for signs of irritation. Which there were, both direct and indirect. My mom recalls volunteering at an elementary school bake sale and, while writing out price lists, blanking out on how to spell the word *brownie*. Laughing aloud, she turned to the woman next to her and asked for help. The lady didn't miss a beat. "Why don't you ask your daughter?" Pow. Yep. A lot of adults reacted that way to me. As a parent myself now, I balk at the pettiness of it. Either they were insecure themselves or saw my very existence as being in competition with their own son's or daughter's . . . in which case, it was insecurity about themselves by proxy. No matter what, I happen to think any adult who's threatened by a child is just pathetic.

Outside of Hollywood, there's a quick descent from "isn't that cute?" to "what the heck is up with *that* kid?" But pondering your own identity isn't exactly par for the course in grade school. And it's definitely not gonna win playground popularity contests. An only child, I mimicked adults. That's who I was around the most, after all. Besides, think about it. When you're a kid, whom do you want to please at school? The teacher. The principal. Whom do you want to please at home? Your parents. (And yes, I do notice now that neither "myself" nor "other kids" registered as possibilities.) Adults. The thing is that I didn't watch and generalize what the adults said or did. I copied it. Exactly.

It's the "exactly" part that gets you. What I hadn't learned yet is that playing well with others isn't about imitation. Imitation is rote and void of nuance or context. No, social success is about *improvisation*. Spontaneity within certain, unspoken boundaries. Break the rules in any other direction, and you *will* be called out. Fast. Upset the apple cart of social homeostasis, and nobody cares *what* you have to say. They'll be too busy paying attention to the way you've said it to listen.

Learning how to keep up appearances was something I'd learned by trial and error, myself. My first audition for that talent scout was for Wonder Bread. My mom and I drove into New York City, about forty-five minutes away, and made our way to the casting director's waiting room. Behind the door was, to quote my mom, nothing short of eerie.

Redheads make up only about 4 percent of the world's entire population. Of course, in some parts of the world, we're a lot rarer than that. One of my high school classmates, who also happens to have red hair, taught in Japan after college. While riding on a public bus in Tokyo, she noticed a small boy staring at her. Hard. Guessing that maybe he'd never seen a Caucasian in person before, she waved and smiled—and was completely thrown by what came next. Instead of smiling back, the little kid opened his mouth as wide as he could and let out screams of blood-curdling terror. Turns out that in Japanese folk tales, witches have red hair. He thought she was smiling because she'd decided to eat him.

Context. I'm telling you, this whole story boils down to context.

Needless to say, even outside of Japan—where it seems I might be mistaken for a child-eating witch—you're never invisible when you're a redhead. My parents and grandparents loved the extraordinary-ness of my packaging, and their enthusiasm absolutely shaped my self-concept, even to this day. In fact, the first words of *Asperkids*, the first book I ever wrote, were the following:

The Unexpected Redhead

"She's got red hair!"

This was, apparently, the first thing my mother ever said upon seeing me. She was merely surprised, she has always explained. She hadn't expected a little redhead (even though she says she had been "Titian-haired" as a girl). But then again, what we expect and what really is are often not quite the same, are they?

The ginger hair did continue to be my calling card, though. I learned throughout my childhood that this unique feature was the source of quite a lot of attention. It was a pretty, coppery color which adults constantly admired, and as I got older, turned quite a few glances my way. Per cliché, perhaps, I was perpetually cast as the femme fatale in school plays, [and] wrote my high school thesis on the history of redheads. . . .

Being different can make you special. A standout. Desired. It can be part of your identity in wonderful ways.

But I know of many other redheads who had quite different experiences. They were the butt of jokes, called names, or simply hated the attention their ginger locks brought them. For them, the "different" that nature endowed upon them (quite without their request, mind you) was altogether unwelcome and maybe even resented.

Different can do that, too. It can cast you in a role and include you, if you'll play along. It can discard you instantly when you don't.

And such is the label, "Aspie."

Long belabored point: see a bunch of brunettes together, and honestly, it probably doesn't register. But think of the Weasley family in Harry Potter. J. K. Rowling's artistic choice to make them all redheads was, indeed, a purposeful choice. Even outside of Tokyo, by virtue of pure math, a bunch of redheads together is . . . kind of weird. Which is probably what made my mother and me so uncomfortable back there in New York, as we'd just walked into an entire waiting room of articulate, six-year-old, redheaded children.

In a matter of seconds, rookie enthusiasm turned to total panic. I was disoriented. No, I was downright scared. Clearly, we'd stumbled into some elementary school version of *The Twilight Zone* where the world I knew had flipped on its axis. The fourth wall had broken. I couldn't be *the* adorably precocious little red-haired girl in a room full of them. Of us. Of me? Really, the agent should have prepared us better. Neither my mom nor I knew the first thing about the (rather dubious) world of child actors and stage mothers. She hadn't realized that casting calls are, necessarily, for a specific "type"—be it cranky retirement-aged men with cleft chins or, for a commercial set to air across the nation's Bread Bowl, six-year-old redheads who looked like "the girl next door." I honestly expected to show up for an experience much like we'd had at the talent agency: just me and a bunch of friendly adults who enjoyed my spontaneous tap dancing and sophisticated verbosity.

I couldn't have imagined being in *this* situation instead. The role I counted on for safety and endearment was a given, here. To my eyes, it had been given away. *I* had been given away. The one way I knew how to be that offered some reliable chance of making people like me—well, adult people, anyway—had lost its value. Now, we had to improvise. Yes, with a script—but with the *same* script.

I had to figure out how to be picked. No. I had to figure out how *not* to be rejected.

And I didn't know how to do that.

"Just be yourself," the director said when I walked into the actual audition. Great advice, except that everyone else was already being me. What else was *I* supposed to be?

It probably doesn't come as a very big surprise that midway through a cold read about how upsetting it was that "my mommy stopped buying Wonder Bread" (only to discover that she was now buying new and *improved* Wonder Bread!), I broke down in tears. The room was so bright and big, and there were loud strangers everywhere. I wanted my mommy . . . and yet . . . I wished the walk back to the waiting room would take forever. She liked when people liked me. But I had messed up. They didn't like me. And I was so ashamed, I just wanted to disappear.

Of course, I hadn't actually *lost* me. In the Existential Crisis of Wonder Bread, I lost my sense of equilibrium because the circumstances changed, and I didn't know how to adjust with them. By age ten, I hadn't gotten much better, either. Which brings us to the crossing guards and footie pajama situation.

Halloween night, 1985, found me standing in the middle of an intersection, directing traffic so that a younger child could cross the street. Ten years old. Directing actual adult drivers behind the wheels of actual cars. And best (or worst), directing said drivers while dressed as a baby—oversized pink footie pajamas, pigtails, and a giant pacifier. It all seemed quite uneventful to me.

However, the next day at school, a girl sidled up on the playground. My nerves prickled. Nothing good ever happened when a kid I didn't usually play with approached me, even if the teachers *were* watching. She got really close, looked around, and smiled innocently, then whispered maliciously, "I saw you in the street last night." My mind raced. What street? After a few seconds of confused silence, she prodded, "I saw you from my house. I know what you did. My dad's gonna tell your mom, and you're gonna be in troublllllllee!" She let the words linger, then snickered and walked away.

Meanwhile, I was panicking. I was gonna be in troublllllllee? Why? I didn't break rules! What had I done wrong? I had no idea, but I did know that if an *adult* was reporting me, I'd seriously messed up. Only . . . how? I knew she lived at the intersection at the end of my road—what had I done there in the street? Surely it couldn't have been helping the kids cross the street?

Of course, it was exactly that, though I honestly didn't understand what I'd done wrong, even when my mom *did* question me. Another "so smart, but" moment from her perspective. From mine, utter confusion. I was an official school "safety." That meant that I'd been chosen, along with several other students, to assist the crossing guard every day at dismissal. I was trustworthy. Had the official fluorescent-orange gear and badge and everything! On Halloween, I'd been very careful to copy her *exactly*. I'd practiced the movements in front of a mirror at home. Not for any particular use, mind you, just because imitating was fun. I *knew* I'd done the same stop-and-go hand gestures just right. So, what was the problem?! I'd been helping!

CONTEXT CLUES

Context. That was the problem. It still is. I pretty much didn't (and often still don't) *notice context*. Had anyone known I was autistic, perhaps they would have recognized my "difficulties adjusting behavior to suit various social contexts." It's actually one of the markers clinicians look for in making diagnoses. Of course, nobody *did* know, so there were no gentle, compassionate instructions coming my way. To anyone who'd seen me, the logical conclusion was that Jenny Cook had either been dumb enough or arrogant enough to promote herself to adult, right there in the middle of the street. In front of moving cars. At dusk. While wearing a giant pacifier. (The irony is not lost.) Since I wasn't "dumb," that only left one possibility. Or so everyone thought. The truth was that I was neither dumb *nor* arrogant. I was just utterly blind to the particulars that made what I did any different from what I helped the actual school crossing guard do every day.

As far as I could tell (and lots of folks said), Jenny was an often-bossy, attention-loving, too-smart-for-her-own-good, overdramatic crisis seeker and hypochondriac. I know now that none of that was true. It was never about good or bad. Too much or too little. Too bold or too shy. It was always an issue of context. Understanding in relation to the surroundings. Or—in the case of how the world saw me—misunderstanding.

Human brains take bits and pieces of information and jump to conclusions. Use what you know to assemble an understanding of whatever you don't. Mental shortcuts. Yes, we know it's not really ethical or kind or generous . . . but it's a natural habit we've developed for survival. You hear a loud, sudden noise in the night. Sure, it could be the Publishers Clearing House van arriving at your house with boatloads of money. Or, it could be burglars breaking in. Both are possible. But, which does your past experience tell you is probably right?

It's all about context. Imagine a constellation. Any one you want. From Earth, we can look up and locate Andromeda by finding Perseus. Or Ursa Major by starting with Ursa Minor. Context. We understand—we see—by making external references. Connecting the dots . . . literally. But travel to Neptune, and the three stars of Orion's belt no longer line up. The Big Dipper isn't any dipper at all. The patterns we know as constant and real simply do not exist. Perspective changes. Context changes. And finally, understanding changes.

There was no alternative context to explain me. Not to other people. Not to myself. I was like that constellation seen from Neptune. Chaotic. Wrong. Without context. Shift the perspective, spot the connections, and everything falls into place. Or it would have, anyway. Instead, I'd have years to wait. Decades before I could make out a picture and make sense of it all.

Where I was, when I was, there wasn't an alternative way for my parents or teachers to understand me. No other context or framework to consider. True. I wasn't all bad. And there were lots of inconsistencies: I was smart but oblivious, wracked with compassion for underdogs but matter-of-fact and indifferent besides, desperate to be liked yet irritating as hell. Lots of disconnected contradictions that didn't add up to anything—didn't align into any recognizable profile or constellation . . . other than this: I was too smart for my own good, smart-alecky, hypersensitive, overdramatic, and difficult to love. It's what I believed because it is—literally—what I was told. And, to be fair, without any other context to consider, it's probably precisely what I seemed.

As a child, how do you know anything other than what you're told? If you can't understand what's different, can't offer another interpretation, if you can't see yourself as others do, how do you know what it is you are missing? How are you supposed to figure out what you're doing that makes you unlikable when even your best perfect imitation of right is wrong?

Short answer: you wait twenty-five more years.

MAKE-A-WISH

Robin Williams said, "You're only given a little spark of madness. You mustn't lose it." I couldn't agree more. A key ingredient in the "how this all came to be" journey was a trip to hell and back, starring my daughter.

I'm known for a "take this poo, add some sunshine, and use it to grow something beautiful" attitude. Which is legit. For me, it began as will to survive through bruised arms and a broken heart. As a parent, it started in children's hospital rooms and ORs, being dismissed as "just another overly worried mother," asked if I was really concerned about my newborn daughter's horrible vomiting or, as a first-time mom, if it wasn't really just "a too-much-laundry" problem.

Eventually, doctors told me that my relentless, unyielding, pattern-seeking, we-didn't-yet-know-it-was-autistic thinking saved her life. Eventually. Which is sort of like apologizing to someone who's been falsely incarcerated for twenty years. Doesn't really change what you've lost along the way. Back then, in 2007, I'd never heard of Asperger's and knew virtually nothing about autism. I'd just lost my father to lung cancer, and my nights were plagued with terrible dreams . . . hyperreal visions of holding my little girl under water, of watching her struggle for breath, eyes wide at me, pleading.

That's exactly how it had felt when I'd had to brace her too-tiny two- and then three-year-old body—a total of four times—for the nurses to insert a nasogastric tube up her nostril, down her throat, into her stomach. When the piping reaches the throat, the child cannot breathe until she swallows. And I'd had to be the one to hold her down for the torture, to see her eyes plead at me, to scream, "Swallow!" at her when she would panic, trapping the tube in her windpipe, unable to draw air . . . and then refusing, for the days it remained placed, to speak.

There are some nights too dark to describe, no matter how bright the dawn. And there are some memories too horrible to endure other than to think, when the doctors finally offered congratulations instead of condescension . . . save her? No. Don't you know? Don't you see? I did this, somehow. I ruin everything good. I always do. Or if that's not the case, how dare so many of you dismiss us if, in fact, there was a life to be saved?

It was about the time she turned four, I think, that I stopped being the good girl. What had begun as failure to thrive had spiraled into layer after layer of rare neurological disorders of her entire gastrointestinal (GI) tract, a feeding tube, months when her entire gut shut down and she had to be sustained intravenously through her upper arm, without so much as an ice cube to crunch. Finally, after four years and specialists seen around the country, one of them listened to a new complication I was describing and ordered an MRI of her lumbar spine. Thank God. It turned out that the bottom of her spinal cord was fused to the bottom of her spinal column, a condition called tethered cord syndrome, and that as she grew, her brain was literally being pulled down out of her skull, like a boat yanked under because the anchor chain is too short.

At the time of discovery, her pituitary gland had been smashed by the downward force pull, and she was millimeters away from the brain actually having descended below the bony ridge, a Chiari malformation. That last bit was good. Just in the nick of time! But, because the brain itself was wedged into the opening at the base of the skull, the cerebrospinal fluid (CSF), which normally moves freely around the spinal cord and brain, couldn't move. Imagine an orange shoved into the drain in your kitchen sink. Now turn on the tap. Like the water you imagined, her CSF couldn't go anywhere. And, as its flow is spurred on by normal bodily processes—like the heartbeat—the force on the fluid never lets up. The CSF just had nowhere it could go . . . so it forced its way through her spinal cord, effectively creating fluid-filled pockets within the cord itself, damaging and destroying certain nerve functions in the process. That's what had led to all of the neurologically based GI troubles . . . all the way back to the first doctor who asked me if the *real* trouble was that, thanks to her vomiting, I just had too much laundry.

No. Can't say that it was. I *can* say that after removing one whole vertebra and two partial vertebrae, and then, using highly sensitive ultrasound, cutting the base of her spinal cord, it jumped two inches—immediately.

How we got to that answer, much like the endeavor to get an accurate Asperger's diagnosis later, wasn't because an "expert" saw the struggling and sincerity and showed us what was happening, or how to make things better. No. Not in either case. If I'm being brazenly honest, then here it is: in both cases, I figured it out.

Back then, much as later on, I did serious, responsible research and spoke with enough authority that every single physician we met asked if I'd gone to med school. Not rudely. They just figured I must have.

Oh, how I wish I'd known to have said, "No, I'm not an MD. I'm autistic, so I can absorb, retain, and access vast amounts of information. In a way that I've only ever encountered among others on the spectrum, my mind grabs onto something, like a little ankle-biting dog, and until the pieces make sense simply will not let go.

But that's no consolation in the middle of the what-is-going-on?? journey—be it medical, psychological, spiritual, emotional, or *all* of the above—there's no way to know what later will bring. There's only the tenuousness of the present moment and the constant certainty that whatever you do, somehow, you're making a mess of it all.

Except for a few, fleeting moments. Now and agains, where all the pieces fit together. When the stars align, and you get to see that there's a bigger plan. There always was. Those are the heartbeats I try to hold. To record the sense of some larger lucidity. They don't last long. But they are powerful and sweet and meant for us to stop and breathe and be aware . . . and be humbled. And they can change you. They should change us all.

In August 2013, I had one of those moments. I'd just been named one of Make-A-Wish's Women Inspiring Strength and Hope award winners. Though I'd never talked in much detail about the hell before I wrote *Asperkids*, that day took me off guard. Made me feel like I was in the middle of a cyclone and everything was converging. The medical road. The *Asperkids* juggernaut, both private and very public. The years and years of fighting—for myself; then for my daughter; then and now for all three of my kids; and forevermore, in a very real way, for every spectrum or spectrummy child, teen, young adult, adult, and for every family member, too, the ones I stand for or with all around the world—caught up to me. Make-A-Wish brought the memories back, the seeds of the work to come—the faces and names of real kids on different continents, and I knew them. Mattered to them, somehow, though never as much as they matter to me.

I thought Make-A-Wish was something long passed. But *Asperkids* had brought me full circle. Now I was in a position to meet thousands of parents who were exhausted and scolded and frightened by experts who seemed anything but. Who said they, the parents, were to blame. Or that they were imagining it all. And on that award day, I couldn't keep it together . . . was literally in the bathroom crying when they called me to the stage. Well, as Flannery O'Connor said, "I write to know what I think." Yep. That. So I did what I do when I need to make sense of something. I wrote:

CaringBridge, online medical journal, January 2010
"You saved her life." That's what the doctors told us days ago after they cut her spinal cord—"By sticking with it, and really digging—being her best advocates, you have saved her life."

Over time we have gone from doctor to doctor around the nation, questioning diagnoses and searching for answers . . . shadowboxing many times, frustrated most of the time. Beyond fighting illness and sadness, we have, in our weary days, battled fear, doubt and fatigue . . . and much worse.

Few people know that this summer [2010], someone who was not brave enough to come to us, but bold and arrogant enough to think they knew better, sent the Department of Social Services to our home in a surprise visit to interview the kids and question our medical care of our children . . . in a moment, our little ones could have been taken from us, and Maura—with enough to handle already—then had nightmares of losing Mommy & Daddy to compound her worries. "Doctor shopping until they hear what they like" they accused us, "Inadequate medical care."

This happened one month before my father finally passed from a terrible battle with cancer.

Though the social worker called it "ridiculous" within five minutes of meeting our little ones, I cannot think of a greater contradiction and validation than that we have just received—the top doctors in the WORLD for this condition have told us in no uncertain terms that diligence, "doctor shopping," faith, and thoughtful, questioning care have literally saved our baby girl . . . any less or any difference in what we did, and she would probably have died.

So today this little girl leaves the neurosurgical hospital with great hope for the future. Her life may still not look like other kids' or it may look exactly the same.

You see . . . before we knew she was an "Asperkid," my daughter was a Make-A-Wish kid. And nothing—nothing that has happened in my life since then would be, without the walk that came first.

A Million Shards of Sand: Sensorial Intensity

Every year, Halloween was disastrous for me. Itchy costumes made me (and my mom) miserable. Trips to the beach were itchy and sandy. But back then, *there was no word to express what I was feeling.* To anyone whose nervous system *didn't* behave as mine (that'd be *most* people), I came across as a bossy, overdramatic hypochondriac who couldn't play well with others. But I wasn't. Like every other child, I was experiencing the world through my senses . . . only my senses didn't behave like every other child's.

Along the spectrum journey, there are three little words teachers and parents hear a lot: *sensory processing disorder.* Or *sensory integration disorder.* Sometimes, this "sensory" junk feels like an overreaction of "helicopter mom unnecessary stuff" that is either a total invalidation of other issues ("oh, there's nothing more than some sensory issues to manage") or some kind of fix-it-all panacea. And in either case, the *disorder* moniker is problematic. But I will concede that sensory experiences can be among the most disruptive of our invisible autistic journey, causing *real* distress, discomfort, and confusion.

Not every person with sensory processing challenges is on the spectrum—but every person on the spectrum does have sensory processing difficulties, that is, challenges with the way our brains process the information our nerves gather through:

- vision
- hearing
- touch (kind, duration, and strength)
- olfaction (smell)
- gustation (taste)
- sense of movement (vestibular system)
- proprioception (our awareness of where our bodies are in space)

The issue isn't one of acuity—it's not indicative of poor eyesight or hearing loss—but of the actual unpacking of the information coming through our senses. *All* developing minds first learn through sensory input—our most primal method of absorption and observation. Knock into a block tower, and it *will* fall. That's also why spectrum kids' sensory defensiveness can inhibit the creation of necessary learning foundations. If you're too put off by the feel of rice, how can you fill up a funnel and watch gravity in action—or figure out how to unclog the "traffic jam" of grains? And though particular sensory issues change from day to day, person to person, even hour to hour, this remains consistent: what we are experiencing is entirely real, entirely overwhelming, and, when we are "dysregulated" (our brains are screaming for either more or less input—or more of one kind but less of another), entirely *awful*.

When we feel either understimulated or overstimulated, we physically *cannot* reason, listen, or think about anything else. We *can't* just ignore it. We *can't* learn. We *can't* be spontaneous or fun. We *can't* rationalize well. And we *can't* hear others' needs, let alone be certain we understand our own. It's like trying to see your own reflection in a pot of boiling water. Nothing is clear.

No one has to teach parents to empathize with hunger or weariness or thirst. When a baby cries, those are the natural go-tos. We expect those problems, so we teach both sensation recognition and vocabulary as we wonder aloud, "Are you hungry?" But we'd never think to teach a child to "scratch" an "itch" that we, ourselves, have never felt. No nonspectrum mom intuitively says, "Aw, sweetie, are you feeling dysregulated?" Along the same lines, I never could make sense of why so many people jangle things at little ones or toss them around to try to stop their crying. If I were a baby, that would terrify me.

That's what happened to my yet-undiagnosed children. They were only made more upset by the additional sensory discord well-meaning adults put "in their faces." Instead of lights and keys and gizmos, my babies all needed deep pressure, rhythmic motion, and white noise. As an (albeit undiagnosed) spectrum mom, I sensed that. What came naturally to me came naturally to them. My boys spun like helicopters. I used to "practice spotting my turns" across the diagonal of my living room, just as I did in the dance studio . . . but no one needs to practice *that* much. Without knowing the word or understanding the action, I was "stimming." Gaining the sensory input that my brain craved—it just looked a lot girlier in a ballet skirt.

There was no "autism" frame of reference during my childhood or for most of life. There was no respite for my parents. No understanding *why* the drama and extreme *everything* are constants. They were just pulled alongside in the constant barrage of emotion, sensation, and rumination that was, and is, my reality.

When I begged for tags to be cut out of my shirts, I'm sure I *did* step on my mother's last nerve. We were probably running late to some lesson or practice; she was probably already rushing, trying to figure out what to make for dinner, trying to get me from point A to point B without losing a tap shoe or baton. And *now* the kid was whining about an itchy tag?? I imagine she wanted nothing more than to pull her hair out and scream, "Oh, for *goodness'* sake, Jenny! It's a *tag*!" But those tiny pieces of fabric were slicing at my skin like knives . . . scratching like some biblical horsehair shirt. "*You* try being polite while something bites at you and no one will help," I longed to rage, feeling very indignant and very small. And, worse, my heart asked . . . why wouldn't she believe me? I wasn't lying. I wasn't trying to get attention. I was in pain. And being yelled at. And I didn't know what else to do.

When my grandmother took me shoe shopping—for *hours*—and I refused every pair she or the salesman offered, I'm sure my tears *did* embarrass her. But—those shoes all pinched. And I was tired. And the lights made my head hurt. I wasn't fussy and spoiled. I was trying to be good. To follow the rules that I *did* know. And I *did know* I'd be in trouble if I brought home shoes that I wouldn't wear. So we left. On the ride home, my grandmother dressed me down in scathing words. I sobbed, hot and angry in the backseat . . . too heartbroken and carsick to speak . . . knowing that was probably better anyway . . . I'd only make it worse if I did.

When a summer storm blew through and I began shrieking hysterically for someone to take down the backyard tire swing, I'm sure my dad *did* curse under his breath. Grumbling and put out, he was being sent into driving rain, heavy thunder, and crackling lightning to detach a *swing*?? From a *tree*?? It had to feel like the most ridiculous indulgence of Jenny's most ridiculous temper tantrum. But—I wasn't throwing a fit for the fun of it. My tire swing made regular arcs, back and forth, to and fro. I knew them. Knew how much pull brought how much lift. Only suddenly, everything was going wrong! The wind was messing up the lovely, predictable motion. And now my poor swing was spinning and twisting and frantically changing directions. It was confused and scared and dizzy and lost—so *I* was confused and scared and dizzy and lost. Logical thought dissolved into primal terror: I pled and cried and begged—stopitstopitstopit!!! Little though I was, I came undone in a big way. Tears streaming down my face, I banged on that sweaty window with as much chaos as the storm itself, hysterical, until, at last, the tire fell, soaked and still.

Oh, and then there was the pool . . .

JUST GO PLAY!

As a young child, I would often go with my mother to the town pool during the summertime. She was a stay-at-home mom and wanted some "grown-up time" chatting with the other moms on beach blankets. That is perfectly rational, healthy, and (as a mommy now myself) understandable. But times were different back around 1980; nobody had ever heard of Asperger's or autism, nor were helpful professionals available to coach parents through the tough times. As a result, my mom was in a real pickle. She had a child in tow who didn't really want to be at the busy, hot pool without friends. Except, she *could not imagine* why I was so miserable there, and she certainly wasn't going to be dictated to by a child. Maybe, she thought, I'd learn to deal with it if I saw there wasn't going to be another option.

Off we went, then, most every day to the itchy, burning anxiety of Cedar Street Pool. Almost as soon as we spread out our towels, my mom would shoo me away with her hand, telling me, "Just go play!" And my heart would sink. The towels were surrounded by itchy grass or hot pavement. The bathrooms were echoing and slick. I didn't have friends there, and I couldn't just join in with some group of strangers. What the heck was I supposed to do, exactly? I was self-conscious and clueless as to where she wanted me to go, and I had a million examples already in my mind of messing up socially—why put myself in harm's way again? The worst part was, though, that I took her dismissal—which was actually her well-meant attempt to push me out of the nest—as rejection. In my mind, even my mom didn't want me. I had no idea where to go . . . or how to be, and without any other plan, I would either head to the playground alone or sit beside her and read—which she said "looked weird." Though she couldn't know, those words hurt more than anything else. Feeling that we have let down our parents is a pain anyone can understand. But feeling that one's innate self is a letdown just slays you.

Neurotypical parents, teachers, bosses, spouses, and friends won't organically recognize the symptoms of sensory/emotional dysregulation—they'll get stuck on the inconvenience or disruptions we cause. Reprimand us for acting out or name-call when we're too afraid or resistant. Complain that we are difficult or "high strung" when we dig in our heels. Just like the summer I went for my lifesaving credentials. I'm a very, very strong swimmer . . . but the smell of the algae in the camp's lake made me gag uncontrollably. I couldn't stop the reflex, and when my mother sent in a note to that effect, they told me to go canoeing instead. No one suggested I use a different part of the lake or a pool, because the instructors just saw a whiner. A quitter, not a kid whose olfactory nerves were in actual hyperdrive. I never, ever got to finish my certification and, without that, couldn't qualify to apply for the job I wanted the following summer. I hadn't the vocabulary—thus, the power—to help myself. If we don't know that our neurology is different, we won't recognize the ways our bodies ask for help *before* a crisis hits. We won't be able to request the simple tools we need to make the world fit us better. And the fair question is, if we adults won't speak for ourselves and for the children, we can't expect anyone to wait around and listen.

So, let me offer my part . . . the kind of calm we need when we reach the edge, and what we sense and think are too big for one person:

Breathe slowly. Smell the roses (inhale, through your nose), blow out the candles (exhale completely out of your mouth). Again. Breathe. You're going to be okay. You've felt this before—these feelings you have right now. Uncomfortable. Anxious. Embarrassed. Afraid. You've felt them, and you have survived. Breathe, and know you will survive this, too, wiser and stronger. The feelings can't break you. They can hurt. They can sting. They can waylay your plans. But if you'll sit with the feelings—notice them, stay with them without trying to run—if you do sit with them and really feel them—you'll discover they have a bottom. They

have an end. They aren't all-consuming. You won't drown in them. They will become shallower . . . eventually, shallow enough that you will begin to walk again. Keep breathing. Keep moving. Soon, you'll emerge from the hurt. You'll be able to turn around and see the far shore where you started. You'll know that you made it through and that you are powerful and resilient enough to float above anything. Right now, that sounds impossible. It feels unbearable. I know. So for now, just breathe. There is a bottom and an end. You will get there. One breath at a time. This moment will pass. It will be over. And you won't be.

Nietzsche wrote, "Those who were seen dancing were thought to be insane by those who could not hear the music." Well, I *am* a dancer. And even if you *can't* hear the music, I'd be glad to teach you the song. Because there really is magic amidst the mayhem. In a few, fleeting moments, a fair few now and agains, the pieces *do* fit together. The stars *do* align. Those are the heartbeats I reach out to hold. Those are the connections I find to a larger lucidity.

Then, without fail, in ways I could never contrive, the world changes. And I get to come along for the ride.

CHAPTER 4

Executive, Functioning: Girls Can Be Professors, Too

On the eighteenth of April, 1955, Albert Einstein died in Princeton, New Jersey. Crowds of reporters and photojournalists swarmed the local hospital, hoping to capture some essence of the man and the moment. But all they found was the same sense of mortality everyone already knows. Nothing about gurneys or midcentury architecture speaks of the *immortality* of a unique mind or creative soul. They had all missed the point. All but Ralph Morse, a photographer for *Time* magazine. Instead of getting lost in throngs at the hospital, he made his way to Einstein's office at the Institute of Advanced Studies. There, in one frame, Morse captured the legacy of the world's greatest mind.

Chaos. Every inch of the professor's desk was covered in paper. Books, magazines, music scores, manuscripts, and torn envelopes were strewn from floor to ceiling. Shelves burst with slipping piles of paper. The chair had been left askew. And, sitting in prominence of place, was one cookie jar. By any judgment, it was a tornado of stuff. Einstein had liked it that way, remarking once, "If a cluttered desk is a sign of a cluttered mind, then what are we to think of an empty desk?"

Of course, nobody was about to evaluate Einstein based on his tidiness. There was something oddly enchanting about a playful genius with unkempt hair and a violin. A certain charm to the eccentricity. An appreciation that different kinds of rules apply to such different kinds of minds. One had to wonder, really, *was* this really mess? Or was this a different sort of mind more interested in *getting messy*? In eschewing

the mundane and, instead, diving headfirst into a tumult of possibilities and ideas?

The idea of simultaneous chaos and genius is a well-established stereotype, so it's easy to recognize and accept when we see it. As far back as ancient Greece, biographer Diogenes Laërtius wrote of the fate of a famous philosopher, Thales. Beset by great thoughts, he went walking through the streets at night, his eyes lifted to the heavens in distracted contemplation . . . and fell into a well and died. Messy, indeed.

Over the last couple of centuries, we've coined a term for the persona embodied by Einstein: "absent-minded professor"—a lovable cultural archetype whose genius goes hand in hand with disorganization, forgetfulness, and social blundering. The brilliant, bumbling character is familiar enough to warrant a Wikipedia entry, chock-full of "absent-minded" examples, both real and fictional. They include the very real Isaac Newton, Nikola Tesla, Archimedes, Pierre Curie, and of course, Albert Einstein. Centuries of popular culture add to the trope: *Back to the Future*'s Doc Brown, *Marvel*'s Professor Edgewise, characters from nineteenth-century Jules Verne novels, the original *Little Orphan Annie* comic strip, and even a Disney classic by the actual name *The Absent-Minded Professor.*

Though not necessarily an academic, he is always possessed of genius, becoming totally engrossed in the minutiae of thought and losing track of just about everything else. So benevolent is he, so unintentional are his gaffes, that not only do we not condemn him, we want to help him. We may roll our eyes and shake our heads at the contradictions, but we do so with smiles. "Absent-minded professor" is not only an easily recognizable descriptor, it's become a term of endearment—a gentle kind of affectionate teasing. I can clearly remember my mom using the name for my dad, who always accepted it with a goofy smile and an "aw shucks" kind of guffaw. Joe, the Absent-Minded Professor. Or, as I called him, Dinky Doodle. It was a nickname I invented while too little to know the "grown-up" words, but clearly not too little to perceive the idea. My daddy . . . my Dinky Doodle. The kind of man who inspires admiration *and* facepalms. *That* kind of man.

That kind of *man*. Except . . . who said "professors" are always boys?

In researching the term *absent-minded professor*, I discovered a pattern so blaring that I honestly can't believe I never saw it before: without exception, the realm of the "adorably discombobulated" is populated entirely by men. In history. Literature. Film. Academia. Science. In the basic overall zeitgeist of it all. Just. Men. I can't help but notice the irony: Hans Asperger described the boys he studied, the ones by which autism was defined, as "little professors." The exact same words used by my teachers *and* my daughter's teachers to describe us. Though I am most certainly my father's daughter, no one has ever loved me *for* being brilliant and bumbling. In spite of, yes. But *for* it? Never.

Fault Lines (Through No Fault of Our Own)

Which is a tragedy, because being on the spectrum is akin to operating on a different software platform. We are, by definition, neurologically distinct. Our minds may create passionately, analyze fiercely, and dream feverishly. And. The same brains that gift us in some ways can also undermine our successes in others. Through no fault of our own, very real fault lines wind through the wonderful.

In the journey from imagination to implementation, we get lost in the weeds. Alternatively driven and stagnant, perpetually distractible, emotionally reactive, organizationally scattered. Cognitive overactivation, they call it. The mind's own busy-ness incessantly distracts *itself* so that time vanishes, meals are missed, deadlines pass, the journey down the hall to the bathroom takes ten minutes . . . or, as just happened to me, you start the shower, get lost in your thinking, and by the time you remember what you're meant to be doing, the hot water's run out.

It's a constant scramble to catch up with fleeting thoughts and forgotten plans and indistinguishable priorities. In the last thirty seconds on my laptop, for example, I've copied a note to my clipboard, typed this paragraph, opened a new tab, and checked a source—but I still haven't hit "paste" because, somewhere in this process, I realized that I'd forgotten to dig up a term needed for the *next* sentence—which, of course, I'd already written but you haven't yet read, because I went back and added this bit afterward. Yes, I can remember the meaning of the word *syncopation*, which I don't think I've used in fifteen years, yet have now completely forgotten what I have hanging out in "copy" limbo, where I was going to put it, or the last time I changed my contacts.

So very many things that are elementary and routine to other people—buying groceries, remembering the laundry, making dinner, keeping track of possessions, paying bills, responding to emails—simply do not come automatically to those with autism, a reality that is not only inconvenient, until we can identify both source and solutions, it's also costly, confusing, and embarrassing. Like juggling five balls while trying to get the mail, walk the dog, and shave the other leg. This, at the same time that the kids are screaming and the phone is ringing and some red-flagged email just dinged its way to the inbox. (Psst! The toilet's clogged, too.)

That's just the practical, exterior, organizational stuff. If you really think about it, as much of life is about processing and regulating our *in*teriors. That is to say, how we manage our thoughts, emotions, and responses, and how successfully we analyze other people's words and the encoded social messages that *underpin* those words.

For example, I turn on the closed-captioning function whenever I watch videos, something I've noticed other people on the spectrum doing, as well. There's nothing wrong with my hearing. I flip the switch because dialogue can move too quickly for me to accurately register the changing facial expressions and body language of multiple characters in multiple settings. By adding emotionally "neutral," unspoken dialogue to what I see, I gain a verifiable reference tool to inform my understanding and the reactions I have to the story.

Real-life emotional and social regulation is just as labor-intensive. Without constant attention, I inadvertently drop the ball on social rules. I forget to be solicitous. I interrupt, knowing my frantic brain will quickly forget the flash of an idea I've only a millisecond to catch. I lose track of pronouns—who's the "he" who's supposed to get "it" from the "there"—and get mixed up and confused and leave people waiting, annoyed. I make generalizations that don't fit situations. I scare people off with ceaseless ideas and "brilliant" but totally disorganized plans. And quickly, I crumble as, more often than not, the goodwill I've worked so hard to earn is undone before my very eyes. Smiling and scrambling. Scrambling and smiling. Constantly. Forget waiting for the other shoe to drop; it's more like frantically wondering where my shoe even *is*, only to realize I've been holding it all along. And then dropping it on my other foot by accident. Which I've *totally* done. This week.

Invisible on the Monopoly Board

Monopoly is probably not a usual stage for life-changing, viewpoint-altering paradigm shifts. But my family has never been "usual." And you never know what life has in store.

There at the corner of yellow and green properties on that world-famous Monopoly board, I was scanning real estate deals. Looking "normal."

Thoughtfully, I checked the properties I'd purchased so far, considered my options, and offered my then-nine-year-old daughter a trade—one utility that she needed (plus cash) for a card I'd need to gain a monopoly. This seemed like a completely legitimate deal until my mom, who was also playing with us, piped up in challenge, first in a joking tone . . . and then with growing indignation.

At first, she seemed to be "needling" me in a way friendly competitors might—so I "needled" back. "Stay out of it, lady!" I joked in an old-timey *Newsies* kind of voice. "This here's between me and the kid." And I smiled.

My mom didn't smile. She scolded. "That's taking advantage of her! I can't believe you'd do that, Jenny!" A combination of shock and disappointment passed over her face, intensifying to anger when I "claimed" to be totally confused. Throwing a hard stare back at me, she instructed my daughter, "Don't do it. Mommy's being unfair."

Apparently, there is a strategy to buying out the two property blocks on either side of a corner. Apparently, this is a highly aggressive, valuable "get" that earns the owner dramatic revenues and bankrupts others quickly. And, apparently, "everyone knows this."

Everyone, I guess, but me.

For the life of me, I couldn't understand why my mother was so furious. What? I asked them. What were they talking about? So, it's a corner? So what? And (now I was shouting) how could anyone—most especially my family—think that I would ever—*ever*—scheme against a child . . . or anyone else, for that matter?! My heart broke as I realized what was being implied about me . . . loudly, publicly . . . by my own mom. If anyone should have known me better, if someone was going to be my defender, I thought, it should be her. But there I was, crumpling under the worthlessness of being "guilty until proven innocent." And there I went, running out of the room in shame.

Children ask how we know that air surrounds us. We can't see it, after all. So we invent science experiments to make the invisible visible. Adults ask the same of God. We can't see Him, either. Maybe there's no such thing. Maybe. I can't prove there is. Then again, I can't prove there isn't. The question really is, must something be visible for it to be real? For that matter, must we understand something for it to be real?

My friend's son happens to use a wheelchair. No one questions the legitimacy of his needs. Another's is blind and deaf. No one sends social services to her door to check whether she's "inventing" trouble. Yet both happened to me as I fought for my daughter's health years ago. She looks so *normal*, people argued then and have continued when they hear she is autistic. There's a situation Emily Post missed. What's the correct response? "What were you expecting? Three heads? An Elvis wig?" Or, how about, "Thanks—so do you." I remember when my daughter was a baby and toddler and was very tiny, mothers would *constantly* ask me where she fell on the weight index charts. Our pediatrician recommended I ask them where *they* fell.

People try. They do. But oh . . . it's so painful to watch. The most common hit I get is the cringeworthy "You're autistic? Well, you must be very high-functioning." Sigh. I understand what they're trying to say. Really, I do. They mean to be kind. The implication is "I don't see many—if any—of the clearly debilitating characteristics I associate with autism when I talk to you. So, good on you. You're not bad off!" Only that's *not* a compliment *at all*. It's a comparison based on the premise that "autistic" is an insult. A stigma. Or at least a bad thing. Because the only reason someone thinks of me as "high-functioning" is by holding me up to someone who is no more or less autistic—just more obviously challenged—and deciding that they are "lower-functioning." Really, it's no different than saying, "Oh! Well, good for you. You're not *too* ugly. That gal over there? She's *royally ugly*." Lack of understanding tied up with a bow of condescension.

Recently, *Jeopardy!* (usually my favorite game show) presented this clue: "Asperger's syndrome is often considered a less severe form of this disorder." The answer was "What is autism?" Apparently, their fact-checkers didn't show up to work that day. Not only is "Asperger Syndrome" a diagnosis that is no longer even given (it was absorbed into a general autism spectrum identification in 2013), there's no "considered" here. There's no such thing as more or less "severely" autistic. There's just "autistic." Maybe *Jeopardy!* also believes in being a little bit pregnant.

In 2014, I participated in a panel discussion alongside a nonverbal young man who used a touch pad to communicate. "Every day," the tablet's electronic voice chirped to the onlookers, "I have to explain that I'm not cognitively impaired. My verbal IQ is 162." In case you're wondering, mine is less. That "low-functioning" man is underestimated regularly because his brain has trouble accessing the words within itself. He is brilliance outshone by perceptible obstacles. And me? I'm *overestimated* just as often because I'm so loquacious. What looks like "high-functioning" is really just "highly camouflaged." My challenges aren't less real. Nor are they less autistic. They're just less obvious.

Truly. No finger waving here. Just explaining. The pain of "so smart but so stupid" is born in the space where ignorance lives. The truth is that we can *all* miss the boat entirely. Even neurotypicals.

Some days after the Monopoly game, my mom and I sat alone in the garden while I (a bit more aggressively than necessary) snipped at the rose bushes. "Mom," I choked, "if you say that I am the most intentionally kind person you know, how on *Earth* could you accuse me of undermining my own *child* in a board game? Who *does* that, Mom? Because it certainly is not *me*!"

Tears rolled fat and hot down my cheeks. I felt ashamed and hurt and blindsided. "Why be good? Why be honest?" I shouted despondently. "Why be kind or giving or relentlessly positive if those who know me best *still* default to thinking suspiciously of me? What—in my entire life—have I *ever* done that indicated I would cheat a child?"

Nothing, my mom admitted sadly. Nothing at all. "I just couldn't . . . can't . . . understand how you can be so completely brilliant . . . but—" Her voice trailed. She couldn't make sense of the conflict. How could I casually, flawlessly discuss the entire lineage of English monarchs from the twelfth century to the twenty-first, explaining in detail the War of the Roses, how it affected the way Shakespeare skewed his historical writing, and the many ways scholars kept up those narratives—how could I be "so smart . . . and not see the corner strategy in a Monopoly game." Or not want to learn about it, if I *really* didn't understand it.

Appearances can be deceiving. Even as my mom witnessed the "glitches" in her own, recently diagnosed daughter—the very distress and disconnects that are *characteristic* of autism—she did not *see* autism. She saw stubbornness. Inappropriate choices. Dramatic hysterics. Default switches can be hard to override. I get it. My mom wanted—wants—things to be easy for me in the ways that they had been for her. I know there were times I embarrassed her. Frustrated her. Hurt *her* feelings. I haven't mean to, but I did. Though never ever intentionally, I still do. We are all just figuring it out and making it up as we go along, after all. Which is why, as the dust settles, my mom and I always *see* each other. Right there. Steadfast. A team. My mom has never read any of my books, but when I wrote the first, she quoted a line from the movie *The Help*. "Sometimes courage skips a generation," she repeated. "You, I think, are courageous." She, I know, is my hero.

But compliments—comprehension—have been, and still are, hard to come by. My mom just didn't understand how *I* couldn't understand everything that was so clear to her. The getting along with people stuff. What did I mean, "Show me how to make friends, Mommy?" You just do it. Inadvertently, my mother's frustrations with her own inability to teach me delivered the same message to me as her mother had lashed at her. I may have been brilliant in school. But in life, *I* gleaned that *I* was "stupid, stupid, stupid." Something about me was obviously bad. Wrong. Irritating. And though you can cover a blemish, hide a rip, or disguise an injury, what do you do when you don't know what to hide? When the trouble isn't one thing that you *do*. It's everything that you *are*.

If you're me, you keep studying, turning to biographies (*lots* of biographies) and to fiction. Characters. Archetypes. Costumes and makeup and body language. You put those mimicry skills to good use. You learn your lines. And you just stop telling the truth.

Even after we are identified, there is no obvious wheelchair reminder to "prove" our naïveté in real time. It's no small thing to accept that what you think you know, you don't. What you think absolutely *is*, isn't. That's a daily chore for people on the spectrum. It's a necessary paradigm shift whose trust we so eagerly want. And need.

Two years after the Monopoly game, I sat onstage amidst an illustrious group of autism self-advocates—among them a Pulitzer

Prize–winning journalist, three acclaimed professors, a scientist, and a renowned artist. All accomplished. All insightful. All *men*.

Once the audience settled and the live video feed began streaming, the moderator addressed our panel. "Please tell us, from your own experiences, what's hardest about being on the spectrum? Anyone may begin."

The professor next to me passed the microphone. "Ladies first," he whispered, irony marking his smile. He had a young daughter on the spectrum. A beautiful, bright little thing whose path hadn't been easy. For that moment, no matter how eloquent and esteemed he was as a professor or self-advocate, this was a father asking me to do what he, as a man, couldn't: give his daughter a voice.

His daughter. My daughter. I remembered that board game and raised the mic. "It's wondering . . . always wondering and never understanding: how can I be so smart and still feel so stupid?"

The room fell silent. Heads nodded. Eyes welled. And next to me, I heard a whisper. "Yes."

Therein lies the conundrum that has plagued my life. How on Earth can I possibly be a mean trivia bowl contender with a super memory bank account that easily retrieves useless facts, lines from my high school plays, *and* the page on Shintoism in my ninth-grade World Culture class . . . yet repeatedly fail to bring out the garbage or return from a quick run to the store with seven things I hadn't planned on buying—and without the one thing I'd actually needed? How could one brain be so good at "hard" things and utterly hopeless at others?

I know full well that I have disappointed friends, family, teachers, colleagues more times than I can count. Made them angry. Made myself sick. Lost friends and even jobs because my innocent inconsistencies were too impossible to believe. Over the years, they've all felt, believed, or said that I was too smart to be so . . . irresponsible, clueless, inept. And when you hear something often enough from enough people in enough places, you believe it. I certainly did. No matter how hard I've tried to dot each *i* and cross each *t*, I've so often managed to screw up the simple stuff with no better idea of how to prevent another disaster. Humiliated, hurt, and lonely, I felt caught in a hamster wheel, futilely running as hard as I could without actually making progress. Defending my heart again. My character again. Hopelessly explaining myself, again, until even I became sick of my voice.

I Can't Believe I'm About to Teach Brain Science in Public

One of the most delightful experiences for my autistic mind is immersing myself in some subject that has captured my fancy. And by "some," I really mean *any* subject. Several years ago, I compiled a "not-your-average" coloring book featuring the art of people on the spectrum. As I sorted the pieces into common interest areas, one jumped out at me: the Fibonacci sequence and the golden ratio. First, I was intrigued because I knew nothing about this apparently famous topic. Second, I've never been interested in high-level math. But this "magic ratio" number sequence thing somehow tied together the patterns of plates on a pine cone, proportions of human finger bones, dimensions of the Milky Way's spirals, features of Mona Lisa's face, intervals between musical harmonies, and the architecture of the Parthenon. Anything that innately integrated some inborn sense of aesthetic beauty with everything from art to religion to space with some kind of almost secret code?—well, intrigue turns to voracious hunger for learning.

It always does. Be it genealogy or the history of the English language or cake decorating, if my curiosity, imagination, and heart are captured in some way, I am *going* to learn and learn and learn and lose myself in the satisfaction of it all. Combine the poetic, the human, and the academic, and it's a veritable siren song to my soul. Less elegantly put, I latch on like a little dog at your ankle and will not let go. Of course, in the meanwhile, I may well forget to pay the power bill until they leave a message on my answering machine (just happened). Oh well. Everything's a trade-off.

I can honestly say that I never expected to become entrenched in the details of brain function. Don't get me wrong. I loved biology in school. Still, high school AP science is a far cry from publishing multiple books on a neurological subject. Though I could (and can) wax sentimental about the poetic, the human, and the academic . . . there is one more, extremely powerful incentive to "lean in"—personal connection. When an issue touches our lives or the lives of people we care about, we tend to get involved. Dedicated. Grassroots, in-the-trenches, blood-sweat-and-tears kind of driven. Love will do that. I know, because "personal" was behind my education-by-fire, hard-won fluency in neurology, psychology, psychiatry, pedagogy, and probably several other "-ogies" that I've forgotten to mention.

About nine years ago, my daughter took a battery of psychoeducational tests as part of the routine entrance process for a nearby Montessori school. Psych-ed assessments provide insight into the many mental processes that form the foundation of our ability to learn. Beginning with a standardized IQ test, the evaluation reflects more and different impressions than pure "academic" smarts. It gives an overall picture of various kinds of cognitive strengths: verbal comprehension, visual-spatial processing, fluid memory, and processing speed. Here and now, don't worry about what each of those means, just know that the Full Scale IQ score is a combination of those five subsections, indicating someone's overall thinking and reasoning skills. Typically, those subscores are within five points of one another. But among spectrum minds, "splintered skills"—discrepancies of more than fifteen points and as much as thirty, forty, even seventy points—are not uncommon (not universal, for sure, but not uncommon, either). To be clear, I know autistic folks with severely splintered skills who are brilliant professors, scientists, and linguists. Intelligence, as we think of it, isn't the issue. What we're looking at is the brain's ability to efficiently, successfully organize and regulate thoughts and emotions.

The thing is, my daughter started speaking in sentences at ten months. By the age of three, she had taught herself how to read and was devouring chapter books at age four. According to my parents, she came by it honestly. No one had taught me to read, either. In fact, phonics annoyed me to no end. I wouldn't pay attention to anyone who wanted me to "sound out" this or that. Bor-ing. The story goes that one afternoon, my mother pointed to a road sign (not a simple one, but those big green things above highways) and asked me what it said. I told her. Somewhat startled, she pointed to another—just in case I'd somehow memorized a word. I read that one, too. Perfectly. I'd never read a word before. And after that, there was nothing I couldn't read. What correlated with that start and the many years to come where I saw my brainpower as my only security? I figured it had to be my IQ.

Back in my day (am I actually old enough to say that?), we only ever saw one score on IQ tests, which I guess was the Full Scale. I still have the school report of mine somewhere. One number. As a mom twenty-something years into the future, I expected the feedback to be just as straightforward. I knew nothing of subsections or multiprocessing scoring or whatnot. I had never heard of "splintered skills." What's more, I wouldn't have cared—until they mattered to someone who mattered to me. My daughter. When that serious-faced psychologist came out to the waiting room with my little girl and started talking about her significant "point gaps" and how I'd need to schedule a neuropsychological evaluation (which nobody told me was code for "she very likely has Asperger's") . . . I swallowed, put on my big girl panties, and started the research that would not only change her life, but my own, and maybe yours.

Almost a decade later, I've traipsed through the darkest corners of medical journals, an infinite number of psychology tests and texts, hundreds of school reports, and hours of evaluations and have had the privilege of knowing some of the premier neuroscientists and psychology pioneers in Europe, North America, and Australia. I am neither a doctor nor psychologist. But I *do* think that forty-two years of living with autism, a combined thirty-six years of parenting children with autism, and all of the aforementioned self-directed learning have to *at least* earn me *some* extra credit to now present to you (drumroll, please) . . .

. . . a *highly* complex, *highly* important set of *high*-level cognitive processes called executive function (EF) and why they drive the discombobulation of all of us absent-minded professors (even the men), and why our less-than-ideal EF is entirely responsible for a lifetime of "so smart but so stupid" and all the damage that follows.

But since I refuse to be boring, I will do so by discussing Santa. Thank you.

SANTA: EXECUTIVE, FUNCTIONING

(I should make it clear before I go any further that everything I'm about to share has been approved by my eight-year-old. There is, after all, no higher authority on Santa than an eight-year-old. So we're good.)

Everyone knows that Santa is the Head Honcho at the North Pole. It's undisputed fact. But have you ever given thought to how much actually goes into his job? He's running an operation bigger than Amazon. If he's going to pull off *the* global event of the year—*every year*—no matter how much of an A-lister Santa may be, he's going to need the help of a whole network of Christmassy departments and subsidiaries.

To truly appreciate the Big Man, we've got to appreciate what he oversees. Let's think of Mr. Claus as far more than a jolly old elf or chubby figurehead. Let's think of him as the Chief Executive Officer of Christmastown, LLC. Consider the Transportation Bureau, for example.

Transportation, I'm informed by my son, would include Reindeer Central and Sleigh Operations—two interdependent branches comprised of specialty-associated departments. Reindeer Central encompasses Stable Maintenance, the Tack Shop, Waste Removal, the Veterinary Clinic, and Flight Training Facilities. Sleigh Operations includes the Body Shop, Navigational Technologies, Historical Archives, Communications, and Toy Integration.

Each of *those* individual departments is crucial to the success of the branch to which it belongs. Reindeer Central is a bust if the Stable Maintenance crew hasn't provided the animals with adequate food and rest. And Sleigh Operations won't be operating at all if Navigational Technologies doesn't pull its weight. (Santa is terrible with directions.)

Which is all pretty logical. What may need some pointing out, though, is how much departments *themselves* rely on one another. Interdependence is what makes magic possible.

For example, Reindeer Central's Tack Shop employs the North Pole's preeminent leathercraft elves. Their handiwork provides leads and saddles used by the Stable crew; specialty harnesses for the Veterinary Clinic; bridles, bits, reins, and harnesses for Flight Training; *and* the special interior upholstery needed by the Body Shop over in Sleigh Operations. Similarly, the elves at the Flight Training Facilities can't teach the young bucks without up-to-date practice gear from Communications or Navigational Technologies in Reindeer Central.

Numerous, highly specialized, interdependent departments, sorted into two associated branches, integrated and combined to form one bureau. And, way up top, in his senior-level managerial role, is Santa: the *executive, functioning.*

BRAIN TRANSPLANT

Time to make some substitutions. We're going to swap out the North Pole and swap *in* the human brain. That's our new location. Instead of specific, specialized, interdependent departments (like the Tack

Shop and Navigational Technologies) sorted into two *branches* (Reindeer Control and Sleigh Operations), we're now talking about specific, specialized, interdependent *skills* sorted into *categories*: Organization Functions and Regulation Functions.

Organization Functions are skills that help us collect, manipulate, and structure incoming data in strategic, useful ways. *Regulation Functions* are more emotion-based and primarily concern how we interact with the people and situations around us.

Combine the categories, as we did the branches, and instead of Santa, we have the brain's own CEO, organizing and regulating our ideas and actions. The North Pole is managed by function of its executive.

The human brain is managed by executive function. And yes, this really does matter. So stick with me.

EXECUTIVE FUNCTION (EF)

high-level skills that control/manage thought and action

Organization Function Skills

- Planning
- Working Memory
- Attention
- Problem-Solving
- Verbal Reasoning

Regulation Function Skills

- Inhibition
- Initiation of Action
- Monitoring of Action
- Cognitive Flexibility

Executive Functions (EF)

Executive Functions are the brain's set of high-level skills that control and manage our thought and action.

ORGANIZATION FUNCTION SKILLS

Organization function skills collect, manipulate, and structure incoming data in strategic, useful ways.

Planning involves evaluating needs, conceiving of options (including the people, opinions, materials, time frame, and circumstances involved), evaluating those options, determining what steps are needed to bring the selected option to fruition, and ordering those steps to achieve a goal.

- Other EF Skills Involved: working memory, reasoning, problem-solving, initiation of action, and cognitive flexibility
- Challenging to Spectrum Minds Because: New, difficult, or large projects can feel so overwhelming to begin that we simply don't; difficult to gauge amount of time and work involved; social anxiety can hamper clear and regular communication with those involved; our focus and attention are easily distracted and hard to return; adjusting to others' input or changes in the situation is extremely difficult and anxiety-producing.

Working Memory is a type of short-term memory responsible for holding on to snippets of information (a phone number, why you walked into a room, what you were saying—or writing) and using them to complete a task.

- Other EF Skill Involved: extremely enmeshed with attention
- Challenging to Spectrum Minds Because: Sensory sensitivities and overcognition make it difficult for us to filter out environmental stimuli (lighting, smells, textures, conversations, music, etc.); we become easily distracted and are unable to refocus on the original task/conversation, leading to nonlinear (jumpy) thinking and disconnected/confusing explanations/storytelling.

Attention is the focus of the conscious mind's energy.

- Other EF Skill Involved: enmeshed deeply with working memory
- Challenging to Spectrum Minds Because: Our selective attention to foundational input (messages uploaded through the senses to the brain) is excellent—but is considered "hypersensitivity" by typical standards, which define "paying attention" by the ability to ignore distractions; our natural physiology is seen as "inattentive" because our brains pay greater attention to, rather than filtering out, environmental stimuli (think about synesthesia—was I distracted or were typical minds simply too busy looking out to notice what their bodies might otherwise sense?); subsequent poor working memory, which actually makes it even harder to ignore sensory input and almost impossible to sustain outward attention.

Problem-Solving is a multistep process of activities related to noticing, overpowering, circumlocuting, and/or neutralizing obstacles in order to reach a desired goal.

- Other EF Skills Involved: attention, initiation of action, monitoring of actions, working memory, cognitive flexibility, reasoning, planning
- Challenging to Spectrum Minds Because: It depends on the success of almost every other EF skill; recognizing that a problem exists (a clear precursor to trying to solve one) is incredibly difficult due to our trouble identifying our own and other people's emotions.

Verbal Reasoning is the ability to understand, analyze, and think critically about concepts presented in words; not limited to vocabulary size or reading comprehension, but equally about discerning a speaker's written or spoken main idea, tone, perspective, and intention.

- Other EF Skills Involved: planning, working memory, attention

- Challenging to Spectrum Minds Because: We have frequent difficulties accepting and responding to assumptions we find illogical or inaccurate (multiple choice and true/false questions are a nightmare—too many unclear nuances and alternate possibilities to even answer. And sometimes open response questions, too. In an advanced placement class in high school American history, I wrote an entire essay on why the essay question *itself* was in error—there was no way I could write three to five pages arguing something I thought didn't even make sense); we often misread or don't recognize the social cues, body language, tone of voice, and social rules that underpin all communication, whether written and spoken; result—sarcasm can be hard to detect, language is interpreted literally (e.g., the period egg), the telephone is detested (no visual cues), texts cause blowups, and I watch TV with the closed-caption subtitles.

REGULATION FUNCTION SKILLS

Regulation function skills are initiating, inhibiting, and monitoring thought and action.

Inhibition is the real-time ability to pause, think, and choose which ideas, feelings, and actions to suppress or allow, whether consciously or subconsciously.

- Other EF Skills Involved: attention, verbal reasoning, problem-solving, cognitive flexibility, working memory
- Challenging to Spectrum Minds Because: The very colors and sounds and textures of the world are so hard to ignore; we have significant trouble identifying our emotions and are overwhelmed before we realize it; we struggle to remember that our experiences and feelings and ideas are not "universal"; what people say and think and feel isn't necessarily what they mean; the directions we hear are often incomplete or misinterpreted; alternate choices don't occur to us; attention is unpredictable; ideas are fleeting; anxiety builds and reminds us of all there is to dread . . . and we blurt and post and hit

"send" and regret it almost immediately, act out impulsively—both emotionally and physically, restrict conversation topics or "brain dump" even though we know other people are bored or annoyed, but we absolutely can't seem to stop ourselves and make hurricanes out of raindrops—jumping to the most catastrophic scenarios, acting on the logic of anxiety instead of possibility, wounding ourselves and our relationships in the process.

Initiation of Action involves beginning any new activity.

- Other EF Skills Involved: problem-solving, cognitive flexibility, inhibition, planning
- Challenging to Spectrum Minds Because: Our minds are more prone to zooming in intensely on parts—of things, of ideas, of conversations or dialogue, of sensation, of writing, of puzzles or equations, of problems—but when we're presented with a whole task or idea or concept (called the *gestalt* or "big picture"), ironically, it can be hard to see those small, more manageable parts, much less figure out how to come up with a strategy or plan of action that doesn't trigger our social anxiety or sensory sensitivities so that we choke up before we start. We're called lazy and irresponsible because we seem to just be procrastinating or uninvested, but really, we are probably overcomplicating things. It's much safer doing what we're doing right here and now, not messing up or embarrassing ourselves, disappointing other people, or trying to adapt to unforeseen circumstances, so . . . even when we *do* know what to do next . . . even when we can't explain it ourselves . . . even when we know that whatever's coming is inevitable . . . change is hard to start.

Monitoring of Action is the error detector and corrector, constantly operating in the background, alerting only when there is an abrupt change nearby *or* taking the foreground in unfamiliar circumstances or when learning a new skill so that mistakes can be noticed and adjustments made quickly and frequently.

- Other EF Skills Involved: attention, cognitive flexibility, inhibition, working memory
- Challenging to Spectrum Minds Because: The vicious sensory processing/environmental, filter/selective, attention/working memory cycle is so very challenging that we tend to find ourselves in a much more regular state of emotional hypervigilance, a state of alert that makes it hard to distinguish a real situation in need of attention from any other moment, leading us to either overreact to the smallest hint of error or become so overstimulated that we need to tune out and "reset" by physical stimming (motor distractions like tapping or bouncing, or mine, running my fingers back and forth over my cuticles), vocal stimming (talking or singing or running scripts/accents), or mental stimming (losing ourselves in a special interest) . . . during which time we turn our monitoring off so completely that we're prone to tumbles, accidents, collisions, and whopper-sized mistakes.

Cognitive Flexibility is the ability to shift, adapt, reconsider, and adjust thinking and/or attention in response to changes in the situation or environment (you've got to drive the repair shop rental instead of your car; the channel is switched; there's a new topic, a change in social circumstances, or in game instructions); also, the ability to consider multiple answers to a question or aspects of a situation at the same time, such as opposing points of view—accepting "and" instead of "but"; last, task switching—changing activities before completion, the ability to stop doing one thing and start doing another.

- Other EF Skills Involved: attention, inhibition, problem-solving, planning, verbal reasoning
- Challenging to Spectrum Minds Because: Difficulties in other EF processes (especially planning and problem-solving) make it harder for us to form new thought and behavior patterns, which are necessary for anyone to adjust to any change of any magnitude; since adapting is that much harder, it's that much more anxiety-producing, so—out of *anxiety and fear, not stubbornness or disrespect*—our thoughts and opinions

crystallize into rigid, unbreakable things, we cling tightly to enforcing rules, following routines and repeating behaviors, activities, and habits (rather than "task switching"); trouble "seeing someone else's side" can be a problem of the brain's impaired EF, not flawed character; diminished "theory of mind" or "lack of empathy" may be reduced cognitive flexibility and a legitimate struggle not to be willing, but *to be able*, to consider multiple points of view.

Thanks to EF, typical minds can readily set and achieve goals; delegate tasks; plan effectively; organize ideas, things, and spaces clearly; initiate tasks; monitor their emotional reactions to situations and people; and adapt to change. In day-to-day life, strong executive functioning means setting an alarm clock, getting up when it rings so that there's time to shower, putting on clean clothing, navigating transportation, and arriving on time for class or work, with all necessary preparations taken and supplies on hand. Daily. While making small talk over breakfast, answering an important text, and making note that the car needs to go in for on oil change. Which will actually take place *before* it stalls on the side of the road.

Typical EF means that a Girl Scout is able to plan out how long a badge project will take—or that a dad will have the ingredients for and fit in the time to prepare his promised bake sale contribution. Moreover, if necessary, these two are able to stop midway, calmly certain that they'll remember to return to what they were doing, pick up where they left off, and finish on time. We, however equally well intentioned, are more likely to sacrifice needed rest in order to arrive hours early and then fall asleep in our cars or at our desks anyway. Or forget to start the grocery shopping in the first place.

Trains and Fireflies

The calling card of autistic brains—the single most omnipresent, most impactful distinction of our minds versus the neurotypical—is the discrepancy between our executive function skills . . . and everything else. Which means what, exactly? How and where *are* we focusing our attention? The answer is trains and fireflies. Though not literally.

Trains: If typical minds are cars, making sharp turns, switching lanes, and cruising easily around traffic circles, then in many ways, at many times, ours are train brains. Powerful, focused forces that require tremendous effort to slow or redirect. When we are truly engaged in a topic, we *do* become utterly oblivious to the passage of time. I can remember many times I worried my family unnecessarily or arrived late to appointments because, in the truest sense of the phrase, I literally lost track of time. Not okay, but true. And worth understanding. Because, hyperfocused on whatever task it is that has captured our attention, we are at our most productive, most satisfied, most brilliant, most content. Please, protect and respect that as much as possible. I know that it can be hard and even downright miserable to draw us away from whatever we're doing or feeling or thinking—to try to overcome our mental inertia. And I know it's necessary. Just, please . . . give us time and preparation. Gently. Like any train, if we have to veer off course faster than we've prepared, we derail. And we crash.

Fireflies: In firefly mode, we are everywhere at once. Mentally, we alight from idea to idea to idea, excited by novelty and energized by the connections we make. New possibilities, new patterns, new *everything* is *everywhere*! There is no time for details or structure. No interest in tedium. We'll lose the momentum of our creativity if we get bogged down in implementing the imagination. It's a fun place to be—*if* someone else is there to organize and systemize those wonderful ideas into life. Otherwise, we'll get going, but before we finish, at least fourteen new sparks have sent us flying. The wind has caught our wings, and we've forgotten what we were doing in the first place.

Our minds slide back and forth along that continuum. Some of us spend more time as trains than fireflies, some the reverse, some are equal-opportunity thinkers sliding back and forth and hanging out in between. In any case, while our measurable skills are not *always* low, compared to those of neurotypical brains, they are low*er* than other parts of our own cognitive functioning. There *is* a gap. And *that* is the frustration we feel. And *you* feel with us. Because our mental energies are spent so differently, tasks that require planning, organization, working memory, time management, or flexible thinking can become mammoth challenges. We're operating in a mental environment that's more like an Apple Store than an office: movement, space, creativity, and lots of hyperlinks, all leading down infinite bunny trails . . . wonderful, inspired stuff—until we look up and discover that three hours have gone by without our actually finishing any one thing.

EF speaks to how well we manage the unexpected, the unfamiliar, and the unstructured. For those of us on the spectrum, "how well" . . . is often not very well. And though our faltering stems from real challenges within our brains, the fact is that the tax collector doesn't really care why we've forgotten to pay, and the neighbors don't really care why we've let the grass go. No matter how wonderful or world-changing our ideas, to anyone looking, we seem like too intelligent, rude, self-absorbed, irresponsible people making excuses. And we will be treated as such. If we don't want to repeatedly disappoint ourselves and the people whose respect matters to us, then we have to understand why it is that we think as we do and struggle as we do. Like it or not, until we grasp the "whys," we won't find effective tools to support the day-to-day tasks that *must* happen in order to keep a job, maintain a relationship, and feel like competent adults.

The reason we feel "so smart but so stupid" is that we are lost, confused, alone, and misunderstood in the space between our intelligence and our executive function. Whether it's a small gap or a chasm, the effect is still the same. We know we should know, but we don't know what we should know or how to explain why we don't know it.

So, on behalf of all of us who really and truly are wired differently—even if we're invisible on the Monopoly board—please trust in this: we *are* trying. And we're really *very* good at thinking and managing information . . . in the ways that come most naturally to *us*. Our normal. Not yours. Respectfully, I'd assert that most neurotypicals would find themselves equally distracted, frustrated, and disappointed were *they* the minority living in a primarily autistic world. It doesn't make us right and them wrong or vice versa.

It's simple logic that we are all much more successful in life if we are encouraged to be, and, in fact, sought after for being, ourselves.

Functional Cruise Directors

Certainly, EF is challenging to both men *and* women on the spectrum. But a 2017 study, published in the journal *Autism Research*, showed that autistic females have more weaknesses than autistic males in both executive functioning skills *and* in compensating successfully with other adaptive behaviors.

It's a problem of nature, yes, but also of nurture. Men who struggle with deadlines or disorganization more frequently find the socially acceptable support of executive assistants, wives, or mothers . . . they *are* the "absent-minded professors," while there is no word for emotional, discombobulated women. At least, there is no kind or endearing word. In our recurring role as the family "cruise director," women are often expected by both custom and peer communities to manage not only our own personal and professional schedules, but also those of our children, pets, and partners, and to shuffle every one of those components at a moment's notice. As a rule, the demands are just more punishing—and so is the judgment.

When we, girls who use big words and think big thoughts and work frantically on next week's project while ignoring today's urgent one, get lost in the minutiae of color coding without actually using the resources, come undone emotionally, miss appointments, or lose what we borrow, of course we're misunderstood. It's no surprise that we are seen as lazy, ungrateful, or self-centered. That we wear through patience and second chances. It's only logical that we lose friends and jobs. That we rack up no-show fees, ruin credit scores, and mismanage savings.

Regardless of class rank or intellectual acumen, our most painful struggle is against a never-ending sense of inadequacy. What good is "intelligence"—what good are *we* when life's most basic, mundane tasks bewilder, stymie, and derail us? After all, most of us don't realize that actual neurological differences, not character flaws, are to blame for our troubles. That we cannot *seem* to do what we actually *cannot do* without informed, intentional supports. Lacking those, we often suffer from chronic depression and terrible anxiety. We try to force control over trivial things, growing ever more rigid in our thinking and brittle in our emotions. We beat ourselves up, self-harming, seeking escape in drugs, sex, alcohol. We find ourselves divorced 30 percent more than neurotypical women and attempt suicide in numbers far beyond our male spectrum counterparts. Many of us stop trying at all. We give up on ourselves. Our homes. Find ourselves cut off from family support. Many of us quit school and accept employment that is neither financially nor intellectually commensurate with our abilities.

There is deep shame in knowing so very much *about* so very much, bursting with complicated, nuanced things . . . and constantly falling short anyway. To our parents, teachers, friends, spouses, and employers, we are confounding disappointments. To ourselves, we are fearful frauds, sure that our ineptitude is as obvious to others as to ourselves. And through it all—as best as our brains are capable—we *are* trying to remember it all. To be on time. Prioritize well. Get started. Remain flexible. And stay calm.

Pivot Point

It makes perfect sense, really, to assume that a child who can recite the name of every Greek god or sing entire scores of Broadway musicals should, clearly, be able to remember where her homework log is. Or where her shoes are. Miss I-Wrote-a-Bestselling-Book-in-Three-Weeks ought to be able to plan enough time for a shower and grocery shopping, let alone remember a friend's birthday, get to—well, *anything*, on time, pay her bills, exercise, bring dirty dishes out of her bedroom, take out the trash, do some laundry, and even go to the dentist. Only usually, I don't. I try. I use alarms and reminders. And I make sure I'm there for every important school event so my kids will *never* wonder if they mattered enough. But *my* mother still helps with playdates and laundry and food shopping. I *know* that I go nonstop. She knows it, too. I *know* I give my everything all day, every day. She knows *that*, too. And we both know I can't do life alone, even though most people looking at me probably believe otherwise.

Being identified as having autism did not rewire my mind, which still darts like a firefly and drives like a train. But discovering the autism answer *did* lift some of the feelings of blame from my shoulders, turning the issue into one of scientific cause and effect. It proved, unequivocally, that I am not now, nor have I ever been, lazy or disinterested, irresponsible or self-centered. From time to time, my behavior may have appeared such. But as descriptors of me as a person or of my intentions, well, nothing could be further from the truth. My struggles with disorganization, poor planning, impulsivity, mental inflexibility, and inattentiveness *are not now, nor have they ever been, nor will they ever be* due to any character defect.

What's more, in hindsight, I'd actually posit that instead of being particularly bad at multitasking, we're actually experts at it. Why? Because we are doing it *constantly*. During any casual coffee date, for example, we are thinking about our eye contact (or lack of it) and trying to match the cadence of the other speaker, gauge facial expressions, absorb, understand, and react to social cues, filter out sensory distractions, process and use new information, respond in ways that won't accidentally offend or sound self-interested, remember to ask questions . . . and smile. Which is simply *too* much for anyone to navigate spontaneously without becoming confused or stressed. We literally blow a fuse. The cognitive demands simply max out our brains, and we're lucky if we even remember there *is* a latte waiting to be drunk.

So much of the internal experience of autism is invisible to outsiders. No one else can see the struggle with our core cognitive differences—just the evidence of things gone sideways. In discovering that our blunders are based in neurology, not defect of character, we are given the choice to let go of judgments past. And passed. EF is a complicated web of knots tied up in curlicues. By learning and understanding the workings of our minds, the power of self-determination becomes much more our own.

Importantly, I have to caution typical folks who read this and think—hey! Now we can just teach her to plan or break things down or strategize or . . . whatever else. It doesn't work that way. When we come to recognize the roots and reasons, the results make much more sense, yes. And yes, there are a plethora of apps, tips, and strategies all designed to support people with executive function trouble. Please notice I said *support*. There are adaptive tools to make life easier for people whose hearing is diminished or sight is impaired—but no one is going to try to *teach* them to hear or see better. To presume to do so would be not only arrogant, it would be ignorant. And insulting. As if, "Doggone it, those danged deaf or blind folks, they're just not *trying*, that's the problem. We put out all of these tools. We're teaching them to listen and look! Guess they're just too . . . stubborn, lazy, entitled, self-centered . . . to try and learn." Phooey.

Mark Twain said that "a man who will not read has no advantage over the man who cannot read." Make no mistake. An autism diagnosis is *not* a get-out-of-jail-free card. *No one is entitled to be intentionally disrespectful of another person.* I'm most certainly not here to say otherwise. The use of supports and adaptations should be a wonderful follow-up to diagnosis—more than that, though, I think it's my responsibility to the people I love, live with, work with, and . . . to myself . . . to use whatever I can to make all of our experiences together as authentic, considerate, and productive as possible. And. As I do for them, I need those same people to understand that *I can't be taught or disciplined out of autistic brain functions.* Sure, I can practice drills and add to my bag of tricks and tools. But every new situation is a new situation, and EF skills are too interrelated and too interdependent to think that a repair here and some fine-tuning there are going to "fix" me. It's not going away. It's not.

Personally, I have no intention of sitting around and mourning that. I'm one of the lucky ones; I'm too busy getting on with living to sit here and complain. All I ask is a little extra patience, even if I look like I have it all together. Camouflage, remember? So, yes, please. Patience. And one more thing: when in doubt about me, default to kindness. I step in it big and bad and—if I had to sum all of this up in one phrase, well, you've already heard it: I pull the rug right out from under myself when everybody's looking. Just trust that I didn't mean to make anyone fall.

My version of normal does not look the same as most people's. Fact. It's an unemotional, demographic tally that means autistic neurology, as an overarching concept, occurs less frequently. Those of us on the spectrum *are* simply less typical. Remember, though, that "normal" and "typical" are *not* synonyms. There is no *actual* difference between a flower and a weed. That's a judgment made entirely by the beholder.

Sure. It's more typical to yank dandelions up by the root, but I'm less typical.

I make wishes.

CHAPTER 5

Mythbusters: Open Heart Emotion

I met the bravest boy in England on a Saturday in October. Oxford Autism UK had brought me to town to give two talks, and I'd just finished the first, explaining "Asperkids" (my word for young people with what was then called Asperger Syndrome) to parents, therapists, teachers, and families from an "insider's" perspective. During the lunch break, a lovely couple walked over with a book for me to sign. They were very kind, enthusiastic about the message and point of view, and excited to have the book personalized. Mom bubbled. Dad nodded. Both tried to pry some semblance of pleasantry out of their rather miserable-looking ten-year-old son, Jack. I grinned at them—and at him. No worries, I assured them with a twinkle in my eye. I wouldn't have wanted to be cooped up in an auditorium on a Saturday, sitting with my parents, listening to grown-ups talking about what was "wrong" with me, either.

No one—especially not a kid—wants to have to hear about all that is wrong with him, about how and why no one likes him, about how much he has to change . . . all of the troubles he causes, the problems he has, the disappointment he is, or the dozens of strangers who will interfere with his life and with his family. I knew that. And Mom and Dad seemed to be able to tell. It's such a relief to get to be real. To not have to always try so very hard to keep up appearances. To have a moment when you can stop worrying, as you always do, that you or your child—or more often, both—won't be liked. Pasting on a smile when you feel so alone is exhausting work.

Looking up from the book in my hands, I half-whispered, "Make you a promise, Jack?" From under the lid of his cap, the boy's eyes met mine for a second. "That last talk was for the grown-ups. Explaining us to them and all. This one is gonna be really useful for *you*. And remember, I told everyone I don't do boring. So you'll be fine. Okay?" Jack considered me and dipped his chin ever so briefly. I did the same. We had a deal, then.

A child's respect is a precious thing, hard to come by, only genuinely won. And in every case, children deserve, I believe, nothing less than unfailing love. Above and beyond that, though, is the entirely different level of commitment that *has* to be made to one whose trust has been broken and soul has been wounded. These are the people I champion. Of all ages and types, really. Because the feeling I get from each and every individual is the same—it's our universal need, often hidden beneath anger, arrogance, disinterest, or distrust . . . a quiet, insistent plea to be loved exactly as we are. That is what I sense. Everywhere. Like a chorus of soloists who don't realize they are singing the same song at the same time.

During the next talk on the "secret social rules"—the directions to the game of life that we, rudely, seem *not* to have been given—I glanced Jack's way now and again, out there, amidst the sea of faces. He'd been playing a Nintendo DS through the entire first speech. But now, he was with me. Watching. Hard. I smiled, satisfied, thinking happily: Connection made. Deal kept. Win one for the good guys. On we go.

What I didn't know—*couldn't* know—was that the real story would be in what came next. That one of the most powerful moments of my life was only minutes away.

After I finished speaking, several local autism advocates joined me onstage for a Q&A session. Volunteers ran about the enormous room with microphones for about twenty minutes before the call went out for any last questions. Much to my surprise and delight, Jack raised his hand. Over scurried the lady with the microphone . . . and we waited. Hundreds of people . . . waited. In silence. That seemed to go on forever. I could see Jack's cheeks flare scarlet. Suddenly, he thrust out his arm toward the volunteer, returning the microphone. She took it, reluctantly, and cast about for some sort of direction. His parents huddled in, encouraging him to give it another go.

And we all waited.

Shaken but not completely deterred, Jack tried again. Out went the hand, again. There was the mic, again. And . . . the silence. Again. All morning, the huge room had been drafty and cool, but now it had gone scorchingly hot as the focus of every single person there honed in on Jack. The entire place pulsed, as though, if we could, we would push that boy right up and through this moment, let him know the force behind him, like a mother whale lifting its newborn calf and breaking the ocean surface for that first gulp of air. But we couldn't. The moment was his, and it was slipping away with every silent second that passed. Jack shook his head, almost scolding himself, then, with slumped shoulders, he handed the microphone back. Again.

"Jack?"

My very American, very amplified voice rang through the silence. A room full of confused-looking faces snapped my way. They had no idea how I knew this child's name, I realized . . . but there had to be a reason I did.

Out of all of the people in attendance, there was a reason that *this* boy and I had made a deal. That *this* boy's name had stuck in my head. I was sure of it. And I was sure it was so that in *this* minute, he would hear me and know that I was totally and absolutely speaking to *him*.

"I don't know if you know this," I began gently, "but public speaking is one of the most common fears among adults. And Jack, here you are, a kid, and you've already reached out for the microphone *two times*! That's something most people couldn't do, and you did it *twice*. I can tell you that I would absolutely appreciate the chance to hear whatever it is you have on your mind, because you probably have some really keen insights and important questions that would be great for us all to learn from. But even if you decide *not* to say anything else, I just want you to know that you have *already* been the bravest person in this room."

He reached his arm. He grabbed the mic. And Jack began to speak.

The particulars of what he said aren't nearly as important as the fact that he said them, or the fact that I have photos taken of the two of us afterward where Jack is flexing his muscles because I'd called him—and the entire audience had agreed—the bravest boy in all of England. Years later and an ocean apart, Jack's mom (or mum) and I are still Facebook friends, meaning that I have gotten to watch as he has grown into an autism advocate and public speaker for Oxford Autism UK, for his school, and for himself. That boy is, and always will be, my heart. Just as are Beth, Louis, Izzy, Ollie, Alex, Nikolai, Hannah, Rainbow, Nina, Anne-Louise, Chloe, and so many more.

How many highly sensitive autistics have been turned away because they don't fit a misinformed stereotype? Because they, like us, *can* sometimes experience transferred emotions so powerfully that we have to escape them? Or go "shields up," shutting ourselves off from feeling? Or live our entire lives determined to save the world? Theirs is the cause I feel in my bones. The one I will forever champion. Because I *do* feel big and love big and try big. And because all of us—young, old, and everything in between—all of those kids and *my* kids and me—are on the autism spectrum, yes. But first and foremost, we are *all* on the human spectrum. Real and alive and so very, very on purpose. Different. Together.

Can You Feel Me Now?

Which leads me to this point: the myth of the unfeeling autistic who cares about no one but herself *is,* in fact, just that—a complete and utter myth. Actually, it's far more and far worse. It's an ill-informed stereotype built on incomplete understanding and bad science, carrying with it serious moral, ethical, and practical implications for millions of people around the world.

So there.

In medical schools, they teach students that the simplest answer is usually right. When you hear hoofbeats, the saying goes, look for horses, not zebras. I am not a zebra, people. Just a horse of a different . . . neurology. Let me be perfectly clear: autism is a condition of neurological distinctions that are based in the brain. We don't *actually* have *different* brains. We have differently *wired,* equally *human* brains. Human functions—like *feeling*—aren't *missing*, for crying out loud. They're just different in brains that are neurologically different, regardless of which way the comparison is made. Or, as Charles Addams put it, "Normal is an illusion. What is normal for the spider is chaos for the fly." No matter who's the fly and who's the spider, it still makes sense.

In Denver, in July 2015, Dr. Temple Grandin, Dr. Patty Gatto-Walden, a nationally recognized psychologist specializing for over thirty years in work with highly and profoundly gifted people, and I were part of a collaborative keynote address that closed the Autism Society of America's national conference. Especially among girls, research was pointing to overwhelming intersections between highly gifted and autistic/Asperger populations. This meant that some of the world's most brilliant people were being held back by their lack of spectrum identification and related lack of psychoemotional support.

Dr. Gatto-Walden spoke first, and though I already knew the substance of her talk, the particular words hit. Hard. "A highly gifted child who is five years old talks like a nine-year-old child, asks questions like a nine-year-old child. A profoundly gifted child [that's someone with an IQ of 145 or higher . . . which includes me] talks and wonders like a thirteen-year-old." By definition, we are asynchronous in our development. We are, I've often said, like Swiss cheese. Strong in some ways with holes in others.

"Add in the emotional sensitivities we see of spectrum children," she continued, "and these girls may act more like a three-year-old at five or a five-year-old at nine—imploding or exploding. They'll often need more or specific types of physical contact. May cry more. Need security objects."

At the head table, I gasped and hoped it wasn't too obvious. I had a security blanket from birth until I was ten. And even then, the only reason Blankie went the way of the garbage collector was that my dog ate it. Ate it and pooped it out on my front lawn, and it was gone before I ever got to say good-bye . . . which I would have . . . even to Blankie poop. A Blankie funeral. Same thing when my mom sold the only family car I'd known . . . fondly called "the Jennymobile." I must have sobbed for a day straight. These objects were my familiar, tangible comrades, even when I couldn't figure out how I'd made my parents mad, or why kids didn't seem to appreciate the "stand out" features adults did . . . people were—are—unreliable. Blankie. The Jennymobile. They stuck by me and didn't ever turn and walk away.

How Do I Look?

Much like our thoughts, our feelings tend to run a bit all or nothing. Bliss or grief, pleasure or pain, ecstasy or agony, intrigue or boredom—though the pendulum can even out somewhat over the years. That's a little gift from our funky EF system again. Emotional modulation that works more like an on/off light switch than a dimmer. A friend of mine observed of me, "When you feel something, it's almost as if that emotion is the only one in your repertoire. The others have all disappeared." I can't say that I agree, really. The whole cadre of feelings is always present, they just pass the microphone and step offstage as needed.

I take the point that I *seem* this way to others, though, at least inasmuch as I've been told the same thing before. Internally, I am swarmed with nuance and texture and highlights and lowlights. Perhaps one of the reasons I love writing so much is that siphoning the words takes just a bit longer than speaking them, gives room for editing and chances to infuse more temperature than hot or cold, all or nothing.

But here's a strange thing. For all of that feeling . . . for as much as I am led by my heart more than my head, I always thought that my head—well, my face—matched up pretty well with whatever was going on in that heart. However. Very, very recently, I have discovered that is *not*, in fact, the case. Apparently, when I am really scared or upset, my expression may convey disgust. When I'm nervous or anxious, I look more annoyed. I've long since become aware that my whole "lack of perspective-taking" trouble makes me more likely to say something that sounds short or dismissive, so I make every effort possible to be as hyperaware of tone and word choice as I can be (although it can be really exhausting).

And yes, I knew that a flat affect—less animated, more generic expressions—could be an aspect of autism. But I am *far* from expressionless. In fact, I've been told that it's tough to take a good photograph of me when I'm presenting because I'm *too* animated to grab in a single frame. So it's a bit disorienting to find that I can say what I mean and mean what I say, but still not feel how I look or look how I feel. On the plus side, those who care about me are now more likely to ask if I feel something rather than being hurt or defensive or angry because they are certain that I do.

I guess the thing with autism is that everything just takes a little more work to make it work.

Thankfully, I've spent decades studying and teaching emotional literacy, so—even though I'm prone to overthinking at times (the natural side effect of cognitive-empathy/perspective-taking fallouts)—at least I've got the verbiage to help explain, negotiate, question, and clarify what the heck we're all *trying* to say to one another. For example, when people say, "I feel that . . ." or "I feel like . . . ," what follows next is not actually a feeling. It's a thought or opinion. And, while no one has the right to argue with a feeling, they have every right to debate a belief or idea. Given their confusion over what an emotion even is, it's no wonder that folks have such a hard time communicating with people they care about. Most people are so busy declaring rather than verifying, creating false realities based on misunderstanding and mischaracterization, and mistaking their own thoughts for emotions that they don't even know how they, themselves, actually feel.

A feeling, you see, is *always* an adjective: giddy, reluctant, timid, inconsolable . . . so much more than the impotent "happy, sad, good, and bad." Those are boring, ineffective words that mostly say how disinterested the speaker is. Or, in the case of a lot of people on the spectrum, how little awareness we have of our own emotions—both in type and intensity. Are you delighted or pleased? Both fall under the concept of "happy," but there's a vast expanse between the experience of feeling one or the other—yet unless we learn to name those experiences, we aren't aware of what is going on within, without, or how we ought to consider reacting.

For example, anger is a Band-Aid feeling. It's real and very much present and has to be moved aside gently because its real purpose is to protect a wound underneath. It's that hurt that needs to be healed—if it's not, you're just going to keep needing bigger Band-Aids. So when someone says she's angry, is she? Yes . . . and no. And while we're at it, is she really furious? Or maybe just annoyed? Is she really devastated . . . or maybe disappointed? Until we know what we're actually feeling, we can't really judge other people's reactions or know how to support their feelings well, either.

How do people learn what emotions they're feeling in the first place? Social feedback. A child points to a book. You identify the object as a book. Soon enough, she repeats the word and either is corrected on pronunciation or usage (in which case there will be more feedback the next go-around) or is told she got it right. Not too much leeway there. It is what it is. Feelings, though, are interior things. You can't see a feeling—you can only see how a feeling manifests as expression and behavior. So what happens if our outside doesn't match up with our insides? Or if our outward expression doesn't show a particular emotion in the way our teachers, parents, caregivers, spouses, or even therapists expect?

Simple. Everyone gets extremely mixed-up. We are told we feel one way when we feel something entirely different. We confuse what expressions are meant to match with which feelings—the ones we feel or the ones they say we feel? Or is that how the other person looks when they feel this way? Or are they feeling what I was actually feeling, not what they said I was feeling?

Ya feel me?

ALEXA, TELL ME HOW I FEEL

"A limited understanding of what causes feelings" is just one facet of alexithymia (also of neurotypicals evaluating autistic people, but that's a whole other story)—not a disorder, but a description of a certain "social emotional" profile that happens to fit the way many autistic people experience emotion. It's good shorthand to explain a multipronged set of experiences . . . as long as those who use it dig a little bit and think about *why* we are as we are.

Alexithymia includes the following:

- *difficulty identifying different types of feelings*
- *difficulty expressing feelings*
- *difficulty recognizing facial cues in others*
- *limited or rigid imagination*
- *constricted style of thinking*
- *hypersensitivity to physical sensations*
- *detached or tentative connection to others*

There are good reasons for why many of us have a difficult time identifying or expressing our emotions. I actually designed a system with colored paint chips to help teach grades and shades of emotion; without being given a word bank of feelings (or lots of fiction books to read), everyone else's confusion about the uniqueness of our reactions confuses us, too. Certainly, we have "tentative connections" to other people (wouldn't *you*, if misunderstanding were such a prevalent part of your life experience?). Yes, "hypersensitivity" to physical sensations is a reality in our lives (sensory differences are actually a *part* of identifying someone as autistic).

And limited imagination? Well, that actually goes to our concrete, literal thinking. And tomato plants. When my daughter was little, she would, on occasion, ask me to tell her a story "from your mouth" as opposed to from a book. Every time she did, I would try to assuage her with a song or tell her a story about herself as a baby . . . in other words, I didn't make anything up. I can look around a room and, in seconds, invent the zaniest, most effective learning tools, party decor, or crafty delights you've ever seen. But I could not come up with a story to save my life. Instead, I began to tell her about my dad, who, when *he* couldn't think of a bedtime story to tell *me* as a child—instead told me the story of the life cycle of a tomato plant.

I could not possibly make this up if I tried. (Get it?)

Confusing and dissected. Intense and intellectualized. The emotional adventures I describe can be excruciating and isolating. They can also be exquisitely, passionately beautiful. Differences set us apart from the typical. And give us access to transcend the typical. To certainty and mission. To the most intimate truths of even strangers' hearts.

Which is lovely and poetic and true. And maybe . . . just a little more triumphant than my track record.

POISON, DIPPED IN SUGAR

Matthew was three years older than me and followed me every day after school. Even now, decades later, I can hear his voice shouting from about two house lengths behind, "Hey, Dictionary Brain! You know nobody likes you, right? You know everybody hates you? Hey! Encyclopedia Head! Are you listening to me?" I'd try to ignore him. I'd try to pick up the pace. I'd try to talk over him to the younger girl by my side, humiliated that even a "little kid" knew my shame.

"I heard you go home for lunch, Dictionary Brain. Is that because no one will sit with you in the cafeteria?!" Yes, it was. Even in the cold winter air, my cheeks burned hot. And when, one afternoon, I realized I'd dropped a mitten along the way—a loss that was sure to make my mom mad—I wouldn't turn back for it. No, I wouldn't turn back for anything.

I'm not sure why Matthew had such a problem with me. Of course, as an adult, I'll sagely opine that it had more to do with his own unhappiness than with me. And maybe that's partially true. But the whole story was bigger. It usually is.

In my little town at my little school, teachers had freedom that modern teachers don't. They knew I was bored in class, so they'd let me go—alone—to the school library . . . for hours. What a gift! I'd just walk in, wave at the always-glad-to-see-me librarian, choose a new shelf, and start reading. One by one, I'd savor each book, exploring long-lost worlds, imagining myself happily entrenched in the time or place—any other time or place—to which I so obviously rightly belonged. To me, the biography section was a wall full of friends among whom I could be necessary, silly, maybe even liked. The dinosaur shelves were my own personal Jurassic Park. The Dewey Decimal was, in a way, my guide to a destination where people made sense . . . and so did I.

The only "fee" for endless time among the stacks was that I had to write extra book reports every now and then. Big deal. As far as I was concerned, I'd scored a major coup.

The teachers thought it a good plan, too. In fact, my report on Christopher Columbus so impressed them that I was instructed—as a second grader—to read the whole thing aloud to the fifth-grade classes as an example of how to write an "excellent paper." One of those fifth graders just happened to be Matthew.

Years later, in high school, I somehow discovered that Matthew was neither a strong reader nor writer. So when a certain seven-year-old redhead waltzed into his classroom to "teach" him, he may have felt embarrassed, spoken down to, demeaned. Maybe it reminded him of dreading being called on in class. Maybe it reminded him of thinking he was stupid. Or a disappointment to his parents. It wasn't my idea to go into that classroom, of course, but I was certainly proud of the invitation. I never considered what it might feel like to be a student in that class. Any student. (Although the teachers certainly should have.) I honestly thought the big kids would like me. Looking back, though, it's hard *not* to see how—with no ill intention—chin-up, clear-voiced, "Dictionary Brain" Jenny embodied everything that little boy may have despised in himself. Or maybe not. Maybe he just found me easy pickings. I won't ever know for sure, but I'd be willing to hedge my bets.

January 12, 1991. I was fifteen years old, and my close friend was having a birthday party. Sometime during the course of the evening, a (very cute) boy named Dan led me to a quiet place at a party (okay, it was the bathroom) and kissed me—for real. He was popular, and I felt pretty and special. More than that, I'd never been kissed before—let alone by an older guy who all the girls drooled after. It seemed like a double win to me: milestone life moment *and* serious social status points scored. And of course, like a typical teen, I gushed (quietly, thank heavens) to my girlfriends later on.

Only . . . there's more. My friend, Rachel, liked Danny. In fact, the reason he and I were alone in the first place was that she'd asked me to tell him, privately. To test the waters, check out her prospects. Which I did—right away. Just as she'd asked, I'd beckoned him away from everyone else and told him that Rachel was interested. Only he'd replied by saying, "She's nice. But—she's not the one I really like. [Fill in more cliché words to make a fifteen-year-old girl turn to jelly here.]" It was *me*. He wanted *me*. I absolutely had *not* seen that coming. And yes. I *loved* feeling wanted. I think, if we're honest, we all do.

In my mind, I hadn't done anything wrong. I had spoken for my friend, as asked, and he wasn't interested. End of part one. Then came part two, which was, to me, an entirely separate thing. Dan made a seriously appealing "counteroffer." And I went right along without ever imagining that doing so would upset her. Of course, it did. Terribly.

I get it—now. A clear-cut case of terrible, self-centered, mean girl-gone-wild. Only it wasn't, really. My behavior came across as naive (at best), and more typically callous, self-centered, and maybe even mean . . . yet none of those was actually true. I never thought for a moment I was doing anything wrong or hurtful. Ever. Empathy: epic-level fail.

Somewhere along the line, I figured out—probably from the cold shoulders and the poison-dart glares—what I'd done wrong. That feeling flattered hadn't been the misstep. My mistake was giving in to my own teenage curiosity and insecurity in a way that caused Rachel to feel rejected and embarrassed. And in her place, I absolutely would have felt the same.

There were twenty years between that first kiss and my diagnosis. Before "she's a prima donna bitch" (an actual quote) wasn't the given.

Twenty more years of sunburst highs, followed, almost predictably, by some kind of social blunder and the inevitable slap of unexpected fall-out. Of schoolday mornings, greeted at my locker the same way by the same boy, "No one wants you here. Just go home and kill yourself." Of falling desperately in storybook-mad love, then eventually hearing the same man whisper in my ear in the midst of a crowded dance floor, "You're a bitch and a whore. They don't know it, but I do. And so do you." Twenty years before I would even begin to understand, for myself, that maybe there was another answer. He was right. I *did* know a secret. One I tried to disguise in cheerleading uniforms and sorority letters. In perfect grades, come-hither eyes, and good-girls-don't smiles. I was poison dipped in sugar. A bomb tied up in a pretty bow. Whatever and whoever came too close, I would spoil, without knowing how I'd done it. And then I'd be despised. Then abandoned.

Over and over. And over.

Why? Because I couldn't see what I was doing.

Cognitive Empathy, Theory of Mind, and Mary Poppins

I've said that typical and normal aren't synonyms. Well, neither are empathy and sympathy. Nor are sympathy, empathy, and compassion. I know, I know. It's a little crazy making, but the language used *does* matter because it drastically affects the way the world views and treats us.

By and large, empathy is basically what we would all describe as giving a damn about anyone beside yourself. More technically speaking, it's the human capacity to understand and share another person's emotional experience. If someone says, "Do ya feel me?" it's empathy that allows us to say, "Yeah, I feel you." Because we *do. Deeply.* On or off the autism spectrum, we *do.* We just get there in different ways. Empathy, you see, is not actually *one* thing. It's actually a combination of two distinct skills.

When my daughter was new to kindergarten, the teacher learned about some of her medical history, about her sensory issues, and about anything important from the ongoing psych-ed testing (the one that led to the autism diagnosis). I can still recall the exact instructions that I "share everything" with her. Largely unaware that "tell me all about it" was a pleasantry—a polite show of interest that doesn't *actually* mean what it says—not a literal request, but interest in a summary or "highlight reel" explanation, I followed directions and *did* share *everything*. I clogged her inbox with simply enormous amounts of information—and then sent a binder into school so that anything lost in the process would still make it in. Oh, but I didn't just send tests and reports. Nope, I also included "helpful" articles, advice, and lesson suggestions that would help my girl play on her strengths while developing areas of challenge. The truth is that I was incredibly proud of what I had assembled, collated, and developed. I could always impress teachers, and in this case, that know-how was going to help my daughter off to a great start *and* maybe even give me a chance to develop some lasting relationships at school.

Except the teacher was disgusted with me. Instead of helpful, she found me presumptuous. Instead of being a resource, she found me overbearing and full of myself. She felt challenged in her authority, condescended to, disrespected, and—worst of all—as a result was completely irritated by my daughter. The next week, I was called in to the vice principal's office to receive a bit of a tongue-lashing from him, too. His faculty had many students to consider and many tasks to accomplish. It really was unacceptable for me to have flooded the teacher's email, to speak with such authority to a veteran educator, or to expect such prioritization of my child. Perhaps she didn't belong there, after all.

What had gone wrong? The same thing that did when I was on the Family Advisory Council of the new, major children's hospital here in Charlotte. Knowing how much the patients enjoyed visits from Sir Purr, the mascot of the Carolina Panthers, one of our chairpersons had undertaken a huge endeavor to create a lovable mascot of our own. There had been rounds of brainstorming, and she had gone on to have meetings with artists and administrators, but the truth is that I really, really didn't like the character idea at *all*, and I didn't think the kids would, either. However, I am one for flash-of-lightning creativity. So, when one of those moments hit, I immediately emailed the council with this new, alternate possibility to consider. We had a common goal—each of us wanted it to be super successful. Well, here was a new creative concept that really made sense and a clearly thought-out explanation of why it would likely be well received all round. Did I mention this was the night before the formal presentation to the hospital board? Or that the chairperson never spoke to me again?

I've been around long enough to know that if someone loses a job, they will be upset. If their flight is delayed, they will be frustrated. I understand that certain antecedents lead to certain results, so I can learn to watch for and recognize likely cause-and-effect scenarios. I observe. I collect information—I read novels, watch for patterns, and pay close attention to the description of feelings. I analyze and study psychology and sociology and history to understand people's reactions to various circumstances as well as the explanations of the emotional and strategic motivations behind them. I gather situational evidence. I think *all* the time—mostly, because I am trying *really* hard to intuit what I can't. Because what I *can't* do is feel along with them. Unless I am also affected by a situation, I don't feel their fear or sadness or excitement. I feel *for* them (we'll get to that), but no, I don't feel *with* them. I don't share their pain or joy. I don't because I *can't*.

Every autistic person I've ever asked has agreed that, while she *knows* other people have thoughts and feelings, those thoughts and feelings just don't seem as real as our own. We're told it's true that emotions as vast and encompassing as our own exist within *every other* human. Interactions have proven that we need to behave as if it were true. All the evidence says it's true. But if we are very honest, if we can be truthful without repercussion for just one moment . . . it seems implausible. We don't tell you because we will be judged heartless, cold, frightening, amoral, even dangerous. Because we will be looked on with disdain. Usually, because we *have* been looked on with disdain. We have learned that this part of us is bad. So we keep it to ourselves.

We are, as the expression goes, "mind-blind," the kind of folks Mary Poppins eloquently described when explaining that sometimes a person we love, through no fault of his own, can't see past the end of his nose. If you can't naturally see past the end of your own nose—that is, step outside of your own perspective—you can't imagine multiple ways to solve problems, won't swerve to avoid unseen pitfalls, and don't change tactics when causing invisible harm.

Think back to Dr. Gatto-Walden and my stories about sobbing over the loss of my Blankie or the Jennymobile. How can it possibly be that I feel so strongly if I don't have empathy? The answer is that I *do* have empathy. Lots of it. It's just that vocabulary is getting in the way of seeing *how*. (Fair warning: that strange thing that happens when you say a word over and over and over, and suddenly it starts to lose meaning? Watch out for the burnout. I'm going to say *empathy* a lot in a short time.)

Do you remember Venn diagram logic statements from school? All cucumbers are vegetables, but not all vegetables are cucumbers. All girls are human; not all humans are girls. That sort of thing. Well, imagine that someone did, in fact, wave around a cucumber and declare, "This is Vegetable!" We'd all be quick to correct him. No, that's a *kind* of vegetable. It's not Vegetable. Psst—somebody alert the peppers before they get mad.

The point is that one type of a thing is not interchangeable with the whole. Remember that we defined empathy as "the ability to *understand* and *share* other people's emotional state." There are actually *two* parts to that definition because there are actually *two kinds of empathy*—cognitive and affective—each of which draws upon its own distinct set of skills.

"Cognitive empathy," commonly referred to as "theory of mind," is the ability to understand the feelings, intentions, and motivations of others without having to have them explained. And that's a problem for us, because, when compared to typical brains, autistic minds are severely deficient. Spontaneous perspective taking, clearly a no-go for me. But the challenge extends further to include fantasy and imaginative narrative. My greatest writing ambition is to write and publish fiction precisely *because* it is so incredibly hard for me to really be able to sustain the perspective of multiple characters. This challenge is also part of the reason for using those captions when watching videos. I need as much help as I can to understand what's going on with the plays if I'm to stick with the plot.

And no matter how much illustrative language an author uses, I cannot actually imagine the faces and places she describes. Never do I get to a movie and think, "Oh, that's not how I imagined it to look." No, I have gotten so that the tang and taste of the letters and words create certain feelings that might go along with the story, but for me, a film shows me what the characters see and gives flesh to their perspectives. Don't misunderstand, my reading comprehension is not at issue. It's simply that I can't imagine experiences, places, and people without personal reference. Once I have enough anecdotal examples, I can generalize. But no plan survives contact with reality. Specifics always change, so in this area, I'm always at a disadvantage.

Then there's strategy, or in my case, a complete lack of it. I've been known to say, on many occasions, that I don't play mean-girl games. And that is true. I absolutely cannot abide when women trash-talk one another. There's plenty of room and voice for all of us, I believe, so it's our responsibility to lift one another up as best we can. As I've told my daughter, "One candle doesn't lose its flame by lighting another." That's the ethical side of things. The truth is that even if I wanted to, I couldn't strategize my way through the complicated webs of "girl rules" and queen bees as a teenager, and I can't do it much better now. Worse, because of my mind-blindness, I manage to set myself up for social problems, then can't see payback coming.

In middle school, I got "best friend" lockets with "Mary," a girl whom I'd known less than a year. Now, I'm going to admit, I was thrilled. Not only did I genuinely get along wonderfully with her, but Mary was also *very* popular, and I was really proud to walk around as the other "half" of a best-friend team. We'd gotten close over the summer between sixth and seventh grades, and by the time school was in, we were "BFFs." We had matching outfits, sleepovers, told secrets, the whole bit. Never did it occur to me that when our other close friend, "Jackie," had returned from summer break, she would naturally feel excluded. Nor would I have conceived of the notion that she would retaliate, sideline me, and walk away with the bigger "social currency" prize. It didn't take long for Jackie to convince Mary that I'd been spreading rumors about her, bragging that I was smarter and richer and prettier (of course, I'd said none of those things).

Part one of the mission accomplished, the two of them grew closer and closer . . . by finding ways to break my heart and making sure the *entire class* knew about it. In one particularly humiliating plot, they arranged for a sleepover party full of girls to dupe me into believing that I had a "secret admirer" *and* that he was actually going to call me *there* . . . in front of everyone! I really should've stopped to consider the unlikeliness of the whole thing . . . but I suppose I was too enamored with the possibility to think clearly. That, and I never could have (let alone would have) concocted and organized such a complicated scheme . . . or even exactly what would most embarrass someone or how to do it in the first place. Anyway, the "mystery guy" on the phone was *not* someone's cousin Kevin from Pennsylvania who'd seen my yearbook picture and thought I was cute. It was one of the boys from school disguising his voice. Only I didn't discover any of that until I walked into school on Monday morning. Mary and Jackie walked up, arm in arm with him, and with giant grins announced what everyone already knew. Everyone, that is, except me.

Some years later, I bumped into the lady who'd been Mary's nanny. Out of the blue, the woman grabbed me and smothered me in a hug, "I'm so sorry. I should have stopped them. I'm so sorry." I was confused. Stopped what? Almost every night for the span of that entire academic year, this woman had listened while Mary and Jackie talked on the phone, devising as many ways as possible to make me cry. Looking back, I'm honestly not sure who bears more of the burden for the hell I endured—the pair of twelve-year-olds who singled me out for chronic emotional torture . . . or the adult who could have stepped in at any time but instead chose to do nothing while a child suffered.

Cognitive empathy, then, is a concurrently occurring, multiple-perspective awareness. Neurotypical kids aren't super at it—but do grow into it naturally. We don't. Ever. We either don't notice or don't understand the thoughts we make others think about us—in fact, we have to learn even to consider that others may have reactions distinct from ours. That what is "obvious" to us isn't a given for everyone. For us, "remembering to look both ways" does not come naturally. It takes conscious effort. Always. It accumulates slowly, one situation at a time, day upon day, year upon year, and always—always—by intellectualizing. It's never "just there." Eventually, if we are explicitly taught, we can spot patterns. Try to make some generalizations. But there are so many variable between moments and people and circumstances, even those go wrong more often than not.

That's mind-blindness. And I promise you, it is as real as the physical kind.

We can't naturally anticipate how others will feel in response to what we say or do. Again, that's *can't*, not *won't*. Nobody would punish a blind person for accidentally stepping on his foot, but there's a very different reaction when a "mind-blind" person accidentally "steps on your toes." To be fair, though, I understand that we seem unfeeling when we mess up. Uncaring. Aloof. Rude. We relax. Let our guard down. We stop concentrating on those juggling balls . . . and *bam!* We pull the rug right out from underneath our own feet. Both chicken and egg, the result of and precursor to every experience we have. For us, fear—anxiety—is one thing above all others. Constant. Primal. There's no logic involved.

Life on the spectrum is a literal roller coaster that whirls from giddy nervousness to completely overwhelming anxiety, a gnawing, jittery, ever-present sensation of waiting for the threat . . . waiting for the fear. It's like living with the *Jaws* music playing. You don't see the danger. But you surely know there's something "out there." That's anxiety. We spectrumites, whose bodies and minds are wired a little differently, live with varying levels and intensities of almost perpetual anxiety.

That may sound paranoid—but it's not. Paranoia is irrational fear. Most of us have been bullied, are constantly assaulted by sensory input, and must fend our way through daily social situations that seem random and chaotic. In other words, our anxiety is an absolutely rational reaction to the experiences we have had.

And it all begins . . . when we do. From the day we arrive on the planet, we perceive and react to our senses in organically, neurologically distinct ways. Even as newborns, we need the sensory regulation of rhythmic movement, of controlled contact and white noise—growing speedily into the calming routines of arranging our playthings just so, of precisely repeating the lines from favorite books or programs, learning about topics far beyond our years, simply because of the pleasure of accumulating reliable, unchanging facts.

Of course, we don't have a stamp on our foreheads or take a blood test that suddenly alerts the grown-ups around us to what's actually going on inside our hearts and minds. Behavior is communication, yes. Except we are speaking a different language. And without a reliable, well-understood profile of what a spectrum girl "looks like," it's generous to say that the motivation for *our* behavior is less than clear. Without being able to see our behavior in terms of the larger autism constellation, parents, teachers, and certainly other children don't exactly brim with kindness and patience when confronted by arrogance, tantrums, meltdowns, perfectionism, interruptions, and contradictions. They don't see need behind silliness, coy seduction, bold humor, or social charm. They don't recognize our behavior as trial-and-error anxiety busters, meant to control chaos. They don't hear the thoughts behind our choices: "This world doesn't make sense to me or I to it. It's scary here."

Why would they? We certainly can't explain it for ourselves. So who else will?

No child possesses the vocabulary or the awareness that her experience of the world is unusual. When her body alerts her to danger, and she reacts to those very real physiological alerts with resistance or rebellion or retreat, how is she to educate the adults who misunderstand her as difficult and high-strung? How can she know that her brain's concrete, literal understanding of language reads as disobedient or smug? Or that she comes across as unemotional or overdramatic because of misbehaving mirror neurons? She can't. We can't. We don't know what we don't know. We have no vocabulary to explain experiences that are innate to us but foreign to neurotypical minds.

We have no neurological translator to interpret the world for us or explain the logic behind the many ways we fight for some artificial sense of control. To tell the world that we are not inherently bossy or bad or uncaring. That we are lonely and, brilliant as we may be, unbelievable as it may sound, we don't know how to do better. So we step on toes and offend others. We seem self-centered when trying hardest to connect. We may blame others. We may raise our chins too high, arrogantly trying to disguise our insecurity. We mimic expertly or hide away. And we learn from experience that there is no one coming to save us, because we can't even explain exactly what's wrong or imagine what would help . . . besides simply disappearing.

We are different, yes. But we are neither stupid nor paranoid. In our positions, who *wouldn't* be a little bit afraid of every morning meeting, every new acquaintance, every change in whatever "controls" make life feel less dangerous, less random? We simply cannot intuit what others do. We misunderstand. And they misunderstand us. We know what it is to be resented, and even disliked by those closest to us from early on. And we don't expect good things to last for long. From classrooms to workrooms, we are accustomed to feeling victimized, shamed, cast aside; to say such things aloud would sound paranoid or suspicious; more often than not, we don't speak up. Not even to ourselves.

Experience teaches, again and again, that while we possess certain unique abilities that can transform society for the better—pattern detection, information recall, laser-like focus—those skills are almost inevitably overshadowed by our social missteps. By our inability to intuit others' perspectives while perceiving our own as obvious, singular, and without need of explanation. By our own impulsivity—hyperbolic, almost heliotropic reactions to glimpses of what may (or may not) be kindness. By believing others to be as transparent as we think we are. By trusting their intentions will be selfless and genuine. By not recognizing how we end up in predicament after predicament. And by not noticing the predators—who see it all and are everywhere.

We, spectrum girls, are playing at the game of life without a copy of the rules, and almost universally, the result is complex post-traumatic stress disorder: a normal psychological response to abnormal chronic circumstances. We develop anxiety that feels ridiculous, hypervigilant, tedious, and exhausting to everyone around us but, in all fairness, is entirely informed and relevant and natural. We have not the social armory to bolster our hearts, or to understand our bewilderment. We have not the sophistication or flexible perspective to judge or imagine a world in which our experiences are validated, much less valuable. Therefore, we fully expect to be undercut, undermined, abandoned, ridiculed, and traumatized. And more often than not, we are right.

People on the spectrum often live in a perpetual state of anxiety over "What? What's wrong? Are you mad at me?" and walk around with either a disarming grin or false bravado. We may deflect broadly—"Whatever—I'll show you how much I care about what *you* think!" (which, we are admitting despite ourselves, is quite a lot). We may lash in slanted, cutting ways that *really* mean, "You hurt me deeply here in a way that hurt me on a bigger, lifelong thematic way. I'm mad at you for that. I don't want to hurt. I don't want *you* to be the one who hurts me. And I feel really bad about me and I need help. Please—don't get scared off. Please be strong enough to find me in the hurting." We are most fragile when we are sharpest. *Vulnerably* angry. *Hopefully* angry. And looking to please, too. We live in the dance space in between.

Inadvertently, we offend or come off as insensitive or somehow inappropriate, *and* we know that very often, we completely miss the first, subtle signs that we've made waves. So we're used to feelings getting big and problems getting bigger before we spot them, always wondering where the next explosion will come from a bomb we never knew we'd set off in the first place. It's only natural that we're in a constant state of hypervigilance. We know, from experience, that until someone explicitly gives logic to their feelings, we won't really know *why* what we've said or did has caused harm or consider how else we might have responded.

That's goes just as much for positives! Not long ago, in the middle of a conversation, someone said, "I love, you, Jenny," to me in a tone of great warmth, sweetness, and affection. Obviously, something I'd said or done had—right then and there—inspired a bubble of good feelings to well up and pop out into the open. Something. Only, I had *no* idea what that something was. So I asked. "Why do you say that—now?"

Let's be clear. If the other person hadn't known I had autism or didn't know what that meant (that I'm often not aware of the effect of my words/actions on others), I suppose my question really could have sounded self-serving. What I was *really* asking was "Please tell me. What good thing am I doing right now that made you feel so good about me—because I want you to keep feeling that way, and I need to know what I should keep doing." Sure, without perspective or understanding, it might have seemed that I was seeking praise . . . or "trying to get attention." But I wasn't. I was "reinforcement-seeking."

Like a physically blind person might ask a sighted one to "paint a word picture" of what she cannot see, mind-blind people need word pictures, too. Typical people easily notice the positive or negative responses to their behavior. It's fairly effortless—as natural as actually hearing someone say "yes" or "no." To them. But not to us. Not only can't we pick up on "subtle" feedback—we don't even know we've missed anything to begin with . . . not until it's too late, and no one is speaking to us anymore.

Over the course of my life, as a child and as an adult, in many, deeply intimate ways, I've been deceived and abandoned because I never saw problems coming . . . and because I believed what was in front of me rather than what logic made clear to others. So it's probably no wonder that I'm now fascinated by stories of long-ago courts where people plotted and manipulated one another to suit their own ends . . . or by profilers and forensic psychology where brilliant minds spar in toe-to-toe dances of tactics and deception. I study out of fascination, yes, and probably, on some level, protection, too. I never learned bridge or poker, both of which my mother plays excellently, and despite the fact that I am a total word nerd, I almost always lose at Scrabble. I just don't do strategy—because I can't. Strategy demands the deliberate use of perspective taking. I can't see ahead enough, can't jump back and forth between the mind of another player and myself. And, though my ideas are never-ending and feedback wonderful, I'm really quite lousy at running a business. I am a helper because I want to be, yes, and also because I cannot effectively do anything else.

Affective/Emotional Empathy: What Happens Once We Know

People on the autism spectrum do not react to as many interpersonal situations as neurotypicals expect (and often as experience has taught autistic people to expect, too). That is absolutely true. The big problem for us is that as long as professionals and the public mistake perspective-taking "cognitive empathy"/"theory of mind" for empathy in general, we are wildly misunderstood as being cold, shut off, and uncaring, when nothing could be further from the truth.

Once we remove the perspective-taking pitfalls, we're talking more about catching feelings than understanding thinking—we're talking "affective" or "emotional" empathy. Formally, it's our ability to respond with an appropriate emotion to another's mental state. Informally, it's how we feel and behave if/when we understand what someone else is going through. Largely, it's what we usually refer to as sympathy or compassion—feeling delighted or afraid or concerned or thrilled *for* someone, doing what we can to alleviate any suffering, and securing them in love. That's emotional empathy. And that we've got in spades.

In our Denver keynote, Dr. Gatto-Walden had explained that "ethically, morally, spiritually, the children I'm describing care so much that they see the world as their global community. See others' pain as theirs to champion. Their responsibility."

Yes, yes, and yes. Instantly, I remembered being a child and racing home to call 911—a squirrel had been run over in the street but wasn't actually dead. It needed help. And there was so much more. As a college freshman, I'd collected all the loose dogs on the campus main green, mistaking them for strays. Prepared to call security with a makeshift leash and somewhat of a chaotic pack at my heel, I'd been stopped at the phone by a *really* big senior. "Hey," he'd rumbled, "um, that's my dog." (Perspective-taking fail *and* giant—if not graceful—empathy win.)

In high school, my tennis teammates nicknamed me "Happy Head." I bounced across courts, constantly singing little tunes, smiling at everyone, getting even the crankiest upperclassmen to smile back. On summer breaks, I worked as a camp counselor, playing in creeks and making lanyard bracelets right alongside the kids. During college, my sorority sisters made me their ritualist—the president was the "head" of the chapter, I was the "heart." And over *those* summers, I taught adult English as a second language classes on the outskirts of Providence. After Brown, I went to Columbia University's Graduate School of Social Work in New York to study the emotional dynamics and communication techniques of family and individual therapy. Every other day, I set out for fieldwork as a counselor in an inner-city high school in the Bronx. Two subway trains, a mile-long walk through open lots, and a pat-down at the entrance, and finally . . . the kids.

My first *paid* job was as a dating and domestic violence counselor. Disregarding important personal boundaries, I answered pages at all hours. I changed diapers. I compiled inspiring playlists. And eventually, I burned out . . . I just couldn't *not* help, even when it meant running myself to emotional and physical exhaustion. So I became a teacher because, for some ridiculous reason, that seemed to be a less emotionally invested career path. Instead, almost overnight, I was right back in the thick of things—honored that mine was the classroom full even at lunchtime, brimming with kids who needed a shoulder to lean on, a bit of social refuge, a place to vent, some extra encouragement . . . and, on occasion, something to eat.

More recently, I've discovered that there's a popular misconception about authors: people think we make a lot of money. Unless you're J. K.

Rowling or James Patterson, that's just not the case. Personally, I've been a social worker, a teacher, a stay-at-home mother to three spectrum children (the hardest job of all), and now an author/speaker/advocate for people with autism. I've probably spent more to do what I am called to do than I've ever been paid. And I wouldn't change a thing.

In other words, yes. We care. We care a lot.

OUCH: YOUR HURT HURTS ME

Affective/emotional empathy is powerful stuff, which is why it can quickly get too big to contain. There is clinical debate over whether "personal distress," or self-focused feelings of discomfort and anxiety in response to another's suffering, is actually a second aspect or experience secondary *to* high levels of emotional empathy; honestly, though, nobody's following us around from day to day with lists of bullet points and psychology textbooks, so really what matters is the reality of the experience and the certainty that it's connected to the kind of empathy we know well. We have such a difficult time discerning the edges of ourselves and others that we may feel as if we were about to be absorbed, paralyzed, and drowned by *their* emotions. So when we "catch" other people's strong feelings—especially if they stir up emotions that have brought us great pain in our own lives—we experience *their* feelings as *our own*.

This morning I left for a business trip in quite a rush, and my older son became terribly upset. Midway to the airport, my younger boy called to tell me that he could hear his big brother crying "really hard and it's really upsetting me a lot so could you please text him or something?" Notice the particular wording: his brother's distress was causing *him* to feel distressed—he wasn't annoyed or frustrated, and he wasn't explicitly asking me to help his big brother. Primarily, *he* needed my assistance to put an end to the overwhelming "emotional contagion." He knew that I could lessen his brother's hurt—in and of itself an example of affective empathy—and that, in turn, would lessen his own.

Inescapable "self-focused" personal distress was the antecedent to the action, yes. But not the exclusive reason for his call. About an hour later, when I *was* able to FaceTime them, I told my older boy about his brother's call—and the two broke into a giant hug. Yes, compassion (or, as I call it, sympathy in action) was *absolutely* involved. Just look at *how* he affected change. He could have screamed for the crying to stop. Or hidden. Or tried to distract himself. But he didn't. He did what his own experiences had proven to make a difference and called Mom. So, yes. Compassionate care can be a way to stave off personal distress. It's just a little bit of a secondary component when you're drowning, yourself.

Transferred upset is incredibly visceral—and incredibly real. I literally *cannot* watch commercials for organizations that work on behalf of suffering children or animals. I'm not saying that they make me uncomfortable. I'm saying that I either have to leave the room, change the channel, or, if that's not possible, clamp down my eyes and cover my ears until someone tells me it's over. The thing is, I'm not ignoring the issue. I sponsor impoverished children, ask for donations in lieu of gifts, and collect old blankets for animal shelters. I just can't deliver them. It seems to me that the emotions that have the greatest potential of overpowering spectrum folks are, not surprisingly, those that have directly and profoundly impacted us in our own lives. Sometimes that's anger. Sometimes it's fear. Sometimes, as is true with me, it's feeling abandoned, unwanted, rejected, excluded, alone, frightened, and—despite every bit of hope and effort that can be mustered—still unlovable. Those are experiences I've known too often and too searingly to escape once they sweep in.

Henry and Kamila Markram of the Swiss Federal Institute of Technology in Lausanne refer to such extreme reactions as "intense world theory." Though an "intense world" is *exactly* what *I* know as truth, I don't agree that we need a new hypothesis to explain it. It's just what happens when our supersensitive affective empathy meets our not-so-fantastic emotional regulation systems. Which is why I have a really terrible time watching a lot of Disney movies. Even though they're cartoons, the emotion is too dangerous. Too . . . raw. When I have cereal for breakfast, I eat strategically—because I don't want to leave one flake or one O by itself in the milk. And when I was about ten, I sobbed hysterically on my bedroom floor, apologizing for hours to my beloved Cabbage Patch Kids, begging for their forgiveness for being such a terrible mother and neglecting them for too long.

Growing up, I was on the receiving end of that dynamic . . . and I will be very honest: it felt awful and confusing and left me wondering why I didn't matter. If I cried about feeling left out at school, for example, my dad would leave the room. Without a word, without explanation, he just left. And I really needed him to stay. The weekend of my college graduation, my ex-boyfriend returned to campus and violated my restraining order. Despite the fact that my dad knew this young man had abused me sexually, physically, and emotionally, when they came face-to-face, the best my father could summon was "You're not wanted here." And again, he walked away. Not because he didn't care. Really, it was just the opposite. Strong emotions overwhelmed my father—although he could handle a courtroom in any country in the world, his child's pain was, it seems, past the limit of what he could manage.

As his little girl—and even as his eventually grown girl—I was not so understanding. The hollowness of my insignificance, the reverberations of those childhood moments echoed in my psyche, saying, "too much—you're a failure—I don't want this." As a young woman, I can only wonder at the choices and compromises I made, believing that the filth I had endured was still not enough to warrant protection. How I wish he had lived to see me come to understand the man he, himself, could not.

Our hearts can feel so exposed, so raw that bearing one more sorrow would break us. So, when we don't have healthy activities to busy our perseverating brains or a support network to help us process, survive, or even harness it, many people simply try to turn down the volume. To numb the extremes through alcohol, drugs, sex, pornography. Through compulsive exercise, cutting, or starving ourselves. Through binge-watching TV, gaming, or getting lost online. In the moment, it can be hard to care about danger if you finally feel relief.

Now a parent myself, I will push through anything for my children no matter how hellish or terrifying. There's a strange distance I can force when I'm needed, and thank God, it's never let me down yet. For people who are afraid and in crisis, for some reason, I can compartmentalize. I can be both role model and respite, putting aside my feelings when I need to so that I can be present when their world feels completely awful. But that is me. And time softens. I know now that while my father couldn't understand the limits of my comfort zones, neither could I understand his.

What my dad and I *did* both understand was Spock. *Star Trek*'s monotone-voiced, logic-driven Mr. Spock (my father's favorite—go figure) is often referred to as the consummate autistic character—or, I would argue, caricature. He comes across as aloof, hyperintellectual, emotionally shut off. Basically, a lot like my dad. But appearances can be deceiving. So it truly struck my heart when, in one of the franchise's latest installations, Spock eloquently explained what others perceived as a lack of feeling:

> You misunderstand. It is true I chose not to feel anything upon realizing that my own life was ending. As Admiral Pike was dying, I joined with his consciousness and experienced what he felt at the moment of his passing. Anger, confusion, loneliness, fear. I have experienced those feelings before, multiplied exponentially on the day my planet was destroyed. Such a feeling is something I choose never to experience again . . . you mistake my choice not to feel as a reflection of my not caring. Well, I assure you, the truth is precisely the opposite.

"I joined with his consciousness." Yes, friends, we *can* do that—and the results are extreme—sometimes to the point that the world thinks we are cold . . . when in fact, we are melting inside. What looks like coldness to the outside world is, in fact, a response to being overwhelmed by emotion and fear of being overtaken by it—a tidal wave of compassion that breaks our hearts, too. We explode or implode—we fight like tigers or flee from the flames when we *do* see and *know* someone is suffering—it's reality we recognize, which we hate sincerely and selflessly, and which offends our deep sense of justice.

Recent clinical research has been conducted to measure and evaluate levels of cognitive and affective empathy among neurotypicals and autistic people. Not surprisingly, those with autism showed comparative deficits in cognitive empathy. That much we knew. *And then came the affective empathy scores.* Not only did tests show equal levels of emotional empathy between groups; in a second, more specific measurement, autistic individuals scored *higher* than their neurotypical counterparts. "Although this finding is at variance with . . . [twenty-year-old] reports of deficits in empathy in individuals with AS," wrote Dr. Kimberley

Rogers, "it is in keeping with anecdotal reports from parents and clinicians that suggest that autistic individuals can be very caring . . . our data would suggest that when individuals with AS are given the information that allows them to understand the point of view of others, they have as much concern and compassion as unaffected individuals."

For years, I have maintained that the most compassionate, most fiercely humanitarian, accepting people I have ever known are *all* on the spectrum. We shout it. We show it. Yes, we may *show* what we feel differently—which can be inconvenient, sure. I speak Spanish, and were I to say, "Me siento muy afortunada de conocerte," some of you would recognize the meaning behind the words, but many would not. Yet, whether or not you got my meaning, I would *still* "feel very lucky to know you."

The misconception that people with autism lack empathy and cannot recognize feelings is wrong. But debunking that myth is *still* news: in 2016, *Scientific American* published an article titled "People with Autism Can Read Emotions, Feel Empathy." The piece itself is positive, making the point that the stereotype of the emotionally stunted autistic "can distort our perception of these individuals and possibly delay effective treatments." Agreed. The disappointing reality check, though, is that a headline is intended to catch readers' interest with the promise of new information. So on some level, I can't help but cry out, Is that *really* a revelation? We are not psychopaths. We are not monsters. We just figure things out differently. Do you know more than one route to your supermarket? If there were an intersection blocked off, could you get to work in an alternate way? And if you did—would you not *still* be at work? Could you not *still* buy groceries? How you get there doesn't matter. It's *whether* you get there. And dang it all, people: we get there.

WHY NOT YOU—OR ME?

The two most important lessons my mother taught me were these:

- When life knocks you down, find a way to lift others up.
- Why not you?

Last one first. How often have you heard "I never thought it could happen to *me*" when tragedy strikes? I never understood the logic of that thought process. If "everyone else" is supposed to be so much better at spontaneous perspective taking, at walking in someone else's stilettos, then why on Earth would *anything* not happen to you—or me?

Fabulous wall art, greeting cards, even coffee mugs entreat us all to "be bold . . . be random . . . be yourself." Hey, I am all for that. Paraphrasing a poster from my old classroom, "Well-behaved women rarely make history." But in reality, blending in is a whole lot easier. It takes guts to play the game if everyone else is playing poker and you show up with Monopoly pieces. Let's be honest, folks—autism is no walk in the park. That's why perspective is so important . . . it's the permission we give ourselves as parents and teachers to whine, to pat our own backs, to occasionally cringe at our own kids' behavior, and to cry at the heroism of the smallest moments no one else even notices. As Boston artist Leigh Standley scrawled into one of her illustrations, "I am fairly certain that given a cape and a nice tiara, I could save the world." Amen, sister.

This life has not been an easy one: illnesses, loss, separation, abuse, traumas, violence, self-harm . . . it's been ugly and terrifying and uncertain. There have been moments I've wished desperately for time to breathe between the waves, but never, ever, ever have I asked, "Why me?" That's not pride speaking. Nor is it some fatalistic statement of pessimism. It's autism, I think. Because, really, in triumph or tragedy, why *not* me?

When I was invited to speak at the White House, I cried at the honor. Literally. Generations of my family have served in the military, and though I'd like to believe I love my country just as passionately, I will never don a uniform. It's not in the cards. So, walking through the Eisenhower Wing, I wasn't proud in the sense of "Yay, me! Look what I've accomplished!" No. It was a deep, deep sense of purpose—of here I am, representing the voices and lives of millions whom I will never meet, asked to do so because the office of the president believes that I have something unique and important to offer my nation. In comparison to risking my life in battle, nothing, of course. But in terms of devotion—everything. This is *my* country, and that house is *our* house. So . . . just as my ancestors might've asked when called up to service . . . in a very small way, I too, say, "Why not me?"

I believe that in times of wonder . . . I hold to it when the world falls apart. And . . . I try to do what my momma taught me: make sense by making it about others.

MY FATHER'S DAUGHTER

My father died on August 12, 2007, of lung cancer. He was sixty-two years old. The instant follow-up question to hearing "lung cancer" is, of course, did he smoke? Yes, he did. And, he still didn't deserve to die. My daddy did what so many people of his generation did—he self-medicated as best he could—which wasn't very well. Clearly the son of an Aspie and an Aspie himself, my dad didn't have access to the antidepressants and antianxiety medications and ADHD stimulants my children and I do (we were diagnosed after his death). There were no explanations for what he saw as his social failings. So he used what he had: J&B Scotch and Marlboro Lights. As a little girl, I would steal the foil-lined packs from his dresser and crack each cigarette over the toilet bowl, watching the tobacco leaves spill over my fingertips and into the water. I would leave notes, "Daddy, I don't want you to die." And when, years later, he knew he was going to miss out on my life and on my children's lives, and "that it's all by my own hand," I did everything I could to undo that guilt. Without understanding of what he was enduring as an unaware, unidentified autistic, he could not have true empathy. I think that's still why people ask if, more or less, he brought it on himself. What crass callousness.

What he did have was my heart. He was sick for just over a year—in which he was not well, got better, then slipped fast. About three weeks before the end, I was visiting my folks with my two little children. I clearly remember sitting at the top of the stairs, tired. It had taken forever, but I'd finally gotten my son down for his nap. Behind me, my dad stumbled down the hall from bed, where he'd been resting, and opened the wood-paneled pantry door, which swung toward him with a loud creak. He stumbled a bit, then began rummaging through the bottles of over-the-counter medicines. Finding the one he wanted, my dad screwed open the top and literally threw a handful of something down his throat.

"Daddy!" I yelled in alarm. "What—"

He shushed me violently. A terrible, splitting headache, he said, be quiet. Those pills were Motrin or ibuprofen or Tylenol . . . he coughed gruffly. I knew something was very wrong, though, and offered to walk him back to bed. Of course he refused and of course I followed right behind. We got to the room, and suddenly, my daddy collapsed over into my arms. Children aren't supposed to lift up their parents. But I didn't cry out, and I didn't let him know I was scared. "No problem, Daddy," I exhaled, trying not to let the strain of his weight sound in my breath. "I got you. Let's just get you down and comfortable." We both knew the truth, of course. And after the EMTs took him to the hospital, there was no denying it. The cancer had metastasized to his brain now. Three inoperable tumors. Time was running out.

Two weeks later, I was back in North Carolina when the phone rang. It was only a matter of hours, they said. He'd gone into the hospital that morning feeling terrible and now was in a coma. I needed to get there. Fast.

Racing against time, the household assembled, but there was only one remaining flight that day, and it wasn't until dinnertime. I honestly didn't believe I'd make it. So, I asked my mother to put the phone to his ear and told him that I loved him, my Dinky Doodle. That he'd always done his best—I knew he had, and he should have no regrets as my father, only the certainty that his Little Red loved him. "I'm so glad I got to be yours, Daddy," I sobbed. Because, he *had* done his best. It wasn't *the* best. At times, it wasn't even very good. But he loved me, and I know that. And when the end comes, isn't that the realest stuff of all?

We did make it, though. That night, I slept beside him in his hospital bed. He never woke up, but I believe he knew I was there in some way. Midmorning, his eyes suddenly sprang open, unfocused, and he began to gasp for air. Quickly, the nurse came in with a dose of morphine to make him more comfortable . . . it was time. His eyes closed gently once more. His breath slowed. My mom chattered—something about it being okay to cry. No, I would not cry. Not yet. I would sing. "Amazing grace, how sweet the sound . . ." My dad wasn't a very religious man; he'd been force-fed a lot of it growing up and never practiced as an adult. But for whatever reason, he liked that hymn. So I leaned in close, whispered, "I'm here," and sang my daddy to sleep.

CHAPTER 6

The Land of Anywhere But Here: Predators and Fandom Families

Attention of one kind or another has pretty much followed me since I showed up on this planet: just imagine a hospital nursery full of tightly swaddled newborn babies—a sea of pink and blue . . . and red. That'd be me, the ginger-fuzzed one. Whether you're born redheaded or autistic, "blending" is pretty much impossible. You can't help but stick out some. It's just something you have to learn to go with. And I went with it. At two, I remember seeing a *Sesame Street* episode where Big Bird was watching some ballerinas perform *Swan Lake*. "Do you like the pretty dancing, Jenny?" my mom asked in that singsong voice adults use on kids. "Yes," I answered, completely matter-of-factly. "I can do that." Of course, my mom thought I was just being cute, but she went ahead and obliged, signing me up for dancing school. The thing was, I hadn't meant to be cute. I'd been serious. And it turned out, I was right. From the start, the teachers were floored—and there they put me, the little redhead, center stage. All eyes this way. Applause and smiles. For a while, anyway. The trouble is that once you're put up on a pedestal, no one can look you in the eye. See you as simply . . . a person. A friend. They're either admiring you from afar, examining you up close for flaws, or trying to knock the base out from under you.

Arrogance and insecurity are two sides of the same coin. The greater one grows, the bolder the other becomes in compensation . . . if there was nothing else I could do right, then couldn't school be my "specialty"? The adults sure liked me for it! Why, then, didn't the kids? It never occurred to me—not for a moment—that in trying to sound confident,

I sounded horribly arrogant. In trying to be helpful, I sounded parental. In trying to make friends, I made a fool of myself. Over and over again. To be truthful, a lifetime of comments between then and now in which people I loved harshly criticized my social skills (with good intentions) has often brought that sense of rejection to bear. In her own way, my mom tried to tell me that I was messing up. She made up stories with my Cabbage Patch Kids in which the redhead was a bossy smarty-pants whom no one really liked; the blonde doll was cute, likable, and funny—everyone's favorite. Did I mention my mom was blonde? I know that her intent was to try to show why one personality was better received than the other. And I know that she really never gave thought to my lonely misery at the pool—she just wanted some (well-deserved) time with adults. At the time, though, I couldn't see her perspective, and she didn't explain it to me.

Everyone was expecting everyone else to read minds, and no one succeeded. I think that's because no matter the circumstance, no matter how certain we are that we know what's what, there's always more to a story. That is the power of perspective. It tags question marks where we think there are periods and undoes absolutes. As C. S. Lewis wrote, "What you see and hear depends a good deal on where you are standing: it also depends on what sort of person you are." And if you are a spectrummy sort of person, your perspective is generally a little bit different.

There's an expression on greeting cards, "What would you do if you knew you couldn't fail?" That's wonderful inspiration. But what about if you knew you would? Or at least were so paralyzed by the trauma of past hurts that you didn't have it in you to try one more time. For us, simply living every day in a world where we miss vast chunks of communication (body language) and endure sensory overload dictates that we *have* to step outside of our comfort zones . . . every single day, multiple times a day. What I am getting at is that the autistic experience *is* different than "the usual." Not worse or better, just different . . . though we don't even recognize our perspective is unique until you give us something to compare it against. Mind-blindness again. To imagine the ways a neurotypical mind works is almost as impossible for me as it is for you to stand where I am. Consequently, it takes a lifelong journey of introspection to identify the distinctions between our "norm" and yours. And though we Aspies are told that we are the black/white thinkers, I would argue that sometimes it is the neurotypical world that labels one viewpoint "normal" and the other "abnormal." I'll agree with "atypical," smile at "sometimes quirky," and cheer for "occasionally breathtakingly brilliant." But "wrong" is just, well, "wrong." Life—its comforts, joys, and challenges—is all profoundly relative. That is, most everything works both ways.

We are taught that off-handed comments like "That's so simple!" make us sound like know-it-alls, even if we hadn't meant to puff ourselves up or put anyone else down. We're told that our casual remarks can really hurt people's feelings . . . and come round to bite us in the end. Yet when neurotypicals declare their own experience of anything—a game, a task, a social situation—as universal (as in "Why are you so freaked out? It's no big deal," or "How could you not know that would cause problems? I mean, it's obvious!") . . . well, that's ironically very mind-blind of y'all. It's also not very nice.

A love of packed theme parks or distaste for grammar is probably very common. I despise the sensory overload of being in the middle of crowds—and adore the rhythm and logic of grammar (um, I *might* have a framed print of a diagrammed sentence). And sure, I'm probably in the minority on those. But I'm not—*we* are not—wrong. Adjectives are opinions. Feelings. They are not absolutes. Annoying, easy, weird, confusing, boring, fun. They're all opinions. So shouldn't we *all* state them that way? With sensitivity and respect toward others who feel differently? It all begins with avoiding assumptions and learning the facts. Someone who "goofs off" or is silly may, actually, be trying to avoid a task that is too hard or too long—one at which she knows she will fail or can't figure out how to begin. Another may talk endlessly about a favorite topic because that's how she feels most socially savvy, not because she wants to be a know-it-all. A cold and an allergy look very much alike. To take for granted that we know all there is to know about any situation is, truth be told, sophomoric. Of course, all of us operate on some basic assumptions. I assume the sun will come up tomorrow and expect to be right. But people are less predictable. If you yell at a child near the road, he may assume you are angry with him. The reality, though, is that you are frightened. Mad and scared look a lot alike. So do shy and stuck-up, overwhelmed and impatient.

There's lots of room for mistakes when we assume to know what is going on in someone else's mind or heart . . . or head.

The Theory of My Mind

Jenny did as she was told. More than that, she—I—excelled in academics, music, dance—and I wasn't too shabby at sports, either. Now, please don't hear that as bragging. It's not. It's reporting. Years later, at my wedding reception, my maid of honor began her toast by saying, "I didn't really become close to Jen until high school. We went to different elementary schools, but even then, in our small town, there were two things I knew about her: she had red hair, and she was really, really smart."

Of course, I know full well that the world is full of bright, creative, curious kids. The difference was that, somehow, I was everywhere. An across-the-board sensation that, eventually, became completely overexposed. Predictably perfect. Or at least, damn near. Academics: a cinch. School plays: the lead. Invitation-only chorus. New Jersey Top Scholar-Athlete. Consummate faculty choice for special privileges, speeches, events, opportunities. I even ranked top of the school when a local grad student came to do research on ESP. Funny, that. I could sense whether the hidden side of a card showed a star, lines, a square, or a heart, but I hadn't the foggiest idea that slamming down my pencil to announce I was first to finish a multiplication drill might irritate the kids around me.

Much to my surprise, during my senior year of high school, my mom informed me that "kids like you used to make me furious." Earlier that day, I'd gotten a test back on which I'd made a 96 percent. Most people, I now understand, would have killed for a ninety-six. That's a totally solid *A* or "excellent" grade. But not me. I was a wreck. In class, my face had fallen, and all I could think about was the stupid mistake I'd made on one lousy question that I should've gotten right in the first place.

Caught up in the "piece," I wasn't able to see the "whole" picture—which included not only my thoughts and emotions, but also the thoughts and emotions my reaction might evoke in other people. To most classmates, my worst grade was better than their best. So my complaining was sort of a high school version of Marie Antoinette. "Let them eat cake" and all. I had meant to criticize myself. But others were, of course, watching. Without even thinking about it, I had sent the condescending message that I believed myself superior to everyone in the room. I'd been disappointed in myself—but from any other person's perspective, I was insulting them, too. My pouting perfectionism didn't just hurt my own self-esteem. It also made other people feel lousy about themselves, then jealous of and completely irritated by me.

Which is key. I wasn't mean. I wasn't trying to insult anyone. And I definitely wasn't being intentionally rude. I was being the only Jenny that got persistent, reliable praise. The relentlessly honed, never-quite-safe, constantly striving Jenny. I won my mother a place of honor with teachers (mine)—and with her parents. I let my dad feel comfortable intellectualizing, discussing the news, or telling me bedtime stories about the life cycle of tomato plants.

Above all, they were the people I very, very much wanted to please. To talk with me. To play with me. To *like* me. My mom: well-liked, creative, president of our parent-teacher association. My dad: brilliant, intellectual, distant, but lovable. They were my world, so theirs was the external approval that I needed—validation that, without my being able to accurately perceive how the rest of the world felt about me, told me that I was good. Not good *at* something. Just . . . good. And the most effective way of guaranteeing that, I found, was to be (or at least try to be) the favorite of the other adults in our world. When my father's top clients would come to the states and visit our house for dinner, I was the "child prodigy" entertainment, delighting our guests by carrying on conversations—in two languages—about everything from nuclear proliferation to fine art. They would laugh and slap my dad on the back, praising him for his "extraordinary" daughter. In style, figure, and academics, I could earn my grandmother's by-proxy approval of my mom, something I knew she'd wanted all her life.

Somewhere along the way, I remember asking my mom to teach me how to make friends. But back in the eighties, my mom didn't know what to make of that. "I didn't know how to *teach* someone to have friends," she's told me, looking back. It's not like "social skills" clubs or camps were available at speech therapists' or psychologists' offices, as they are today. When the bullying and social hell got so bad that my mother truly worried I would take my own life (in *middle school*), she brought me to meet a psychologist for "gifted kids." I spent an hour telling him about all of the awfulness that was going on—about how getting bad bronchitis and missing two weeks of school had been the highlight of the year. When the appointment drew to an end, I fought the urge to smile—prepared *finally* for kindness—compassion—an ally.

He shut his notebook and sighed. "Stop being so difficult," he instructed. "You're upsetting your mother."

Hope broke. No one coming to save me or help me or protect me. Not ever. Of course, I didn't tell my mother that the psychologist said I was the cause of my own misery *and* of her shame, stress, and expense. I couldn't tell *anyone*. The only choice I had was to work harder. To do better. Every compliment I received made them beam. Every perfect report card brought praise. I had the überpolite manners of a "little lady." Enchanted teachers. Made the cut for traveling sports teams. Was the youngest ever invited to elite music programs. Of course my parents enjoyed their child's successes. Of course they encouraged me to pursue natural talents. Of course I enjoyed doing well. But success itself wasn't ever the reward. What I worked for every single day was the guarantee that, though friendships were unpredictable and I always ended up the outsider, my parents would like me. Because if they did, I'd never really be all alone.

Authority hadn't been the issue in 1988, and it wasn't the problem in 2009, when my daughter had an in-school meltdown. She was worn out, embarrassed, lonely, and miserable, and that day, she totally lost it—sobbing and screaming outside the classroom, unwilling to go in. In a phone call later that evening, the teacher interrogated us. "I am just wondering," she asked curtly, "if you ever discipline this child?" Arrogantly, she also added that she doubted the accuracy of the Asperger's diagnosis; however, when I asked her how many *girls* with Asperger's she had actually taught in her thirty-year tenure, she conceded the answer was "none." And instantly, my heart broke for the hundreds of autistic girls she *did* have in class—girls who didn't know themselves and whose "expert" teacher believed they didn't even exist.

"I think," finished the teacher, "she's just a lot like her father. You know, socially hesitant." Six months later, he was diagnosed.

Professionals' careers predicate public confidence in their training, experience, and observation. But how many of us are equipped to see through that power dynamic? The voices in the victim-blaming chorus are loud. And numerous. After meeting my six-year-old daughter for a single therapy session in 2009, a self-proclaimed "Aspie expert" therapist offered me his advice on how to support her social anxiety. "Just be sure to show her who's in charge." Hope broke again. A mother's hope. But I'd be damned if I would let another child's break, too.

I knew the fresh hell of being a hopeless child. Alone in my room in 1988, I cried myself sick and then made a conscious decision. I would not forget the pain. I would not let myself forget how it felt to live within its irregular margins. To feel soul-raped. To feel loathsome and afraid. And in whatever form it took, my life's mission would be to ferociously champion the right of every heart to be witnessed and loved. That decision remains the singular thread connecting my every venture, value, and story. My perpetual pledge. In every way possible until I close my eyes for the last time, I will, quite literally, love the hell out of this world.

Little Blue Men in the Hands of Predators

February 14, 1983, was a terribly cold day. A fact, I suppose, that isn't too shocking for midwinter in the Northeast. But—I mean *really* cold. Bitter. Biting. Inside your bones. In hindsight, it still makes me shiver. Being fair, though, I'm not entirely certain whether my memories have to do with the temperature or with Valentine Smurf and a big, snowy field.

Every Saturday morning, my parents slept in. Being an only child, this meant I was pretty much on my own, which made indulging in my little fantasy world that much easier. I'd pour myself a bowl of cereal, grab a snuggly blanket, and turn on the TV—ready to lose myself in every last minute of Smurftastic adventures.

The Smurfs were big with the elementary school set that year. But Miss Grant's second-grade class hadn't been going too smoothly for me, in terms of other kids. So my little blue guys had become more than a plastic fad. They were a village of almost-imaginary friends. As is true with most passions of spectrum girls and women, my topic of interest wasn't anything unique. The *degree* to which I cared and thought about them *was* different—because the interest *itself* served a function above and beyond the typical. The buffet of facts and names and episode titles provided intellectual escapism. Collecting, organizing, and contemplating facts was a *relief* from the other perseverations on which my mind got stuck.

Throughout the week, I would set my ever-growing collection of figures and plastic mushroom houses into little tableaux, scenes from the previous weekend's show. The Smurfy world was so easy to understand. There were no worries that the nice girl would turn out to be mean or that you'd think the other kid was making jokes when he was actually annoyed. Nope. Who they were is how they were—the Smurfs' names made everything clear. Like a handy-dandy character-trait highlighter. Brainy, Vanity, Jokey . . . and of course, Smurfette, a bit of a minivixen in tiny heels. Which meant, I concluded, that what she was—and *how* she was—fulfilled the characteristic "girl." (The fact that no human being actually has a one-dimensional personality somehow didn't cross my mind. And I definitely missed that everyone thought Brainy was annoying.)

Mostly, I was too busy enjoying the clear-cut categories, the simplicity of the labeling, and trying quite hard to mimic Smurfette—to the point that I insisted on being her for Halloween with blue body paint and 1983-quality blonde wig. A chipping, itchy face and shedding, scratchy artificially shiny yellow hairs stuck everywhere. It was a sensory disaster. But still, I'd been *her*. And that was amazing . . . because the *whole village* loved *her*. Whereas my whole class hated me. Just recently, the "leader" of the girls had told everyone that they weren't allowed to play with me, which was bad enough. Worse was the fact that I couldn't figure out *why*. She and I had been friends since kindergarten. In fact, when she and her "boyfriend" formed a version of *Grease*'s T-Birds and Pink Ladies, she'd made me Marty to her Rizzo. So what had gone wrong?

Years later, she said that she'd wanted everyone to "hate" me because she was jealous. Her family had emigrated from Scotland not long before, so, ever the accent- and word-lover, when I played at her place, I spent most of the time trying to talk to her parents—to soak up their burrs, listening more to the speech in the air than playing with their daughter. It was just that I found her world so different and interesting. She had two rebellious teenage siblings, and to me, an only child who followed the rules, they were equally terrifying and mysterious (especially her sister's super-sexy wardrobe).

Looking back, I realize that their home was actually a rented half of a two-family home. That it was dark and smoke-filled. That everyone shouted at one another. That her father was unemployed and always had a beer in hand. That to this little girl, my wide-eyed staring and suddenly timid demeanor spoke not of detached fascination, but of judgment. As she told me years later, when she looked at *me*, at my nicely dressed mommy who came in her Cadillac to take nicely dressed me home to a bright, quiet spot where I didn't have to share anything with anyone, she wasn't interested or fascinated. She was embarrassed and jealous. And dang it if my do-everything-I-could-to-impress-everyone behavior (my attempt to get people to like me) didn't make our disparities that much sharper—didn't feel shaming and stuck-up.

Everything that she wanted, I had, she thought. Everything, that is, except for one thing. She was popular, the kind based in bullying—a social status built on fear, intimidation, and control. The kind of popular that isn't really about being liked or admired, but about building herself up by tearing everyone else down. The kind that's all about power. She had it. And then, without realizing the tipping point, I'd gone and challenged even that small bit of power when I didn't let her lean on my shoulder, like she did with the other girls. It was a move I understood only because I remembered seeing the boy leaders do it in *Grease*. A power thing. Dominance. But we were *friends*. She wasn't my boss. The teacher was. That was the rule. So I said no. And she unleashed her power.

Seven-year-old me was already tired. I had no idea what had gone wrong. No idea that she was strategizing in ways, even now, my mind cannot comprehend. That her end goal wasn't really even about me, but about securing herself as someone who mattered. All I knew was that when she told the girls (and some of the boys) to give me the silent treatment, they did. When she told them not to invite me for playdates anymore, they didn't. When she decreed that I was no longer allowed to join in the games at recess, they "locked" me out. And when they wanted "extra credit," all the kids had to do was make me cry.

During that awful second-grade year of locked games and silent treatments, my mom did whatever she could to cheer me, including making frequent trips to Rainbow Heart Throb Gifts & Cards (again, the eighties) for new Smurf collectibles. Whatever the occasion or holiday, she made certain that the perfect figure arrived to celebrate. Usually, I kept her gifts safe in my room, but on bad days, I would—with great TLC—bring a little blue friend to school and perch him or her on the corner of my Formica desktop. Left-hand side.

That cold Valentine's Day morning, Cupid Smurf was waiting by my breakfast cereal. I must have been going through an especially rough patch then, because not only did I decide to take him to class with me, I even tucked him carefully into my pocket come recess and brought him out to play. I had given up trying to get the girls to talk to me. Now, I was debating whether to ask the boys if I could play kickball with them or just try to build a little snowgirl on the edge of the macadam. It had snowed the night before. Beyond, the grassy field lay covered in deep piles of brilliant white, gleaming so brightly that you could barely look out in their direction.

In the early morning hours, plows had cleared the hard surfaces where the kids played, pushing the powder into huge mountains at the field's border. A tall, frosty crust to what might as well be an endless arctic tundra. Somewhere near that precipice, I took Cupid from my pocket. I don't know whom I spotted, but I do know I was trying to show off my new toy, hoping it would draw the other child in . . . and then, out of nowhere, a boy ran at me. In one fluid motion, he snatched the Smurf from my pink-gloved hands and turned toward the field. I saw his arm pull back and knew what was coming. "No, don't!" I gulped.

But it was too late and probably didn't matter anyway. He had already released my little friend into the icy air, arcing far, far out, over the plowed border, above the blanket of white. Without a sound, it was gone. Really gone. Lost. There was no way to find a two-inch plastic toy in an entire snow-covered field. No way I'd be allowed to try. And no way any adult would bother.

I didn't tell the teacher. It would only make things worse for me. Instead, I just began to cry, quietly, so no one would pay attention. Mourning the loss of the only friend I had in my classroom and wondering how much longer before I could just go home.

Fast-forward to seventh grade, the worst year of my life to date—the year my dance class traveled to Manhattan for a major competition. Though I was three years younger than everyone else (which was pretty obvious in our leotards), I'd been specially placed in the group—and then made captain. Two hours before our big performance, I finally got my turn in our hotel room shower. I'd just stepped in when a burst of cold air rushed through the suddenly open door. The lights went out. Confused, I grabbed at the slick shower curtain and opened my mouth to scream when I heard laughter—and a bucket full of ice came raining down over my naked body. Stunned, I stood shaking in the dark and began to cry. I just wanted my mom.

Maybe it was a joke, she said after the performance. Just playing around. But I knew it wasn't. I'd danced since I was two. Had been invited to come to the school for the performing arts. It was my passion. My soul. Now, I couldn't stop shaking. I'd made them hate me, too. I'd just been me. I'd been naked. And that day, dance became another place to scare me. To hurt me. That last day. The day I decided to never go back again.

Had I imagined an alternative, I would have refused to go back to school, too. Academically, things were fine. I adored my English and history teacher—like Miss Grant had been, Mrs. Greene was old school. Tough. Clear. Organized. I knew what to do to impress her, and when and how to do it. But life on the other side of the expandable wall was pure hell. There, things were a lot more casual, which for most kids meant more fun. The math and science teacher was a long-term substitute, the mom of a classmate. As an adult now, I can see that she had every best intention, and that her laid-back classroom probably gave a nice foil to the higher-stressed environment in Mrs. Greene's room. But not me. I despised every minute. Relaxed meant spontaneous. Casual. No time to plan how to . . . be—toward her, toward the other kids. It meant more chances for kids to crack jokes and to not know how to react. More chances to make an already terrible year worse.

One afternoon, in that science class, the teacher announced we'd be playing pretest Jeopardy. Actually, the idea seemed fun at the start. *Jeopardy!* was a favorite show of mine anyway, and (here's the real and rather sad-sounding truth) I thought, maybe . . . maybe . . . I could score some points for my teammates. And they'd be glad I was there. And that . . . that would be nice.

Then, it was my turn. And I answered. And I got it wrong.

Which shouldn't have mattered much. In the scheme of the world, middle-school biology is not a concern of Earth-shattering proportion. It did count for an awful lot to me, though. The only value I brought to that team—the only reason I'd been wanted—was my brain. Now that I'd made a mistake, I was worthless.

I tell my daughter that's why pencils come with erasers and keyboards come with delete buttons. No one was so kind to me, though. From his seat in the back of the class, a boy began to sing, "Ding, dong, the witch is dead! The Wicked Witch is dead!" Over and over he chanted, eventually even skipping around the entire room in one giant circle, landing back in his seat with a thud. The class exploded in laughter. And I turned, quickly, to the adult. She would stop it, right? I—it wasn't okay . . . to do that, was it? Up front, the teacher stifled a giggle while shaking her head at him. Nothing more. Next question, Team Two.

Twenty-three years later, I can still see his shirt untucking as he skipped. I just sat, trying not to cry, expecting someone to make it stop. No one did. I have heard that up to 85 percent of bullying goes unobserved by adults. That is true, I am sure. More often than not, it's much more subtle, quiet, understated. Teachers can be right there in the room or on the playground and often be totally unaware of the social dynamics playing out in front of them. Michelle Dean and her research team report that

> strained interactions can be difficult to detect. Because of girls' interactional styles, the subtlety of their social negotiations can fly under the radar. What appear to be obvious exclusion practices in this study in fact pass very quickly and were only discovered upon repeated, close inspection by the researchers. Thus, it would not be realistic to expect adults to catch these social subtleties and intervene in the moment. In fact, some argue that such efforts would increase the occurrence of even more subtle aggressions between girls.

Years later in a chance meeting, my mom told Mrs. Greene about how bad that year had been for me; the poor woman broke down in tears. She had never known a thing was wrong. And yet, everything had been wrong.

I was naive, I was different, and I came off as pretentious and arrogant, I know. That's not *because* I was either pretentious or arrogant. It's just that smarts were how I garnered praise. And my ability to accurately imagine another's perspective was so off that I thought if I tried hard enough and did well enough at everything, kids might like me for the same reasons grown-ups did. After all, parents and teachers frequently asked others to "be more like Jenny" right in front of me. Mind-blind as I was, I truly thought that by constantly displaying how smart I was, starring in school shows, *and* making competitive-level athletic teams, I would earn my peers' respect and friendship, too. Didn't quite work out that way. As my mom asked me once, "Why doesn't anyone you want to be friends with want to be friends with you?"

I had no idea.

That same year, my gym teacher had offered me "the one hundred percent I know you'll get anyway" if I'd grade everyone else's written tennis exams (and of course, I agreed—I'd be allowed to use the *red* marker—as long as no one recognized my handwriting). The year before, our teacher had awarded me the "special honor" of proofreading, editing, and rewriting the six-inch-high stack of research my thirty or so classmates had turned in after studying the Constitutional Convention. From that pile, I was to write a full-length play—on behalf of the class, not myself. Everyone would be required to learn the lines I composed. To follow the guidance I gave (did I mention I was also director?). And finally, to put on an entire performance for our families and the administration.

Looking back, I wonder what I possibly could have done, in the positions those teachers created, to avoid being hated. Targeted. Ridiculed. If I'm being nakedly honest (and why not at this point?), the way they behaved reminds me of the way sexual predators groom their young victims. Several state attorney general websites report some version of this idea:

> A predator will usually introduce secrecy at some point during the grooming process. Initially, secrecy binds the victim to the predator: "Here's some candy. But don't tell your friends because they'll be jealous, and don't tell your mother because she won't like you eating between meals."

They swore me to secrecy all right. Tucked away in his quiet, private back office. Sent to work on my own in the behind-the-desk rooms of the school library. I had privilege and I had peace and quiet. An escape from the social melee. What's more, they explained, I was doing a *good* thing. I was helping to protect the other students from feeling bad about their own work (aww . . . wasn't that nice? And even if they did find out somehow, wouldn't they all be glad that I'd helped?). No one had to offer me candy. All it took was a guaranteed *A*, a red Sharpie, and a chance to wear pretty colonial clothes while showing my parents and grandparents what a good job I could do on stage.

No, wait. That's not fair. It was really so much more. We know from every Oprah special and Lifetime movie that the adult in power chooses a target carefully, and that a child who feels unloved and unpopular will soak up adult attention like a sponge. I most certainly did. The ultimate seduction, for me, was the feeling that someone liked me. That even though I went home every single day and cried, never understanding what I'd done wrong, these two—a cool teacher, sort of a popular, jock type and super-strict only-likes-you-if-you-are-completely-excellent former nun—had smiled down upon me. Trusted me. Only me. And I was proud. I felt . . . special. Chosen. Wanted. Which, apparently, is also completely cliché. This is how the spiral begins. The very one that, later, will lead so many unidentified spectrum girls down darker paths.

When the other kids were handed their lines to learn for our play, it was clear their own work had been heavily overhauled. And when they found me setting stage blocking, I suppose it wasn't hard to figure out who'd done the rewrites. Our teacher just smiled, tight-lipped, at the administrators who came to watch us and turned a deaf ear and blind eye to whatever might befall me in consequence. I was on my own. In gym, someone recognized my red-marker handwriting on his quiz and made a (rightful) fuss. I'll never forget the only look Mr. T. ever again granted me, once the principal had been alerted. One glance, heavy with heart-wrenching disappointment. I'd failed him, his face said, tragically. And he never looked my way again.

Typical kids need help steering clear of those who would take advantage. Their fear of people is still maturing, fine-tuning, and based mostly in stranger-danger scenarios (which are a whole lot less likely than abuse by people they know). Those typical kids are still forming what will become self-protective "gut instincts," still uploading enough experiences, information, and perspective to eventually intuit ulterior motives. To build up a sort of internal database that will alert and keep them from harm. But we on the spectrum don't do that. Not fully. Not ever. We are mind-blind to the strategies and subterfuge of those who would hurt us. We can't intuit perspective. And so, in many, many ways, it's no surprise that, without the benefit of diagnosis, we will not receive the explicit social teachings, keys, clues, and self-esteem reconstruction that absolutely can secure up our coming of age.

Adolescence is not a pretty thing in the best of circumstances. It's why, when I chose to teach middle school, parents often joked that I was either crazy brave or masochistic. Neither was true. I just knew that's where I was needed. Above any curricular or practical goal, I believe that every teacher, counselor, parent, and caregiver has a part to play in showing Aspies what we need to do to compensate for that which our brains are just not hardwired to do otherwise. I don't care how superbly you teach math, develop sensory integration, or cook your kids' favorite dinner: if a child is lonely, every other aspect of his or her life (and yours, too) suffers.

On the contrary, an adult who takes the time to notice a need can save a young heart. Back in that miserable seventh-grade year of mine, that is exactly what happened to me. My middle school had a program called "Advisor/Advisee," a weird name with a good intention. Basically, it was a regular time when students and teachers put away textbooks to discuss the issues endemic to adolescence: peer pressure, drugs, and so on. For the most part, I'm guessing it felt like a colossal waste of time to the majority of students and teachers involved. Sort of like a live, mandatory after-school special. But for me, something amazing happened.

Unlike most kids, who were assigned to "talking groups" with our main teachers (in my case, that would've put me right back in the "Ding, dong, the witch is dead" crew), I somehow managed to get "assigned" to the music teacher (whom I loved). Mrs. Silbert just seemed to sense that I needed some serious lifelines thrown my way. So, without any official fanfare, she simply casually extended "AA" into the following period, lunch. Besides myself, three other students—a new girl I enjoyed, a *Star Trek*–loving shy guy, and a popular football player—stayed, too. Though there were times in years to come that we each disappointed one another, we became more than just good friends—we became family, giving phone tips on what to do (or not to do) in social situations, broadening social circles. Heck, I even took one of the guys for a makeover, and we two girls taught him to dance. Families vacationed together, and years later, we were attending (or actually being part of) one another's weddings. Even Mrs. Silbert, the teacher who created our "Breakfast Club" of sorts, was tearing up the dance floor at mine. She changed my life, plain and simple.

Catching the Rain

The year was 1982. Ronald Reagan was in office. "Don't You Want Me, Baby?" was on the radio, and the smiley face emoticon was born. But, like, what I most clearly remember about, like, that year isn't Valley girl speech or, like, Ms. Pac-Man. It is E.T., the Reese's Pieces-eating alien who I was absolutely sure was hiding in my closet.

Try as they might to counter my certainty that there was not, in fact, an extraterrestrial lurking in my bedroom, my parents couldn't convince me otherwise. So I clutched my teddy bear for reassurance and sat there in my bed—scared. Now, I'm not talking nervous or "trying to sneak into bed with Mom and Dad" scared. No, I mean pit-of-my-stomach, cold sweat, freak-out-if-you-touch-me terrified.

I'd venture that most everyone reading this has felt that kind of fear at some point in his or her life. But try this for me: allow your body, not just your mind, to remember that feeling—your heart thudding, mind racing, stomach lurching, your little self ready to run or fight against any shadow. That's what fear actually is, you see. It's not a concept or idea, it's not a topic to be discussed rationally. Everything about fear is primal—irrational . . . and bodily. There's no logic involved.

Anxiety is little bit different. Imagine the volume of that fear is turned down just a bit so that's it's not so immediate a threat or so acute a danger. Instead, it's replaced by a gnawing, jittery, ever-present sensation of waiting for the threat . . . waiting for the fear. It's like living with the *Jaws* music playing. You don't see the danger. But you surely know there's something "out there." That's anxiety.

What most neurotypicals don't realize is that we spectrumites, whose bodies and minds are wired differently, live with varying levels and intensities of almost perpetual anxiety. That may sound paranoid—but it's not. Paranoia is irrational fear. But thanks to lifetimes of bullying, exclusion, abuse, heightened sensory perception, and social anxiety, we often think we are at the top of our games when, in fact, we have unwittingly engineered our own heartbreak.

In other words, our anxiety is an absolutely rational reaction to the experiences we have.

So why does this matter? Simple. Pull at a weed and simply tear off the leaves, and what happens? Nothing new. The weed grows back. Similarly, if teachers, caregivers, therapists, spouses, and friends focus their energy on tantrums and meltdowns, obsessions or rigidity, they've only torn at the leaves. Nothing will change—either in the behaviors or in the heart of the loved one.

But grab that weed near the base—dig at the roots, and pull—gently. What happens? Yes, another weed may grow elsewhere, but this one is gone. Anxiety is that root. It is the seed from which our topical fixations and "overly sensitive," routine-driven, black/white, obsessive behaviors arise. We are trying to catch the rain. We are trying to create predictable order in a chaotic, often random world . . . by asking a million questions, by challenging exceptions to rules, by scripting dialogue we know was funny (once) or dictating play. It's not that we want to be unlikable or difficult or dominate the conversation with topics you don't enjoy. We just want to feel secure, safe—and to be able to stop the endless waiting for unwelcome surprises.

There was no alien in my bedroom back in 1982, of course. But I've met very real danger in places and with people that should have been as familiar and safe as a childhood haven. Those of us on the spectrum want to be liked, we want to please—even to impress. We certainly don't want to *be* the problem. Courage is, after all, the choice to feel fear and to master it—to do the "scary stuff" anyway. Those of us on the spectrum have to choose to be courageous almost every day . . . like that little girl in the bedroom back in 1982, when we *are* afraid (even if that fear is unnecessary), we certainly don't want to feel condescended to or be punished. We need understanding, respect, patience. Like I did years ago, we need allies—stuffed or otherwise—to cling to until we can steady ourselves . . . until we can see, peeking through the fear, the safety and calm of an unsullied tomorrow.

Unlikely Heroes

Folks on the spectrum know what it is to feel that the "odds are never in our favor." We love "losers" and underdogs. Flip through the "geek chic" categories on Pinterest, Tumblr, Etsy, and Google, and you'll see a definite trend: Doctor Who, Twilight, Star Wars, The Hunger Games, The Avengers, Harry Potter . . . all stories of far-from-perfect, "you and me against the world" heroes. Misunderstood, marginalized, well-meaning underdogs. We "get" them. Heck, we *are* them! After all, for those of us on the spectrum, "otherness" isn't fiction. It's reality. The way we think, speak, dress, feel, even move may be "a little different." And if it's not, that's probably because we've learned, though a lot of trials and a lot of errors, how to "pretend to be normal."

Our deeply felt connection with unlikely heroes makes sense. We've been hurt. We want to protect ourselves. To feel safe. But often, because we are unrecognized, misunderstood, and unsupported, we are in a battle over our heads and against our selves. Individual incidents of trauma build up, like layers of grime on a window . . . obscuring the view of the real self and locking us in to a perpetual state of heightened flight/flight/freeze arousal.

This is what's known as "complex post-traumatic stress disorder (PTSD)," a severe (and, actually, very logical) effect of real trauma that holds its victims captive by the very complexities of their own situations and forces us to confront present-day stressors while attempting to resolve triggers from the past. It's an exhausting state of constant emotional arousal colored by insomnia, quick temper, less-than-clear decision-making, exaggerated sensory experiences, avoiding situations that feel hurtful or frightening, broken relationships, emotional dysregulation, microaggressions, and misplaced trust. Many who are subject to regular bullying or abuse, like I was, may not have any way out of what they perceive as a trapped situation. Day-to-day life is filled with tiny terrors embedded within larger cracks in the psychological war zone of our minds—a release of prickly "shock" hormones that says either "Run!" or "Destroy." It's wearing, depressing, and worst of all, we can't escape it easily—because for us, hypervigilance may seem like our only form of self-protection because, so often, reporting incidents tags us as troublemakers and tattletales and gives the bullies more material to work with.

Evolutionary scientists say animals respond to fear in the way their successful ancestors learned to cope with threats. Generally speaking, mammals will first try to avoid danger—that translates as avoiding social situations (parties, dates, job interviews), depression, emotional withdrawal, keeping to ourselves at school or at work . . . or even at home. We may feel that our futures are constrained and try with all our might to fly under the radar . . . or to be so perfect and so commendable that (we pray) no one will criticize, condemn, or chastise us.

If we can't get away from social rejection, we get aggressive. It's the old "your best defensive is a good offense" plan. What looks like an angry outburst or a zero-to-sixty temper may actually be a protective reflex built upon emotional scars and real insecurities. Heightened memories of past threats will increase the wish to disappear, to hide, to avoid the conversation, or just to flat out quit ("flight"). Those same memories—of feeling like a failure, unwanted, or hurt—also make us quicker to anger, and with greater intensity. That's our shield. We are trying to immediately stop what feels like a threat.

Which is because our fears *are* born of repeated exposure to very *real* threats—either to our bodies, our minds, or both. We "mess up" without realizing it and then have to deal with the fallout—just when we may have thought we'd finally gotten our "act" together. Without a clear understanding of the whys or whens, we negotiate daily social situations that seem random and chaotic, building families, marriages, and incomes upon the relationships we are able to reap in those environments. It's easy to see why we'd feel as though we need to keep our guard up. We're walking through a social minefield with blinders on. Trouble with theory of mind, reading tones and interpersonal cues, understanding perspectives, and detecting hidden motivations mean that danger feels random—chaotic—and ever looming.

That's where the "disorder" in PTSD comes in. Traumatized by real experiences, we end up using coping mechanisms that are not in line with present circumstances. We detect threats when none exist, avoiding the unfamiliar to avoid danger . . . hearing challenge and accusation in the voices of loved ones . . . interpreting sincere offers of assistance or kindness as insults and ridicule. It's very hard to know where people are coming from and to fight the fear that they mean us harm. As the saying goes, we are listening to "old tapes playing in our minds" rather than to the present situation. We think we understand others' intentions, so we are curt or avoid social situations altogether. No one will get the chance, we reason, to disappoint or hurt us . . . nor, unfortunately, will they get the chance to delightfully surprise or encourage us.

Why? The truth is that we don't really know what others will say or do in any given situation. We just *think* we do. So, we don't bother to communicate. We assume. We misinterpret. We push them away. We flash fierce. And in the process, we cause heartache (for others *and* for ourselves) that needn't exist in the first place. Overriding triggered emotional responses isn't easy. Where there is fear, there cannot be trust—"one cannot live while the other survives." And without trust, there can be no love . . . no possibility, no hope. There *are,* in fact, questions that are not threats. There are critiques that are not insults. But life doesn't pause for us to unpack and heal. We're figuring out which is which and what is what while living every day. And I, for one, am still trying.

Long Ago and Far Away

As the torture of seventh grade drew to a close, I was ready for escape. Like a long-lost friend, a memory returned of a place where things were better. It was a story that Miss Grant had read to us in second grade, *Little House in the Big Woods.* For most of America, Laura Ingalls Wilder was a girl in a house on a prairie, back in some vague pioneer era. But I gathered photos, read biographies, memorized timelines and travel routes. I still remember that she was born on February 7, 1867, that the television show was basically hogwash (though, duty-bound, I watched every syndicated episode anyway), and that in her very real, historical world, family was everything, everyone belonged, and the simplicity of a tin cup or regular weekly chore routine could bring great worth to the life of a young girl. Those books gave me an alternate destination when I was wishing the world might just crack open and gift me a here and now other than my own.

Though they didn't always, diagnostic guidelines for autism now recognize the omnipresence of a "special interest," though the descriptor—"highly restricted, fixated interests that are abnormal in intensity or focus"—belies a prejudiced ignorance of the function special interests serve. Though I take great issue with the subjective attribution of the word "abnormal," I understand that from the outside, seemingly endless, unrequested regurgitation of information on topics that only mildly—if at all—hold interest to anyone besides the speaker is . . . less than enjoyable. Tedious. Obsessive. Self-indulgent. Isolating.

From the inside, the view is totally different. Our passions are like lightning rods, immersive and sacred, deeply enmeshed with our sense of self and life in a neurotypical world. They are windows into who an individual is, who she wants to be, and what she wants most out of life. They offer the purest way of touching our hearts—and the most powerful way through which we will try to reach yours.

Consider a very young child who shows you her favorite plush toy. Let's say it's Cookie Monster. Perhaps she holds him out to you. To other children. At first, that seems nice. But should you try to play with the fuzzy blue guy, she will shriek or cry. You're not to hold him, that much is clear. Siblings or playmates protest and eventually become disinterested. She doesn't share. She doesn't seem to care about the other children's favorites. She just wants to show Cookie Monster to everyone. Who wants to watch her hold her own doll? Where's the fun in *that*? Adults exchange looks. Not very good at taking turns, is she? Eventually, even the kindest grown-ups are sick of the thing. Maybe she's ill-mannered. Or maybe . . . she was me. And autistic.

Because of my limited theory of mind, I have always felt as though my thoughts were transparent. That what I knew, everyone knew. That what I felt, everyone felt. When I see Cookie Monster, even now, there's a wordless sense of affection. Of friendship. Of silliness. *Those* were what I thought I was showing when I showed people my doll. I expected they would see him and experience, by my hand, all the good things he made *me* feel. No, I never explained any of that outright. Why would I? You don't explain the obvious. Here's Cookie Monster. Enough said. I'm sharing the feelings with you. Those are unlimited. But he's coming with me. I can't give *him* up . . . because I don't want to give up what he makes me feel.

Though most listeners would never realize it, when an autistic person "shows" (i.e., talks about, or shares photos, links, articles, music, or memes about) topics on which she is expert, she's not showing off for showing off's sake. She's trying to "infect" a potential friend with shared enthusiasm—trying to achieve a level of social confidence and transferred emotion. The awful irony is that we become our own undoing. Impulsivity and a tendency *toward* perseveration but *away from* reciprocity lead us to dominate the conversation, redirect the topic back toward our favorite, and interrupt other people frequently. Our limited theory of mind makes it difficult to register when we're boring or running off those around us—and executive function differences make it incredibly difficult to stop or redirect even when we do. As so often happens, we confuse attention for affection, prioritize accuracy over pleasantry, and instead of interesting and charming, we've managed to convey ourselves as self-centered and one-dimensional.

Which is not what anyone wants in a friend.

So we turn back to our interests, confident that they will distract, transport, and transform us—hence, the prerequisite for a topic that encompasses a vast (preferably infinite) amount of pertinent information. Dates and names, chemical symbols, a pantheon of characters, divisions of species and genus, the roster of the *Titanic*, an entire brain full of Harry Potter or Star Wars or Disney factoids, the entire body of poetry of Emily Dickinson, etymology, jazz music, breeds of dogs, ancient mythologies, or Broadway music. Evocative, important, telling. My daughter's complete mental catalog, at age five, of every My Littlest Pet Shop animal and present catalog of every line in *Hamilton*—a carbon copy of my fourteen-year-old expertise on *Les Misérables* and the tears I cry today whenever the theme to *Outlander* plays. Facts are merely petrol for the engine. Maybe, instead of Pokémon, our love is fairies or Barbies, especially if those Barbies are quietly acting out a historical event or favorite Greek myth.

And don't be surprised if, when we play "princess," we're *not* Cinderella. We're being Juliet. Young women will often try and piece together their growing, emerging selves by fiercely identifying with facets of various archetypes from literature, mythology, pop culture, theater, or even gaming. Whatever the specifics, give us an encyclopedia (or Wiki page) of information, and we have something to *do* with our fidgety, restless brains. Memorize. Categorize. Draw. Write about. Dream about. Reenact. Even the very act of collecting information is joyful. The focus is relaxing, like a meditation. The rigor invigorating, like going on a great run. The reliability comforting, a buffer against the mercurial nature of people.

Special interests are cracks in what is. As we accumulate and ingest information, our passions become more and more tangible. Accessible. Transportive. They flesh out into nuanced, inhabitable realms—times, places, species, or social scenarios where interpersonal rules and customs can be studied and mastered—the seduction of belonging somewhere, a place of safety where we cannot mess up and we won't be left out . . . the sense that somewhere (even if it's far-off or fictional), we have the very real potential for social success.

Just dive into a Wiki board, and you can find out everything (and I do mean *everything*) you'd ever need to know to succeed in whatever "world" we please. Maybe the distant past or the far future. Maybe the adventure of superheroes, the endless possibilities of mythology, or even gaming. Dictionaries for futuristic alien societies. Wiki boards all about hairstyles and social strata from a specific time period. These are all "worlds" where we can imagine ourselves thriving socially—worlds with fixed, clear customs, clothing, and languages that leave a whole lot less room for mistakes. Worlds where no one will ever skip and sing in celebration that we are "dead."

My love for history and genealogy was absolutely born of that transportive yearning. At age twelve, Laura's artifacts even offered me her favorite scripture verses, found beside her bed in a handwritten journal upon her death. It seemed to me that, through those private notes, my distant friend was actually reaching out to help me. Psalm 27, she wrote, was one of her favorites when she felt alone. It spoke of being kept safe from enemies who surround and attack, of feeling special, not condemned, of being protected and loved. It was as if, very much alive somewhere in time, Laura knew I needed her. I was no fool. I knew full well that I was twelve years old, growing up an only child in late-twentieth-century suburban New Jersey, not a member of the Ingalls clan on the mid- to late-nineteenth-century frontier. But maybe, just maybe, there was a way out. As Wendy McClure wrote in her book *The Wilder Life*, "Sometimes it felt like there was a trick to it, that if I held this thing [from Wilder's time] long enough I'd somehow be more human than I was now." There was a part of me—a very real, very deep, and very powerful part of me—that hoped if I could devour enough names and dates and places, I could fall through time to a place where I truly belonged. Obviously, this wasn't it.

As an adult, my love for history has only grown, though now, I look back further and across an ocean. I'd already become quite thoroughly versed in the royal history of England, Ireland, and Scotland, largely because I am so fascinated by the ways women used savvy social manipulation to affect power in a time when they had so little—especially because I could never conjure such complicated strategies or interpersonal chess games, even in a time when women *do* have power. In 2017, the story broadened, and I thought of the days I'd longed to find a tangible connection to Laura's past . . . as I delved into my own ancestry. To my *total* surprise, I found that I am actually *descended from* many of the *very people* I'd already studied—from the peerage, royalty, and nobility in ancient England, Scotland, Ireland, France, and Viking lands (Denmark). It is a treasure trove from which I hope never to escape—libraries full of information about my own ancestry, historical fiction based on their families, and endless archeological and anthropological feasts. My spirit will never run out of places to wander. In writing books, I have been gifted a way to inhabit the future. In my ancestral research, I have discovered connection points to real people and places whose languages I study, about whose contemporaries I learn, whose places I visit . . . and sense a resonance I cannot quite explain.

What else? I become giddy over historical fashion and am a fairly reliable repository of all things Broadway. Why? The fashion—it's a peek at who women have wanted to be and feeds my imagination as to which parts of my own self might be better expressed by pinup couture or the steadiness of button-up boots. And Broadway? Because . . . my heart, my soul, my body speak music. My mind speaks music like a language—swells and syllables and sentiments that are entirely nonliteral, purely emotional—and unhindered by rules. In fact, special interests do present us with the power to articulate an emotional vocabulary we often lack—à la expressing anguish by saying, "It was like Snape seeing himself with Lily in the Mirror of Erised." I actually did that in a major talk and the entire audience filled with heartbroken faces and a resounding, compassionate, "Awwww. . . ."

Each of these interests leads toward fandoms, which are, for all intents and purposes, our people. They are part of Geek Culture. That strange mixture of lowbrow pop culture and highbrow discussion where Shakespearean insults show up on gum wrappers, *The Princess Bride* is quoted like religious texts, and Jane Austen comes as both air fresheners and action figures. Geekdom. Global cultural communities (just peek at Tumblr or Pinterest), which create space for instant, intimate connections. Born of the zeitgeist, certain favorites emerge most prominently for women on the spectrum—mythology, Disney, faerie lore, historical fiction, fantasy (with strong female characters), vintage pop culture, time travel (*Doctor Who*, *Outlander*), musical theater, and magic. Want to know if someone's got the making of a true friend? Forget Myers-Briggs personality tests. Find out her Hogwarts House. Which POP figures does she have? Ask whether she speaks fluent show tunes, Disney pop culture, or Marvel heroines. Ask if she never misses *Once Upon a Time*. Or has a favorite wife of Henry VIII, Greek goddess, or episode of *Bones*—and why. They're social shorthand. If you see a stranger wearing a Tardis dress, and Dr. Who is your passion, you've got an instant connection . . . a conversation topic in any crowd or even foreign country.

Because fandoms *are* family. They're legitimate havens, true subcultures with language, music, stories, art, and even clothing that carry deep meaning. To us, they feel sacred. Which means they should be respected. In fact, they should be harnessed as the greatest glimpses into who we are, how to inspire us, and what we'd like our lives to become. In spirit, that is. And maybe at Comic-Con. When we talk about our passions, it's sort of like showing that Cookie Monster toy and asking you to play. A gesture at friendship. It may be clumsy, but it's genuine.

Differently wired brains mean differently wonderful tomorrows. If our families, friends, and teachers catch on and encourage us, our special interests can even become springboards for the future. *If* we see our differences are gifts. Coding classes for gamers. Fine arts for lovers of anime. And girls like that one who wanted nothing more than to dive into her favorite book? Well . . . she may write her own book. Or seven. And other girls may carry her words around in *their* hearts. Who knows? You may even be reading her words . . . right now.

For us, girls and women who often spend their entire lives thinking we are the "only ones," fandoms are how we find one another—how we discover that we aren't alone. That we can build *real* friendships and relationships, have meaningful dialogue, tell jokes that other people will actually find funny, and be valued for being our most real selves. They are the magic of authentic living—made very possible.

CHAPTER 7

The Statue of Venus: Friends, Rules, and Red High Heels

I began kindergarten at the age of four. Midway through the year, our class welcomed a few new students—a brother and sister who didn't speak English. Intrigued by language and the opportunity to be "teacher" without coming off as bossy, I took it upon myself to "adopt" them. Like pet projects. Which sounds so demeaning. But really, it was the beginning of a lifelong social strategy wherein I could build a friendship free of prejudices. Find the underdog and help. New kids didn't arrive with preconceived notions about me, so I could start fresh and become essential—apparent bossiness, which was really flaming insecurity, came through as important, appreciated, and nurturing. Which was, in fact, precisely how I meant it. You might say I looked like a duck, sounded like a duck . . . but was, in fact, a platypus.

The Teachers' Lounge

The next year, I gained another ace up my sleeve: a counterpart. Teddy read like I did (voraciously and years ahead of our ages), was moved on to long division like me. We were our own reading group, guaranteed playmates who, because we were a "we," didn't seem . . . like a problem that needed solving. But, at the end of first grade, catastrophe struck: Teddy was moving to St. Louis. Without a "partner" to diffuse the social scene, everyday life changed quickly for me. Somehow, I'd known it would. And I was miserable.

Teddy and I had shared an unspoken mission—of delighting our teachers, of making our principal so very proud, of winning poetry prizes and art prizes and accolades and validity for our school. There was a buzz that came from making all those grown-ups so happy. Think of a high school football player who goes out there and shines on the field, bringing as much glory as two young shoulders can bear. The crowds cheer him, pat him on the back—and they *hug one another*. They celebrate "us" and "we" as if they'd been on the fifty-yard line. All because of their champion. A way to be part of the "we." It's that bit that had me addicted.

I'd discovered the intoxicating power of making people feel good about themselves. Like the folks in the stands, the adults saw my successes as partly their own. And that was fine by me—because in their smiles and in the little privileges they doled out (you know, line leader and obvious-choice-to-trust-with-this-errand-to-the-office or whatnot) . . . all those little things added up . . . and, by proxy, made me part of a "we" celebration, too.

There was talk of closing Harrison Elementary. And with Teddy gone, as far as I saw it, I had a clear mission to tackle . . . on my own. Though it was new and lovely, the enrollment was too low to justify keeping it running when several other perfectly good elementary schools in our district were literally within walking distance of almost every child in attendance. And as my mom was president of the parent-teacher association, I knew she was working particularly hard to keep Harrison open . . . which meant that, beyond the morale boosters we'd delighted in giving the faculty, every ribbon or trophy, every photo that appeared in the town newspaper, every gold star and good impression our school made to the public and to the board of education mattered tenfold. Which is pretty much exactly what I meant when, on the day Teddy moved, I told my mom, "It's all up to me now. It's all on me." So the responsibility, I believed, was mine. The weight of proving our school viable. Of making sure the faculty knew they mattered. Of saving an entire little community—and above all, making my mother proud that her little girl had been by her side to do it.

While it might seem like hubris, the problem wasn't one of inflated ego. It was an inflated sense of responsibility. More of a matter of trying to matter to the people who mattered most to me. To make the crowds cheer, too (first figuratively, then literally)—for me, okay, a little bit . . . but ever so much more, for the idea of being essential . . . to "we."

We, that is, largely meaning me . . . and the grown-ups. They were the pack I wanted to belong to. According to research conducted at UCLA, there was (and is) a very good reason for my preference. Psychologist Michelle Dean writes,

> Social interactions contain rapid verbal and non-verbal cues that can be difficult for people with ASD to interpret. Further perpetuating social difficulties, people with ASD often struggle with monitoring the quality and quantity of their turn in conversations. Since children with ASD experience exclusion from peers in school, they often prioritize adult interactions . . . [when] conversations are facilitated . . . [a greater sense of] social competence is achieved because adults are "generous interactional partners" who make linguistic and social accommodations that children often do not.

I felt better about myself around adults than I did around other kids. Unlike the children, adults were more tolerant of—and, in fact, often praised—my "little professor" precociousness, expected less conversational reciprocity (back-and-forth), and had more patience with my blunders. That's why I wanted to hang out with my mother and her friends at the town pool instead of trying to "just go find someone to play with" and likely failing. Why I loved entertaining my father's clients. And why, to me—in a building where I was literally ensconced in social anxiety—no lunch club was more coveted, no membership more longed for . . . than the Teachers' Lounge.

Dollars to donuts, that was about the last place in the entire building the other kids wanted to go. And let me be clear, in hindsight, I am in no way under the illusion that the faculty saw little pig-tailed me as their peer. It was more the other way around. I didn't see—more accurately *couldn't* see—the social hierarchy in full swing around me. I just liked being around adults a whole lot more than braving the completely unpredictable terrain of recess or the cafeteria (shiver). Anything could happen there. It got loud, and when the other kids shouted, it seemed that they were mad or maybe about to be mad or maybe going to do something they weren't supposed to and then what??

Adults were a whole lot safer. Not to mention a lot more interesting. I really didn't care who could make the loudest fart noise (I still feel all impolite and embarrassed now, just writing the dang word!) or that someone could burp the entire alphabet. Everyone else laughed. I thought it was disgusting. And bad. You were *not* supposed to make bodily noises in public. This, I knew, was the rule. As my father would say, "Act like a lady," napkin in lap, elbows off the table. Definitely not belching your ABCs.

Years later, as an actual *teacher*, I *did* get to have lunch in the Teachers' Lounge. It turned out, though, that bouncing up and down with joy, telling a lounge full of cranky veteran teachers that I'd been nominated for Disney's American Teacher Awards in my first year of teaching, did not garner team enthusiasm. As colleagues, I'd thought we would celebrate one another—never realizing that my news probably felt like a slap in the face. Never considering that unhappily single female colleagues wouldn't care much for the bubbly new chick who fits into the cheerleading uniform and does splits along with the fourteen-year-olds at the faculty-versus-student basketball game.

This is the social blindness that wins us enemies. That loses jobs and ostracizes friends. That denies us the privilege of the benefit of the doubt. That makes it plausible for a boy to stand beside my freshman locker every morning with the same message: "No one wants you here. You should just go home and kill yourself." That makes it equally plausible for me not to tell a soul.

Before my spectrum identification, I had no answer to "why the kids you want to be friends with never want to be friends with you." Neurotypical folks are constantly taking the social temperature. Without even realizing it, they monitor one another's body language and tone of voice—able to correctly detect what others think of them. And if they sense they are causing uncomfortable or confused thoughts or feelings, they can change their own behavior in time to keep everyone comfortable and happy. Typical people easily notice the positive or negative responses to their behavior. It's fairly effortless—as natural as actually hearing someone say "yes" or "no." To them. But not to us.

We either don't notice or don't understand the thoughts we make others think about us. Not only can't we pick up on "subtle" feedback—we don't even know we've missed anything to begin with . . . not until it's too late, and no one is speaking to us anymore. Feeding a perpetual sense of waiting for the proverbial other shoe to drop. Mine was a life of never-ending could-happen-at-any-moment catastrophes where being everything to everyone felt like the only way to keep the sky from falling. When my mom offhandedly mentioned that I didn't know how to flirt (I was fifteen), I even tackled that "failure" with such gusto that, a year later, *flirt* was my nickname. Literally.

In other words, whatever it took to get people to like me, I tried to do—perfectly. So many of us do. The trouble is, "people" aren't a big blob of brainwashed clones with the same idea of what "likable" is. We're tilling at windmills. Chasing shadows. Just be yourself, we're told, but usually, it's the survival of the generic out there. Our classmates resent us. Or maybe taunt us. Insult us. Our coworkers leave us out—or hang us out to dry. And the people who are supposed to cherish us may love so cruelly that we lose all perspective on what kindness is even meant to be. And, even if by some miracle we *do* manage to pull off the "she's got it all together" persona—smart, accomplished, witty, charming (with effort), interesting, generous, physically attractive—we're doomed because if you're the best at everything (or, more likely, people *think* you are), everyone else feels less by comparison.

One of the who-knew-*that*-was-a-thing-back-when-I-did-it trends among people on the spectrum is that we tend to have far greater social success with (and thus prefer the company of) people who are older or younger than ourselves. Clearly defined subordinate/authority roles reduce the room for accidental blunders. Among peers . . . well, who's in charge? Is that across the board or situational? Are there vested interests at play in strategies we can't see? Who says what is right or wrong? Whether we're students divvying up responsibilities for an assignment or neighbors divvying up responsibilities for a block party, "group work" is the bane of our existences. It's chaotic. Ripe with blind spots. Worst of all, it's dynamic—evolving in real time, demanding social fluency and a strong theory of mind. And more often than not, we either come away feeling unheard or spoken over or, sure that our perspective is *the* perspective, have unwittingly taken control and burned bridges in the process.

Sitting in the corner of my darkened classroom, I might as well have been in a perverse time loop—as a fourteen-year-old eating by myself in the woods outside of school, darting out of my last class precisely at noon because I always ended up as an afterthought or forgotten entirely. And there I was, eating lunch alone again. How and why was it that *I* was always me on the outside? That it was always *me* who was, time and again, celebrated publicly and bitterly cut down in private? What was the dark poison inside me?

I could seduce the world en masse, it seemed. Be witty. Charming. And smart. But one on one, the enchantment always turned toxic. Somehow. I didn't know why, but I knew this . . . give me long enough, feel strongly enough, stay close enough, and I would make anyone hate me. Guaranteed. As a kid, I'd had a terrible time with other kids, faring much better with and flocking to the adults. Now, *as* an adult, the table had turned. Kids were my biggest fans, and my adult peers were the mean ones. The girls who edged me out of conversations. Who made up stories and made sure I knew I wasn't welcome. I'd made it to the Lounge. And I'd left.

When the change-of-class bell rang, I'd turn my classroom lights back on, fix my lipstick, and get into character: vivacious, young, fun, smart, caring, silly, the favorite-class-of-the-day teacher who makes a difference in every single student's life. All 137 of them. No matter what, I would be waiting—brimming with (very genuine) you-can-be-amazing, I-believe-in-you, hey-we-can-do-this-together enthusiasm. No matter what had happened "backstage," I would know my lines and smile in the spotlight. No matter what, the show would always go on.

There's a psychological theory that says we each carry a core maladaptation—a little liar who takes residence in our noggins before elementary school (like *Inside Out—the Nightmare Version*). Some days we may work to confirm the lies are, in fact, true. That the Voice is right, and that we are very wrong. On those days, life seems to whisper, "No one will ever truly like you, let alone love you." I remember my ninth-grade history teacher, who saw me talking to another student on the front lawn of the high school and shouted—for all to hear—"Oh, Miss Cook! I didn't know you *had* friends!" And then I remember how, only a year later, one weekend as the lingerie-clad lead in the school musical skyrocketed me to overnight "hot chick." So I flash wild, all copper hair and Scorpio sting. If they won't like me or love me, then I'll at least make sure as hell that they see me shine and want me badly. And I'll dance as fast as I can and live for the devil-may-care day.

Other days, we do everything in our power to prove the Voice wrong. We overcompensate. If we believe we are weak, we flare in rage. If we believe we are destined to be misunderstood, we talk ceaselessly, explaining and dissecting every word. And if we believe that we are too difficult to love, too much trouble to like . . . well, that's, apparently, when we . . . I . . . pour every ounce of my soul into a worldwide, high-profile, feels-as-though-everything-I-am-depends-upon-proving-I-am-worth-more-than-the-trouble-I-cause (and still totally, sincerely heartfelt), do-good mission.

The other option is—unsustainable. If I believe the Voice, I can either submit to tears and loneliness or brazenly play some version of Evita Perón. Or, said one friend, be like a statue of Venus. Beautiful and sure, the embodiment of Woman. That is—and always has been—me on stage. I am safe. I am poised and funny and poignant. (Well, that's what they tell me—I'm a little too busy to notice.) But up close to Venus, you see that she is covered in tiny cracks. She is porous. And vulnerable.

That part I could recognize on my own.

That's What Friends Are For

Psychologist Dr. Tony Attwood observed that when asked what makes a good friend, people on the spectrum usually answer with negatives. We define a good friend by what he or she *doesn't* do, rather than what he or she *does* do. While that may not sound too significant, if we consider the same dynamic from a slightly different angle, the real impact becomes clearer. Imagine asking a child what makes a good parent. Instead of replying, perhaps, that a good parent reads bedtime stories, says "I love you" a whole lot, makes sure she gets good food, or is involved at school, the child answers, "A good parent doesn't hit me or starve me. She doesn't leave me alone all night. She doesn't make me scared in my own house." Red flags would wave and alarm bells would sound, because we define in terms of what we know. A child defining good as the absence of bad knows bad—but isn't familiar with good at all.

Ask a person on the spectrum (who has not had the benefit of self-awareness, cognitive behavioral therapy, or social skills) what makes a good friend, and that definition, too, will be in terms of what she knows. Odds are the answers will be stated in the negative—something along the lines of "She doesn't talk behind your back, doesn't lie to you, and doesn't leave you out of conversations." In fact, I'd add that many positive answers would *also* be reactions to our negative experiences, such as "She responds to your texts" (because we've been ignored or shut out) or "She invites you to parties" (versus being left to hear about the fun we weren't invited to share). Unfortunately, we haven't had enough good experiences to give us a solid idea of what friends *are* supposed to do. We know we want friends; often, though, we don't really know how to choose good ones. Or that choice even exists for us.

When you are lonely, feel rejected, or are afraid, the want of companionship can feel bottomless. Since we can't recognize them, we continue to accept impersonators. Even the most adept autistic person is not as adept at social nuance as her neurotypical peers. We expect the rest of the world to be the kind of friends we would be in return. We think, naively, that other people's intentions are as pure as our own. We are oblivious to hidden agendas or manipulation. It is our biggest weakness—we can't see another's perspective, so we cannot imagine they would want to hurt us, when all we want is to be friends. And over and over, we are brokenhearted when our false friends show their true colors.

I have watched well-intentioned parents sit back, happy that their child has *any* friends at all, no matter the quality of the others' characters. I have also witnessed parents try to "buy" friends by throwing the coolest parties or planning social excursions. Honestly, I've been guilty of the latter myself. Heck, I've even seen my mother try to help her granddaughter by "setting up" friendships and pen pals. But our little girl didn't possess the drive or empathy to maintain those relationships, built largely on a false, neurotypical persona "created" (though lovingly) by her grandmother. In the end, everyone (including the other child) is let down.

"Faking it" or engineering inclusion only leaves us believing that without pretense, no one would choose to be her friend. And that, I can tell you, is a terrible place to be—and is totally opposite of what the family members are trying to create. It may take us longer to find or make a real, true friend. We may even find we are more successful in long-distance friendships (my two best friends live across an ocean) where the day-to-day maintenance requirements are less intense. Regardless of the particulars, if a friendship is going to lift us up, it has to be real to count.

Which leads to another problem: they say the best way to make a friend is to *be* a friend. Our hearts are always in the right place. Our words and actions aren't quite as well put. So how do you make friends if you don't really even know how to *be* one?

Imagine moving to some other country and being expected to speak their language, know the customs, and follow every one of their super-complicated laws—without anyone ever explaining them to you. And if you mess up, you could (and probably would) get fired, be laughed at, left out, bullied, or even arrested. Would that be fair? Of course not. But that has, literally, been the story of my life—and so many others, trying to follow a set of hidden social rules without the rule book. To us, not really rules, but secrets. Just like neurotypicals might have to buckle down to remember a timeline or equation or factoid known by rote, we have to "do our homework" to learn the social rules that run our mostly neurotypical world.

That process is even more complicated for girls and women—especially for those of us on the spectrum. In her research of gender-specific friendships, psychologist Eleanor Maccoby concluded that female relationships require more intimacy than male friendships, and that "autistic characteristics conflict with the dominant features observed in female bonding, which includes engaging in reciprocal conversations about thoughts and feelings," which our executive function skills naturally preclude. Michelle Dean expanded on the dilemma, explaining that

> because stable female friendships often include the additional responsibility to protect secrets, girls are less likely than boys to initiate new friendships and more likely to use relational aggression to protect the boundaries of their relationships. Therefore, subtle nuances and exclusivity that characterize many reciprocal

> female relationships present formidable challenges for girls with ASD. With a heavy priority on interdependence, social conversations frequently address and exclude girls that are different or "weird. . . ." Furthermore, language and social communication deficits associated with ASD are more detrimental to girls.

That is to say, female friendships rely more acutely on verbal interactions like concise, well-timed, relevant storytelling and emotional and conversational reciprocity. But our nonlinear, jumpy thinking style, impulsivity, and easy distractibility tend to stall conversations instead of furthering them. And because we can't organically shift perspectives or recognize social hierarchies, we unwittingly tend to dominate airtime, return conversations to special interests, neglect to ask open-ended questions—it's a dynamic for which we, on the spectrum, aren't naturally hardwired . . . but that we, nevertheless, must navigate, primed for victimization by our most fundamental differences.

In female cliques, picking someone apart—judging her clothes, her sense of humor, her intelligence, her body, her love life—is a super-common way of bonding. Of connecting. Sort of an unwritten, horrible social rule: when girls can't think of anything to say, the trick is to talk badly about someone who isn't there. To share something you've overheard. To "worry about her"—which is code for "form a little jury and pass judgment on her." Through incredibly nuanced criteria (usually based on body language and social intuition—spectrum blind spots), judgment is passed. And torment begins.

Now imagine walking these minefields, while blindfolded, speaking a different language, distracted by sounds and lights and unquiet minds, all while wearing a supersensitive bodysuit. That is our reality. Navigating the subtleties of backhanded compliments, of "group work," of playing the role of "female" well—but not *so* well as to intimidate or put off peers—of recognizing and adapting fluidly to different expectations from different people in different circumstances that even differ from one day to the next so that you must relearn the rules of dress, speech, candor, trust, and propriety for every new station in life and in every single relationship . . . while wired to be straightforward and impulsive and driven and compassionate to the point of emotional shutdown. Now pay attention to making the right friends, dating the right people, looking the right way, or learning how to self-advocate. Oh—and heaven help you if you're pretty, because just by that stroke of nature, so very much more social sophistication will be expected of you—there will be so many more ways you are vulnerable to abuse and misogyny, so much more that you'll have to learn, intellectually, just to survive.

If you fail, you will be alone. If you succeed, it won't be done correctly anyway. That's the lesson. The constant, lurking threat. The omnipresent anxiety. And with it, responsive, heightened reactivity, imprisoning us from living the broad, expansive lives we desire, and breeding cycles of self-defeating, self-destructive, and even suicidal thoughts that drag us down into depression and self-harm. Obsessive-compulsive disorder, panic disorders, cutting, eating disorders, emotional isolation, almost-manic impulsivity, sexual exploitation, financial and professional dependence.

We're each individuals, of course, but there are most definitely common themes—one of which is that we are amazingly good at thinking all is well at our job, in a friendship, with our dress, when, in fact, we've managed to upset, anger, or embarrass other people. What happens next? We tire people out. We annoy them. We hurt or offend them. And a lot of times, we end up alone. Is it really any surprise, then, that one of our most universal, persistent thoughts is: why do they always end up hating me? Most of us on the spectrum have had "eras" of friendships but never really seem to be able to keep them going over time. Either we don't know how to make friends to begin with, or we are "super hot then super cold." We charm everyone, only to eventually find ourselves "blown off" or downright "kicked out" in the long run. And, after enough cycles of that pattern, you can't help but wonder how long until you pull the carpet out from under yourself again.

As a college freshman, I consciously found pleasure in the number of people who would recognize me and smile or say "hi" while crossing the campus. Friends even commented, half-bemusedly, half-annoyed, that they couldn't keep a conversation going with me because of the number of greetings I'd need to return. I'd engineered it that way, collecting and shoring up a social spot. Almost like Neil Patrick Harris says in *How I Met Your Mother*—"When I start feeling sad, I get awesome. True story."

Back then, the quantity of pleasantries, rather than the depth of relationships, was what mattered most to me—it was validating to someone who'd often felt left out before. Even today, I feel great satisfaction in helping establish positive relationships and great security knowing that, if folks appreciate my involvement, it means they will probably be nice to me, too. You might say I discovered the power (and sincere joy) of being a social yenta. It is vicarious success—an illusion of proficiency that keeps me included *and* maintains a safe social distance, protected from exclusion or rejection.

That all said, I did, years ago, come up with a sort of "by-proxy friend" strategy, without ever realizing it. Being on a stage in my work now or in theater growing up, I could (and do) feed off the energy of the crowd. Off the tears of weary relief, I can feel free, and the bouncing steps of hope, confidence, and "she's in here with us" sense of team. Of being part—at a distance—of "we." An emotional, social strategy for guaranteeing inclusion on my own terms.

Maintaining those friendships is an entirely different story—because it is an entirely different skill. There are scripts, rules, and, most important, patterns to follow in establishing relationships—both platonic and romantic. Reciprocity is expected. Thoughts of people and events out of our immediate day-to-day experiences are there, for sure. But our attention is fleeting, and one recollection is quickly replaced by other fast-paced ideas. It's a working memory thing, not a lack of affection. And if a relationship is established, we may get way too attached; friendly and friend are fuzzy boundaries, confusing and variable with lots of room for embarrassing gaffes. The new person may become a special interest—something on which to happily hyperfocus, though perhaps with preconceived plans for get-togethers, playdates, or relationship trajectories that don't accurately include the other party's perspective. Then, unable to manage the reciprocity comfortably, or doubtful of the genuine affection we may have won, we may dramatically break off or politely drift away.

Something Beautiful out of Something Broken

None of which means that we want to be all alone. Nor that we will be. Life changes when you first discover a person who loves you for you and simply won't allow you to drift away because she thinks you matter and are of value *now*. You may never agree with her. You may think she was, quite literally, "seeing things" instead of seeing you. But you'd be wrong. Which is why no friend was ever more precious than my Lori.

May 15, 2013

My best friend, Lori, and I were sorority sisters—but more than that, as two precocious only children, we each became the real sister the other had never had. And in our seventeen years of friendship, I learned that I didn't have to be impressive all the time to make an impression, that real friends can disagree deeply and in the open without fear of reprisal, that sometimes your girlfriends are the *only* people you can call with those *really* personal questions, and that being silent next to someone you love speaks more than a thousand Hallmark cards.

In short . . . I guess you could say we grew up together.

A week before my senior year in college, I left a physically and psychologically abusive relationship. And, typically me, I tried to seem "together" even when my mind was crashing in . . . Lori wasn't fooled. She, alone, drove hours to be by my side. There was no blame or expectation—only presence. And so, she taught me that I was worthy of the love of a friend even if I wasn't chipper and happy and bubbly. I could be human—I could even be a freaked-out emotional wreck—and she still saw me as "brilliant," "courageous," and "wonderful." Words I never would've used to describe myself, if speaking honestly.

We had boyfriends and broken hearts. We earned diplomas. We moved out. We became women. We sat in judgment of "the one" before giving our seal of approval, each for the other . . . we became wives. We became mothers. We talked about breast pumps and houses suddenly filled with trucks and trains. We juggled careers and kids and guilt. She sat next to me at my father's wake. I held her firstborn son when he was less than two weeks old.

When I graduated from Brown, Lori gave me a mirror she had framed herself—a mosaic of pottery shards in pinks and golds and greens and white. The truly ironic thing was that I, too, had made

> her a "memory mirror" . . . except mine was *really* ugly. Lori's was gorgeous. And then she said, "For my friend, Jen, who has made something beautiful out of something broken." I hung that mirror in my daughter's bedroom before she was even born—and it's now in my stairwell, so that we both look in it before we face the world each day. Because "Aunt Lori," as she is known to my children, made it. "And Aunt Lori is really smart."
>
> Except she was wrong about one thing. It was Lori who made something beautiful out of the broken pieces. Her name is in the acknowledgments of every Asperkids book for a reason. She held up a mirror and let me see that I was beautiful—not in spite of my jagged edges or chips and cracks, but because of them.
>
> For two years, she has battled a largely private war against aggressive breast cancer—and I consider it a privilege that I was allowed to be one of the very few people who knew what was really happening. Tonight, she left us. For many people, it's news they never saw coming. For me, it's news I've been expecting but willing *not* to happen.
>
> Aspies don't need lots of friends. It's a quality-not-quantity thing. Lori was—and is—the closest thing I will ever have to a sister. I will look in that mirror every day for the rest of *my* life. I will see the wrinkles come and be grateful for the time that brings them. With every new morning that passes, I will look into that reflection and say, "Today, I will make something beautiful out of something broken." Because in a very chipped, cracked, mismatched, and imperfect me, Lori already did.

While neurotypicals will, of course, feel terrible loss, as I did, should some terrible reality snatch that person away, the likelihood is that they *will* have a remaining circle of friends. None can replace your most precious, but the others *are* there to bolster your spirits, take group girls-only holidays, buy you crazy hats and drinks, and, well, be your "clan." I don't. I won't. I am the pretty girl without a date to the prom. The one whom people, now, chase into cars for autographs in their books and ask, very nervously, if we could possibly take a picture together. Facebook fills in a major social void for me, connecting me with very close spectrum friends I've made overseas. But. In day-to-day life, time passes and invitations don't come very often. I'm "fabulous," says the world. Ah, well. More often, I'm fabulously alone.

Bottoms Up

At age thirteen, I completely freaked out. I was a high school freshman and had elected advanced geometry for my math course of the year, a bold placement that had to be staff approved. I wasn't being arrogant; I knew I could tackle this challenge, I wanted the transcript that went along with it, and I enjoyed pushing myself to learn new things (I still do). However, for the first time in my life, a class was about to throw me completely.

Suddenly, we were memorizing random theorems about abstract rules, which seemed unimportant and disconnected. For example, we read that a trapezoid is isosceles if, and only if, the base angles are congruent. Okay, well, I understood the words, and the little picture in the textbook looked right, so, if they said so . . . but, trust me, there was no real learning happening. Then, to make matters worse, we were expected to apply these random theorems in real time when solving problems that didn't look anything like the original instructional illustrations. I was lost, and, worst of all, I truly didn't understand what I didn't understand. But how do you ask for help when you don't even know what's confusing you?

Looking back, I can see that it wasn't the material that didn't make sense to my brain. It was the way the information was being presented. Geometry, you may recall, involves a lot of "proofs" that begin with a diagram of some lines or shapes, provides some "given" facts about the picture, and, finally, tells what conclusion must be proven—step-by-step—using the information provided and a combination of mathematical "laws." As far as I could tell, the only thing this kind of problem had going for it was that at least I knew where I was supposed to end up. On the other hand, how the heck I was supposed to move forward from step 1 almost always eluded me. At the time, I had no idea why this was so hard. And, certainly, my instructor couldn't understand why I wasn't acing her class as I had previous math courses—so the teaching approach didn't change . . . and neither did my frustration level.

By now, you've probably gotten the hang of the way I explain new ideas. Generally, I tell you about an experience (or two or three) from real life, then connect them with one, bigger idea, like assembling a mosaic out of bits of tile. It's a bottom-up approach to thinking that usually feels more natural to those of us on the spectrum. Neurotypical minds (and geometric proofs) work the other way around: top-down, based on deductive reasoning, which is usually thought of as a skill that develops without any teaching or training. And for nonspectrum thinkers, that's mostly true. They see a fact—maybe a facial expression, maybe a social situation—and easily link it to a clear, logical conclusion. Our spectrum minds operate differently; we don't make the same mental leaps others do. So "obvious" to them isn't "obvious" to us.

Generally, we understand things, people, ideas—life—using *inductive* reasoning. We go from the bottom-up, starting with specific, concrete experiences, facts, and examples. Then, we spot trends, notice patterns, and discover bigger concepts that link it all together. All in all, having different methods of thinking is a good thing. If we lived in a world where everyone arrived at the same conclusions, we would be without creativity, problem-solving, or curiosity. There is, however, one complication. The world is trying to support us and teach us everything from geometry to how to play well with others . . . *backward*. Neurotypical teachers, friends, employers, mentors, and parents are all showing us how to set and achieve goals (be they personal or professional) in the most opposite way to how our brains actually work.

However, if we let our minds think as they were designed, we can become some of the world's most observant, adept social anthropologists. Collecting individual observations, noticing otherwise invisible trends, and building them up to larger statements of truth will lead us to the most important "given" of all: because of who and how we are, not in spite of it, we have more power than we've ever imagined.

How to Be a Girl

The pervasive global perception is that girls and women on the spectrum have no interest in "looking girlie" in the "expected" ways . . . makeup, dresses, flirting. That is absolutely true for *some* girls. As it is true for *some* girls/women of *any* group of people. But let's be very clear: asexuality, androgyny, and autism are *not at all* universally wed.

On the other hand, some of us like sex. A lot. Some of us are *very* eager to get classic, traditional ideas of "being girlie" right—as much as our perfectionism drives us to get everything else "right," too. "How to be a girl" instructions are damned confusing. And externally prescriptive. And contradictory. Be "this," not "that" (except for sometimes *do* be "that," just don't be too obvious about it). Regardless of the confusing guidelines, other spectrum women just enjoy "old-school glamour" because we like starting with rules, playing around with them, and then inventing our own, fresh versions of the classics (probably why you see so very many of us in theater or literary study—we're surrounded by characters to sample), or simply because we like the aesthetic. For me, both are true.

Magazines tell us how we're supposed to look. Movies tell us what we're supposed to say. Teachers and parents and even adult peer pressure tell us how we're supposed to think. And behave. And feel. The truth, though, is that as long as we construct our version of "femaleness" based on a world of conflicting directions, it's only natural that we'll feel conflicted.

Which is probably why, as an undergraduate student at Brown, I somehow managed to design my course of study in response to my yet-undiagnosed autism. I even wrote my honors thesis on Barbie, spending two years researching, studying, and writing a book about Barbie as a "didactic tool of postwar modern femininity in America." That is, I literally made an academic course out of learning the expectations of my own society and my own era. It made me feel safe . . . which is not, I point out, the same as saying I'd checked my brain (or sass) at the door. I didn't read people easily. I held too rigidly to rules and ceremony. I was apt to come off, alternatively, as parental and bossy or giddy and happy. As aloof or naively sentimental. As flirtatious tease or sexy playmate.

These were tender spots, untrue extremes I almost never noticed in real time, not until I felt foolish and exposed. A few people took the time to see that the real me existed in the middle of the Venn diagram, not in any extreme. But for the most part, I was playing the game of life without a copy of the directions. Though I called upon uncanny skills of mimicry and theatricality, I was faking it socially. In truth, I was mind-blind—unable to naturally read and respond to others' intentions or glean their perspectives. I couldn't see myself as others did, couldn't recognize one day or feeling or conversation in relation to a larger situation.

Fifteen years or so later, I was diagnosed, had written my first book about how to teach and reach and love kids on the spectrum, and was waiting for it to hit the shelves. Exposure to more and more people like my daughter and myself confirmed that we, on the spectrum, simply were not programmed to constantly take the social temperature of a room, or conversation, or relationship. However, I came to realize that in trying to help my children navigate social ambiguities, I was actually using my bottom-up thinking and highly analytical autistic brain to create a road map of sorts for them. And, if I could do it for young children, why couldn't I do the same for myself?

In the Middle East, to show the bottom of your shoe to another human being is considered deeply offensive and rude—in Japan, not taking off your shoes upon entering a home would be the insult. In Bulgaria, nodding your head means "no" and shaking it from side to side says "yes," but the opposite is true most everywhere else. Argentinians expect you to arrive about thirty minutes after a set arrival time; many other cultures would find that disregard for time to be costly and arrogant. And in the United States, driving five miles over the speed limit is technically against the law—yet it's also expected, and sometimes even necessary if you don't want to tie up traffic. Rules are relative, from one place to another. Expectations change over time (like women going to work), and from one situation to another (talking on a cell phone is fine, but not in the middle of a restaurant).

If I could be a sort of social anthropologist—if I could really focus on my own culture as if I were a visitor, unfamiliar with customs and mores—I might find life a lot less scary or sad than it had been. So I began watching "people patterns," and quickly, it became clear that, taken up close, the neurotypical world wasn't quite as random as I'd thought. In fact, through careful study, it even seemed possible to infer and then "play by" a set of unwritten social rules. There was, I began to discover, even a discernible rhythm to it all—a predictable pattern into which we could insert ourselves with a much greater chance of reducing social anxiety and increasing personal connections: think, feel, do. People of all kinds observe one another, then think about what they've seen. Those thoughts lead to feelings. Those feelings inspire action . . . which is observed. And the whole cycle starts over again.

Anyone who has ever lived in unstable or abusive situations will tell you that the greatest source of anxiety is never quite knowing when the storm will hit. We walk on eggshells, on constant alert for signs of danger. Which is why discovering the existence of the think/feel/do pattern changed my life. Suddenly, I had power and choice that, beforehand, were utterly unimagined. "Secret" rules are just part of that big cause-and-effect deal. How "well" you follow the rules (the cause) determines how most people will treat you (the effect). Do what others expect, and the reward is that you are accepted by the group. Behave in unexpected ways, and other people felt threatened, uncomfortable, even embarrassed or scared (though I might see it as frustration, uncertainty, or confusion). When that happened, they would employ social consequences—isolation, gossip, bullying, teasing, practical jokes—to get me, the person who'd created the negative feelings, to either go away or change. But, if I could learn how to better match my intentions with my receptions, I could improve the ways I understood and reacted to other people *and* the ways they understood and reacted to me.

I decided to be my own test case. In a blank notebook, I jotted down some "apparent" rules, tried them out . . . and lo and behold, they worked. No, the responses weren't huge celebrations or applause. I knew they worked when neurotypical's *didn't* realize I was doing anything *at all.* And when my therapist discovered what I was doing, she suggested I propose it to my publisher as a second title (though the first was not yet on shelves). I was dumbfounded, but decided to give it a whirl, and began as I would have years ago . . . had I only understood *why* I didn't understand:

> 1990
> Dear Journal,
> What the heck? How is possible to be so smart and so clueless at the exact same time? It seems like everyone else speaks a language that I don't. I watch them. I listen. I imitate. I act—a lot. Have you

heard my newest nickname? The tennis team has taken to calling me "Happy Head." They actually mean it to be nice. I think I've become the seniors' pet. The cute little redhead with the smile plastered on her face—it's plastered, all right. And plastic. I'm completely petrified of feeling left out. Again. It's probably just a matter of time, though. We both know that I always manage to blow it somehow. Just give me long enough and I'll screw up any friendship. Seriously, I wish someone would just give me some rules on how to be "normal" . . . let me know when *that* book comes out. It seems to be the only one I haven't read.

Love,
Jenny

2012
There wasn't a rule book, then, like I wished. There was no peek into the secret rules that I knew had to be there, but couldn't ever figure out. There were rules, I was sure of it. Everyone else seemed to get them. But not me. Over and over, I'd mess up without even realizing it. Then try to cover it up. Then have to find new friends. For thirty-four years, that was the cycle, until I learned a new word: "Asperger's." And all of a sudden, I made sense. It all made sense. No, there wasn't a rule book then. But there is now. Part code cracking, part doodle pad. Completely honest and all yours. Well, ours . . .
Welcome to the (Secret) Rule Book.

The manuscript was off in the editors' hands when I asked my therapist doubtfully, "Do you really think anyone will want to read it?" My mind-blindness, apparently, had been just as extreme as every other person on spectrum, trapping me, too, in the belief that I was truly alone in my disconnection and confusion, unable to make sense of people, much less help anyone else do so. Eighteen months later, over forty thousand copies of *The Asperkid's (Secret) Book of Social Rules* have been sold—with at least a third of the readership being adults. It hit number one on Amazon multiple times in multiple categories; experts shortlisted it over and over again to top-ten book lists around the world. When I traveled to speak, teens hunted me down by Twitter posts just to say "thank you," and in 2015, the Autism Society of America awarded it the Dr. Temple Grandin Outstanding Literary Work of the Year Award. So, I guess the answer was and is . . . yes. When you speak truth, a whole lot of people really *do* want to listen.

Red High Heels

The next few years were an absolute whirlwind, and by 2014, I'd been featured as one of the world's "Top Aspie Mentors" in a book by the internationally renowned psychologist Dr. Tony Attwood. To celebrate its publication, we "mentors" were invited to participate in a global panel where we would discuss some of the highlights.

Several wonderful men—dressed in baseball caps, sweaters, sandals, Hawaiian T-shirts, and suits—were on the stage with me, as were two other bright women. One wore all black and a cowboy hat, the other wore a loose-fitting pantsuit. Then there was me.

Clothing is about comfort and practicality, sure. But above all, it's about respect. Self-respect. Respect for an occasion. A host. About consciously learning and acknowledging what is appropriate for the formality, culture, import, and environment of a situation. Fashion is something different. It's clothing raised to art form. An evolution. It's respect infused with perspective, personality, voice, humor, and intention. Which is why I'd paired a lovely 1960s-style black-and-white floral pointelle dress with my favorite "happy" wardrobe item—red high heels. Classic elegance with a pop. Smart, sassy, a little bit daring, and a lot bit playful.

You can see for yourself. It's the picture that ended up on Wikipedia.

The panel lasted for about an hour; afterward, one of the members of the audience—a woman in her late fifties—came up and said, "Jennifer! I saw you walk in here with those red shoes and thought to myself, 'Now there's a confident woman!' Keep it up."

I beamed and thanked her for taking the time to say so. I'd fought hard for the confidence I have. Yet soon afterward, I learned that another person (a professional) had taken great umbrage at my shoes, complaining (and even calling colleagues to report) that they were a terrible distraction . . . my too-sexy, unprofessional attempt to draw attention to myself and away from the conversation.

She was, apparently, uncomfortable watching as I "seduced the entire room." I'm not summarizing or inventing. Those were the actual written words on her evaluation card.

I'll admit. At first, I was embarrassed. Hurt. I excused myself, hid in a bathroom stall, and started to cry. Like a filmy residue, shame sticks to your soul, and before long, it actually feels familiar. It feels right. Even when I'd scrubbed and scrubbed, it took only a word—a glance—to cover me in filth again.

All of a sudden, though, a question occurred to me: Why did no one comment on the "professionalism" of the men's clothing? Are *red shoes* less professional than a Hawaiian shirt? Or Teva sandals? Or than another woman's ten-gallon cowboy hat? No! We were all *okay* being *us*. That was the entire *point* of the book, after all. Each in our own various way, we "top mentors" were expressing ourselves as much through our clothing as through the deeply sincere life experiences we shared onstage.

When we *respond* to a name, a title, a cruel insult, or a loving nickname, we are agreeing that some part of the name fits. That it's appropriate. That somehow, we recognize ourselves in the words we hear—*Too sexy. Too butch. Too girlie. Freakishly neuter. Prude. Slut.* I knew that. And, as I calmed down, I knew I had done everything *right*. Had nothing to defend. That I'd sat on that stage along with my colleagues and had been so professional, dynamic, and engaging that I'd already received two invitations to keynote elsewhere.

During a radio interview a month earlier, I'd been asked whether I'd "come to prominence so quickly because of [my] looks." Worse than the original, invalidating implication is the fact that, despite enormous evidence to the contrary, I hesitated. Unsure. I actually wondered whether that's all I had to offer, after all.

Think. Feel. Do. Now I'd come to my senses. The issue wasn't me. The issue was my red high heels. A hint at female sexuality. At an intelligent woman's self-possessed power. And that scares people.

Gender expression is, arguably, more actively played with by spectrum girls and women, who are, as a rule, less confident in every aspect of their own identities. In many ways, we're waiting to be told what to like, whom to like, how to feel, how to act. Spoken or written, other people's words etch themselves into our souls, shaping and reshaping the ways we understand who we "actually" are. Which means that even when we try to listen to and figure out our deepest selves, it can be really hard to tell which inner voice is truly our own. That confusion can get particularly mucky when we try to understand our own sexuality—our individual ways of "being female."

At the end of the event, the moderator thanked me for the kindness and humility he felt my words had carried to anyone listening . . . and I know I must've done something right from the achingly beautiful letters I received from mothers, teachers, teens, and twenty-somethings who heard me speak. But you know what? I can't recall a single thing I *did* say that day . . . sadly, what I most remember from a personal, professional pinnacle are my shoes . . . because again I saw that if a woman can't be taken down by attacking the content of her work, the next (but totally irrelevant) target is her sexuality.

One month after the panel, I was at another conference when I learned about the insulting, truly sad red shoe "back channel" talk. So I took a minute to think about what to do. And I *did* respond. Just not as expected. I promptly went back to my hotel room and changed *into* my red shoes. I also added some bright, 1950s-style red lipstick. And I walked out the door—with my head *and* red heels high.

Sometimes, I've been able to manage that confidence. To giggle as Temple Grandin rolled around on my hotel room floor doing "butt stretches" and accidentally rocked right over those red heels. "I don't know how you can wear those things, Jennifer!" she exclaimed, shaking her head. "Temple," I laughed, "I'm pretty sure I could *not* rock a bolo tie like you. I'd say we're both okay."

Indeed. There is a spectrum of ways to "do female" even on the autism spectrum.

The last time I checked, how we dress—how we look—has nothing to do with our value as humans or our successful "executions" of "femaleness." However we package ourselves, understand ourselves, or present ourselves, there is *no* right way—and no wrong way—to be a woman. Spectrum sisters . . . and sisters on the human spectrum.

I don't care if you dress in trousers every day
and never ever put on a lick of makeup.

I don't care if you love high heels and vintage perfume bottles.
I don't care if you are attracted
to boys, girls, both, or nobody in particular.
What we wear isn't what makes us women.
Whom we want to kiss isn't what makes us women.
Tell me this, if you'd tell me what kind of woman you are . . .
Are you being kind to others? To yourself?
Are you thinking new ideas? Are you exploring?
Are you trying new things?
Are you showing courage and curiosity and generosity?
Good. Because those are the things real women do.
No matter what shoes we wear.

CHAPTER 8

So This Is Love: Autism by Gaslight

Content Warning: *This chapter contains explicit descriptions of my own experiences with sexual assault and/or violence that some survivors may find triggering. I respectfully offer the power of forewarning and the choice to read or move to page 212. Whichever decision feels best is the right one.*

Minnie Mouse shattered on impact. Reduced, for the most part, from shiny ceramic to chalk dust. The only recognizable chunks were from her skirt. Glossy, pale pink shards, speckled with clean white polka dots. Jagged edges where curves had been.

There were whispers growing in the hall. Piling up outside my door. My sorority sisters had heard the shouting. The crash. Somebody knocked. "Is everything alright in there?"

"Honey . . . ," closer to the door, more quietly. "Are you ok?" Fine, I answered. Of course, they knew it wasn't fine. Of course *I* knew it wasn't fine. But we were young. And this was so complicated. And really, none of us knew what to do next.

This. Wow. This.

It was April 1996. I was twenty. A junior at Brown. From the outside looking in, everything about my life seemed perfect. I was making all *A*s in the prestigious Ivy League and had recently been approved to write a senior thesis, meaning that I would graduate with honors. I was a staff writer for the newspaper. Cheerleader for both football and basketball seasons. Part of the university dance company. Proud officer of Kappa Alpha Theta, the nation's oldest sorority. Volunteer adult ESL teacher. Cover model on the bookstore's catalog. And the "pinned" sweetheart of a fraternity president—a guy who was also a varsity athlete, a musician, who had played Jesus in the church's Easter reenactment, and had JFK Jr.'s old bedroom.

These were all markers by which I defined myself to the outside world. Privately though, more than anything on Earth, I wanted to feel powerfully, recklessly, unconditionally wanted. That, if I'd told the truth, was more important to me than any "perfect score" or list of achievements. Just imagine a desert mirage of an oasis: you can see it out of reach . . . what you want most in the world—what seems almost possible—but it's just an illusion. That's happiness—that's "who am I?" built on other people's approval . . . shaky, without substance. For those of us who've spent a lifetime on the edges of "lovable," the want—the need—to be wanted and liked and included is too powerful to resist. Experience had already taught me that being attractive opened doors. And being publicly "chosen" by a man (especially a good-looking, popular one) carried more social currency than any bullet point on a résumé ever could. Sadly, it's a conundrum we still teach our daughters. And reteach ourselves. Modern women, we can be anything. Do anything. True. Anything, as long as we look young, slender, and alluring while we're at it. But not too alluring, because then whatever happens is our fault. Basically, be Grace Kelly. Not Rita Hayworth. In which case, you'll be wanted by lots of men, rejected by lots of women, and none of them will actually know who you are—or care.

Thing is . . . I *am* Rita Hayworth. Or Jessica Rabbit. I'm not bad. I'm just drawn that way.

We'd met the year before at a Greek council executive board event . . . he was an upperclassman with a (casual) girlfriend, and I was just a Jennifer Who? freshman. Besides introductions, we didn't actually speak until sometime in late January, when we'd bumped into each other at the athletic center. He'd been finishing up track practice, and I'd just wrapped dance rehearsal with my cheer squad.

"Coming to the game tomorrow night?" I asked with a smile. "I'm dancing." He looked at me squarely, considering, cocky. "No, don't think so." Silence. "See ya round. Bye." And off he walked.

First, I was taken aback that my trademark smile and intentional mental image painting had been so easily dismissed. A minute later, I was offended. Didn't he know how lucky he was? Guys were always trying, and I never spoke first! Then, last . . . and most lasting . . . I was completely embarrassed. Damn, I thought, what a fool I'd made of myself. And boy did that sting. Maybe two weeks later, I was invited to a cocktail party at his fraternity house. I can still smell the final dashes of the perfume in my half-up/half-down, softly curled hair, can still feel the clingy, bouncy crepe of the little black dress with white keyhole accent—all of it. The party had only just begun when, from the dance floor, I noticed him watching me. Determined not to be the one left out of the power play, I marched over, said something sassy, gently grabbed him by the tie, and led him back out with me—honestly not sure what I'd see when I got there and turned around.

A-ha. There it was. The amused smile that said, "Oh really, little girl, let's see what you've got." Dare accepted. What I had, of course, were serious moves. What I hadn't expected was that he could dance, too. Like, really well. Like—before we knew it, a literal circle had opened up around the two of us as if we were in *Footloose* or the boy-meets-girl moment from a teen romance movie. Breathless and laughing, we looked at each other and knew. This. Wow. This.

Hands Off, Boys

He'd kissed me soon afterward. "We Belong" was playing, and I can only tell you that later, he'd said it was if a star were collapsing in on one point and exploding with all of the gravity in the universe. *That* kind of power. (Hokey? Sure. Then again, let's be fair—what nineteen-year-old girl wouldn't feel a little bit lightheaded to hear a boy say that about kissing her?)

Later, at an after-party, I knelt in front of a CD tower, arched my back, and turned to look at him over one shoulder. "Is there anything you like?" Yes, I knew what I was saying, though I pretended not to. And yes, I was striking poses on purpose—I'd copied them from every TV show and movie and magazine I'd ever seen. Mimics like magpies are we. But no, I did not know, for real, how dangerously powerful were the messages I was sending. *I* felt powerful. In control of the game. Womanly. Vixen-like. I didn't feel vulnerable. I didn't understand, as most girls like me don't, that certain kinds of "power" are the illusions others indulge until they are tired of the game. That my movie siren copycatting and coquettish play could ignite things that flash over and singe and scar before you even feel the burn.

He didn't do anything untoward. Not at all. Naively, I hadn't imagined he would—even though the semester before, a boy had pushed his position with me and shrugged: "You can't blame a guy for trying." Except you can. And I said "no." And when he complained that I'd created the situation, I figured he must be right. Just a few years back, my psychiatrist heard the stories I told and matter-of-factly said, "So basically you were a major cock tease." I blinked once. Paused. And looked down. "Yeah, I guess so." That's what I'd believed. Too many bad things. Too many moments. One common factor. Me. And every authority I'd tried to tell agreed. A dozen or so comments and a new therapist later and I learned that this was inappropriate, as were, apparently, many others. In fact, my psychologist strongly suspected that his thoughts about me were not entirely of a clinical nature. Strange what happens to my life when it's examined from the perspective of one who can, in fact, see other perspectives. And sad what happens when over and over, I'm the one who can't. The day after the cocktail party back in 1996, I was honestly surprised to learn that this new boy had thought he was going to have to do his best "to keep [me] at arm's length." He hadn't wanted "to mess this up by going too far too fast"—and was only too delighted when I, in fact, had been the one to put brake lights on quickly and firmly. Come-hither sexy and a good girl all wrapped up in one (with so many layers of gender power issues, it's dizzying). Yes, please. He was hooked . . . and honestly, so was I.

For those of us whose very nature seeks emotional intensity, registers the world in binary extremes—love is made of superhigh highs and heartbreakingly low lows. Success or failure. All or nothing. Agony or ecstasy. Certainly, I never contemplated that there were gray areas, that like everyone, I may have made mistakes. That I probably did. Then again, if your rejections have been soul-deep, you seek out affirmation of equal volume. Dig a big hole, and you'll need a lot to fill it in. We'd been together for just over a month when spring break had rolled around. Several girlfriends and I were going to Cancún, Mexico, and before we left, he'd given me a gift. It was a "cover-up" for the beach: a hand-painted white undershirt that read "Hands off—I have a boyfriend" on the front and "Taken" on the back. God help me, but I thought it was the cutest, most romantic thing ever. I even had a friend take a photo of me wearing it to bring back as a souvenir. Eighteen months later, the girls told me they had thought that shirt was "messed up." But at the time? Nothing. I wonder, hungry as I was for unconditional love, if I would have listened anyway. Smack in the middle of our vacation was "bubble party" night. My mom, a former travel agent, had heard about a "can't-miss" event that "all the kids just love." One particular club actually flooded the dance floor with soap bubbles—which sounded crazy and silly and . . . she wanted me to have fun, probably envisioning a land of happy little bubble machines like the ones at weddings or gala celebrations. Bless her, she even bought us all tickets ahead of time.

I've been told, after the fact, that almost any guy would've predicted the disaster that followed. Soap plus dancing girls and thumping bass basically equals a live porn fantasy . . . but not me. I walked right in. For a few minutes, everything was fine—then the lights went out and the soap machines started . . . and it was everywhere. Where were my friends? I spun quickly—too quickly—in the sudden slippery darkness and fell beneath the waves. By the time I got back up—the strobe lights were on full blast—I couldn't see—there were bubbles punishing my eyes and clouding them with tears whenever I fought to open my lashes . . . so I tried to call out to my girlfriends—I heard one of them laughing—how were they having fun? what was I doing wrong? God, I always felt like such a troublemaker. Stick-in-the-mud. Drama queen. "Where are—" I started to call, but suds filled my mouth. I was choking and gagging . . . and between gasps there were hands . . . cupping my breasts, stroking my bottom with middle fingers extended . . . wordless murmurs against my neck . . . crotches rubbing up on my thighs. I was in hell. A frantically lit, insistently thrumming hell where giggles echoed and I wanted to disappear—and my mom had said it would be fun so why did I always have to ruin things and no one could hear me and I thought I was going to puke and my body was a lubed-up playground for anonymous, horny strangers.

I did make it back to the hotel, in the end. Everyone else was still out having fun. But me . . . I showered off the filth, curled up in my T-shirt, and whispered its charm against the darkness: Hands off, boys. Hands off.

An "Us" instead of a "Them"

He was not my first boyfriend. But he *was* the first man I'd ever met who kept pace with my mind as well as my sense of passion and fun. Who made me feel like a treasure. Which is why I was still standing in that room. Why I was so desperate to preserve the girl whose self-worth was dependent on being an "us" instead of a "them." Why I was, as I'd done many times before, praying that I might be able to convince him to forgive whatever I'd done wrong. Whatever I'd done to make him hurt me. I have yet to meet a woman who was diagnosed as an adult (virtually all of us born before 1990) who has not been sexually violated, abused physically, emotionally, verbally, or all three, by a romantic partner, or is a survivor of rape or incest. And sometimes, several of the above. As young girls, we are so very, very hungry to be included, wanted. To be elevated. To feel essential. That we are *someone's* favorite. We learn not only to tolerate but expect degradation in the name of love. Like the proverbial frog that never jumps out of the ever-so-slowly heating pot of water, those of us who are used to being disrespected and bullied feel unalarmed by power mismatches in close relationships. Multiple times every single day, we are misunderstood. We misunderstand others just as often. Every conversation, every gesture, every moment has to be edited and defended. Explained and examined. As children, we discover that, to be treated with any kindness, we *must* exist in a constant state of hypervigilance. Life is a perpetual feeling of fight or flight. So when self-doubt, criticism, and guilt enter intimate relationships, the walking-on-eggshells dynamic is painfully familiar. In fact, it's what we've come to expect.

We are shown unequivocally that, when everything falls apart, we're the destroyers of the goodness. Of the trust. The secret bond. The special privilege. We've ruined it. And then comes the death knell . . . for me, what remains the kryptonite of my heart. The purposeful withholding of affection or approval. The vacuum of abandonment. The certainty I feel—have been taught to feel since I was tiny and sometimes still battle today—is that if I come to trust or care or love, it will always end. And it will always be my fault. I will ruin everything. Somehow. And in a desperate chase for emotional survival, I will compromise any remaining ounce of dignity to win the softness, the pureness back. But it can't be soft or pure. Only sullied and shameful. And precarious. And never, ever "good" again.

It's a pattern-and-repeat I'd been groomed for since childhood.

Over the years, I'd been told outright that I was difficult to love. And when you've come to believe that, as I had, you're willing to love for crumbs, no matter what degradation comes along with it. No one consciously trades in her dignity. No one surrenders herself without reasons that seem, in the moment, clear and right and convincing. We misunderstand jealousy and control as proof of how much we're wanted. Are seduced by the foreign prospect of being adored, essential.

Women, in general, are expected to be more emotionally connected and inclined toward intimate communication; I easily accepted the yoke of maintaining the health of the relationship—in every capacity. My boyfriend explained that a priest had told him it was necessary for a man to ejaculate every day. I added that to my mental checklist and made sure I bought his favorite-color lingerie. He began suffering from insomnia, blaming my affinity for pillow talk. One night, I awoke from a deep sleep, startled and confused. The bed was shaking. Rolling over, I realized he was masturbating next to me. "You didn't take care of things today," he said, noticing my gaze. "And thanks to you, I couldn't sleep. Again." I felt so very hurt, and even, somehow, that I'd been violated while lost in the safety of sleep. But I loved him—and I'd caused him to overthink and hadn't done what I'd promised I always would . . . the failure was clearly on my part. With a lump in my throat and tears in my eyes, I pulled him on top of me. "I love you," I whispered. "I love you, too," he replied . . . and that's what I thought about for the rest of it.

Many times, he'd jump up in a fury just before I was ready to drift off. I was selfish, he'd yell. A stuck-up bitch. He wanted nothing more to do with me. I begged him not to go, but he always would, my dorm room door slamming behind as he rushed off into the pitch-black New England night. Left behind, alone, I crumbled to the floor. I'd done it again. Why couldn't I just make people happy? Why did I always make them hate me? I'd sob and start calling his room. Sometimes he'd answer, and I'd usually be able to convince him to come back to me. But I can just as easily remember, after one terrible fight, creeping into the darkness of early morning, sitting in wet grass under the moonlight, waiting for the world to wake up so that I could tiptoe into his fraternity and slip an apology note under his door.

When cracks began to show in our relationship, when he told me how much he hated me—what a bitch I was, that the ruin of all we'd been was my fault—I never doubted him. It progressed to the point where the mere "stress" of being with me was responsible for his increasingly regular constipation. Or so I was told. I prayed every day that he would come and tell me he'd "had a satisfying shit," knowing the tenderness and affection I so enjoyed depended on the right answer. Soon there was no escape from the evidence of how loathsome I was. He'd gone home for a long weekend and come back with his head shaved. Surprised, I'd put on a very deliberate grin and asked why he'd made such a big change. "I did it to remind you of how much I hate you," he answered. "Every time you look at me, you can remember."

A Cumulative Panic

I'm certain that I reacted to the intensity of the relationship in emotionally volatile ways. I'd been studying popular culture for most of my life, trying to mitigate the social blind spots that plagued me. From *Romeo and Juliet* (which, as I have taught my daughter, would be better named *Romeo and Juliet: How Not to Write a Love Story*) to *Beverly Hills, 90210* to *Gone With the Wind*, the story was the same: great love is synonymous with great pain.

Remember that rigidity is partially the fruit of anxiety born of years of accumulated rejection *and* of our brains' comparative executive function deficits. We trust easily because we don't see strategy or others' self-serving behavior. We take things at face value, expecting a lover's promise of eternal devotion to be reliable, intransigent fact, never hopeful hyperbole. For those of us who aren't used to kindness, who feel we are more endurable than lovable, who don't know what "healthy" or even "friend" looks like, the now-or-never, this-person-or-all-is-lost feelings are what we're taught to expect out of love and romance. I sure did. That's why over-the-top fallouts didn't scare me. When a guy got jealous, I felt special. When I heard, "You're the only one who'll ever understand me," I finally felt necessary.

My life plan took shape around the dreams we dreamed together, around his effortless charm, around the bold declarations he made to his family. My "diffuse" sense of self and difficulty with emotional regulation melded into a perfect storm of "this is what love is and we are without borders between us," and, as Offspring was singing that year, the more I suffered, the more it showed he really cared.

Every exclusion, every abandonment, every insult triggered a cumulative panic in the deepest part of my soul. My goodness, how this man could love me. *Did* love me! Loudly and boldly and proudly. And his logic was dizzyingly brilliant. For example, he'd pointed out that while, yes, I was getting straight *A*s, all of my classes were in the humanities. He was in the sciences and had not done nearly as well at school, despite being every bit as smart. Obviously, I was outperforming him because my classes were much easier. I was a fraud, a pretense. I'd come to understand what he did: that whenever he got angry or walked away, it was because of something I'd done . . . or something he'd done in response to something I'd done. Meaning, in the end, that whether love was preserved or destroyed was my responsibility. And because I *did* love him, I believed him. I just no longer believed in me.

To rebound from such an existential break would take more ability to adjust than my mind had flexibility, healthier boundaries than a life of constant correction creates, and a stronger ability to modulate emotion than my autistic self could muster. Whatever clout or respect I had would be gone. Whatever associative social currency I carried would disappear. I'd be a public failure and private disgrace if I couldn't simply keep happy a man who thought, as his best friend had said, that "the sun and moon rose and set in [my] eyes."

Though on that night in April 1996, I seemed to be anything but heaven-sent. Earlier in the evening, just after a big cookout on the fraternity porch, a drunk pledge had tripped, pitched forward onto me, and pinned me against a wall. I'd smiled broadly at my boyfriend, willing him to see humor rather than the panic and perpetual sense of guilt that were welling up fast. No harm done! How silly, right? Can you believe this kid? As I was a pinned "sweetheart" of the house and the president's girlfriend, underclassmen tended to get nervous around me—the First Lady. No one was going to do anything disrespectful intentionally. I figured it'd end up as a joke. Nobody there was stupid or rude enough to make a move on me. The kid was in a less-than-graceful state and utterly mortified. That was all. No harm, no foul. Right?

Wrong. I could see it in my boyfriend's face. There would be trouble as soon as we were alone.

My smile melted.

An hour later, the crowd had dispersed, and we were behind closed doors. I'd discovered almost immediately that he wasn't mad at the pledge. For a brief second, I'd breathed a sigh of relief. At least in *this* case, I didn't have to worry that *I'd* done anything wrong. Drunk guy falls on me. Clearly not my fault. Except, somehow, I was being blamed *again*. The pledge had only been able to fall on me because I'd gotten so close to him in the first place. If I hadn't been so busy flirting instead of paying attention to my own boyfriend, I wouldn't have made such a fool out of him in front of all the guys. For a heartbeat, I saw his point. I was about to cave.

Then he grabbed the rose.

The Poor Flower

Earlier in the evening, he'd presented me with a beautiful, deep-pink, long-stemmed rose, sang me a song, and kissed me the way every Prince Charming ought. I'd not had a chance to put the flower into any water yet. It was still lying where I'd left it before the party. Now, he grabbed the rose and, aiming a look of pure hatred my way, bit the bloom off, chewed it up, and spat it in my face. There was saliva in my eyes. Dripping down my cheeks. Petals were plastered to my skin. This was a man of symbolism who wanted me to know that the love he gave could just as easily be taken away. Was tinged with hate. Was a weapon. That once again, I'd taken something beautiful and tarnished it. And for that, I was filth. Many, many times, I'd withered in shame before him. I'd traded my body for hope. I'd been afraid of the heartache. Tonight, for the first time, I was mad. I think he could tell there was something different in my eyes. I wasn't whimpering or pleading or apologizing. I just stared back and let the rose-polka-dotted spit shine.

Of course, I had no idea that, legally, spitting in someone's face is physical assault. And yes, by that point, I would have liked to know because, truly, I don't think I had any gauge as to how I should expect to be treated . . . by anyone. Honestly, that's something I still wrestle with. Most neurotypical people seem to have an internal barometer that tells them when something is "off" or "not okay." All you have to do to find the right path—the right way to be or say or do something—is to "trust your gut."

But what if you've been teased, insulted, abandoned, rejected, and manipulated your whole life long? And what if the consequence for speaking up to the "authorities" was more ostracism? What if you were told that you must have misinterpreted . . . every time? What if the authorities themselves ridiculed you? Or stood by and watched in amusement? Or chastised you for being too sensitive or overdramatic? Why couldn't you just take a joke? Or do this instead so you'll be liked more and treated better? What if you *can't* tease apart your thoughts from countless years of corrections and consequences and condemnations? What if you can't figure out which are *your* feelings? How do you know what your gut is saying, then? For that matter, if you've spent a lifetime *trying* to "trust your gut," only to find, over and over, that your instincts about other people are more often right than wrong . . . why would you, instead, not be more inclined to do precisely the opposite of what your gut says? I didn't tolerate awful things because I was needy or insecure. I was needy and insecure because I'd had to tolerate awful things. If you believe you are worthy and strong, you will live up to that truth. If you believe you are unworthy of love or happiness, you will live up to that truth, too.

Without a system, I still can't tell how bad a situation was—or is—or whether it really even *was* a situation at all. Bullying and rejection, neglect and ridicule, verbal abuse, public humiliation, victim blaming. These are the hallmarks of trauma—little *t* traumas—not life-threatening, but absolutely soul-threatening, linked to PTSD, depression, anxiety, self-harm, and substance abuse. What's more, they are the first, most indelible, and most recurrent social realities for girls and women growing up on the spectrum. They are the constants in our life stories. The inescapable patterns we expect—then, unwittingly, seek. Fault, internalized. Love and hurt, intertwined. Bound up in tendrils of power and control, creating a template for the adult relationships ahead.

A Kiss Is Not Just a Kiss

Not long ago, a man parked outside my therapist's office asked me for a jump. The question was legitimate—his wife was bustling about trying to get the engine to turn—but I didn't have jumper cables, and I didn't like the language he was loudly using in front of my fourteen-year-old daughter. Since we had to walk directly by him to reach the door, I politely asked him, "Please stop the profanity. There's a child present, sir."

His response was to call me a filthy bitch and whore, and to tell me that what I really needed was to get laid—would I like to suck his cock? With no one to tell me what to do and other recent traumas adding to the load she and I were carrying, all I could think of was calling the police to file a report and show my daughter that her mother would take no more. Which is precisely what I did. Except I had it all wrong. My daughter wasn't inspired; she was humiliated. And when I shared the story over dinner, my mother wasn't proud; she was livid that I'd not seen how foolish it was to have engaged at all.

I cannot tell when to do what. What I should object to. What I bring upon myself. Or whether that even matters. So these things . . . they keep happening.

Recently, I went to dinner with a close friend and his longtime friend and career-long mentor. After three minutes into the meal, I felt utterly naked. This stranger (to me) had long since undressed me with his eyes and, at least as far as I could tell, was doing a lot more now. His conversation was genteelly peppered with innuendo, dancing from polite niceties to knowing smiles about "the addictive power of fiery redheads" and back again before I had time to think, from asking about my work to dashes of advice on exactly *how* he believed I should go about relieving stress. At the end of the evening, I went to give a hug good-bye—I didn't want to be rude to this friend of a friend. But where I expected a cordial back pat, this man I'd never met (who was decidedly not drunk) swiftly took my face in his hands and kissed me on the lips. And what did I do? I shouted, "Hope to see you again! First of many!" I am so ashamed to admit it.

After that dinner, I got to my car as fast as possible, driving off alone and already crying. I was home in fifteen minutes, by which time I was now nauseated and shaking, my body under the assault of as many of its own memories as was my mind. It was late. My kids were asleep. There was no one around to talk to, and the phone would wake the children if my sobbing didn't.

I had no idea whether what had happened was actually bad. None. I was coming apart . . . and I didn't even know whether I had a right to. I tried searching Google: "kissing acquaintance on lips appropriate?" No pertinent answers. None. Two days of shakes and somatic hell later, I had to travel out of state to deliver a keynote address. Over four hundred people and I chatted yesterday, and somewhere during the ninety minutes, I slipped in the dinner story—for example, yes, and as a straw poll of sorts (which I admitted). What was the reaction when I got to "the kiss"? Everyone gasped. Seriously, the gasp was so audible and decisive that the oxygen level must have fallen entire percentage points. To the rest of the world, there seemed to be little question. It wasn't a kiss. Groping or kissing a person without his/her consent is sexual assault. As Kristen Houser, chief public affairs officer at the National Sexual Violence Resource Center, explained in the *Huffington Post*,

> There are a lot of different ways that people can be sexually violated and exploited that don't need to require any physical contact, let alone sexual penetration. Sexually violent acts fall along a continuum that go from no contact to very brutal physical violations such as rape or sexual homicides and we absolutely include any unwanted touching, kissing, and groping on that continuum. . . . We never sit back and say someone was overreacting to having a gun pulled on them just because the trigger wasn't pulled. This is the same kind of thing. You can't qualify whether or not the amount of fear a person feels is appropriate—it is what it is.

Much as I needed multiple layers of objective verification that my synesthesia wasn't a product of my imagination, it seems I still need an auditorium full of cheerleaders and a national agency to do what my lack of self-possession prevents. "Your experiences have always been enough to count," said the friend who originally invited me to dinner. "Yes, Jenny . . . #YouToo." I cried when I read that text. Not in grief over being victimized, but in relief at hearing that I'd been long since hurt enough.

A SISTERLY ASIDE

Allow me to pause here for a very brief digression—a sisterly aside to the ladies, offered with the utmost conviction in sincere solidarity.

In the 1800s, white American women did their sisters a great injustice. Many suffragists believed that having women of color involved in "the cause" would weaken their chances of winning the vote. Public support for women's voting rights was hard enough to come by, they argued. *Black* women's rights were an even harder sell to the nation—including to many of the white suffragettes, who had no interest in being associated with "*those*" women.

In 1851, Sojourner Truth took the stage at the Women's Rights Convention in Ohio. Bravely, humbly, she asked them to consider whether we, gals, oughtn't see ourselves as more alike than "better" or "less":

> That man over there says that women need to be helped into carriages, and lifted over ditches, and to have the best place everywhere. Nobody ever helps me into carriages, or over mud-puddles, or gives me any best place! And ain't I a woman? Look at me! Look at my arm! I have ploughed and planted, and gathered into barns, and no man could head me! And ain't I a woman? I could work as much and eat as much as a man—when I could get it—and bear the lash as well! And ain't I a woman? I have borne thirteen children, and seen most all sold off to slavery, and when I cried out with my mother's grief, none but Jesus heard me! And ain't I a woman?

Women, then, fought as they do now—against one another, instead of for one another. Divided, they didn't gain the vote in the United States for another sixty-nine years. Instead, they wasted time and energy. They jostled to be recognized—to be heard—as if there weren't room enough in this world for *each of us* to have a voice.

—*Sisterhood of the Spectrum* by Jennifer Cook O'Toole

My commitment is to "all for one and one for all." I'm told that's what the world holds for me, too. If that's so, then it's a strange thing to note that across the board, the people who have listened and shaken their heads in horror, *and* who have judged me most for "taking it," *and* who have publicly humiliated me for making "an indignant fuss over nothing" because I'm "too serious and think all men want [me]" . . . are women. Neurotypical *and* autistic.

And . . . I'm sorry. With tears in my eyes this moment, I just don't understand. I *want* to. We say that it doesn't matter how she looks or how she dresses, she doesn't deserve to be victimized. I agree! But what if by "it doesn't matter how she looks," we mean that she *is* pretty by conventional standards? Ignorant men question why "unattractive" women are targeted—as if the issue were about anything but power. Humbly, ladies, I have to attest that women undermine the "hot" girl. Let me be absolutely forthright. I am the girl who will always look in the mirror and see awful 1980s glasses and a perm that would make Annie cry.

I don't think I am the object of global desire, for crying out loud. I am neither so arrogant nor ignorant to think myself any more or less likely, because of my appearance, to be the subject of assault or harassment or rape. I *do* believe that I am more vulnerable because of my neurology.

No one bit of anticipation for this very book has meant more to me than its being named to Book Riot's list—several months before publication—of "24 Amazing Feminist Books We Can't Wait to Read in 2018." I am a proud feminist, by which I mean that I value the wonderful and equally important contributions and presence of men *and* women. Please hear that in my voice when I ask . . .

How am I, a woman who wears high heels as much because they make her feel like Ginger Rogers as for the sake of fashion, supposed to *ever* feel safe believing in myself when more often than not, ladies, *you* don't? Do you *honestly* think, as one person wrote of me on Amazon, that my voice is nothing to put before your daughters because I am "smart, pretty, popular, and life has come easily" to me? Has anyone *read* the words I've actually said? When it comes to intimate violence, are we, women, not the perpetrators of *at least* as much, if not more knowing, selfish damage to the universal female psyche, spirit, and potential? If I may speak only from my own experience . . . yes. Yes, we are. So, forgive me for hijacking Ms. Truth, but please indulge the question: Ain't *I* a woman, too?

(A Little Rough Sometimes)

In that little room in Providence, twenty-year-old me *was* hurting. And spit-covered. Then, he moved me. That is, he did something that we referred to as "moving me." A few times now, he had grabbed me by the shoulders and not-quite-shoved-half-lifted me to the side because, he said, I was preventing him from coming or going (hard to do when you're smaller than the other person), daring him, even, to do something about it. Though he had already put his everything everywhere, when he actually put his *hands* on me, something registered in the literal part of my brain. Something different from everything before.

We'd been together at a party a few weeks before, and I'd come upon one of the cheerleader girls, sitting alone, crying on a couch. I was doing my best to console her, but no matter how hard I tried, I just couldn't figure out what she was saying through all of the sniffling and sobbing. The only words I did manage to decipher were the name of her boyfriend and "mean." Enter my lack of perspective shifting. Had he done something to her? I understood. My boyfriend got a little rough with me sometimes, too. Suddenly quiet, she wiped her nose with the back of her hand and looked at me, eyes wide. No. Someone had been mean to her, and she *wanted* her boyfriend. Oh. God. Please don't . . . Okay, I assured her, I would find him and scurried off to look before she could whisper another word.

Now, he again felt "constrained." And again, he "moved me." This time, though, for whatever reason, I moved *back*. For once, I knew—*knew*—that I'd not done anything wrong. "No!" I stomped. He wasn't going to just walk out. He didn't get to leave me feeling the pain and fear we both knew would overtake me after only a few minutes. We were going to discuss this.

The ante had been upped. Though I perversely imagined his dwindling respect for me increasing in this moment, things were actually going from bad to worse. Intimate violence, like every other kind, isn't about sex or love. It's all about power and control. When I'd said, "no," I'd challenged his authority—challenged the way he had interpreted the evening, and, in doing so, challenged my tacit agreement that he was always right and I was always wrong. I'd put the focus back on him, and whatever he saw did not align with the gentleman-scholar-athlete he believed himself to be. So he'd taken control of my entire being, including my heart. While it pounded and raced and quivered . . . it was also breaking with grief. You can't go back from beyond this ledge. You can't unsee this side of truth.

He grabbed me again, hard, hands gripping my upper arms like vices. These hands, the ones that held mine so lovingly, that lifted me so effortlessly, the strength of these same hands now made me cry out in pain as, this time, he threw me down onto the bed, hard. For a moment, I remember being surprised. One minute I'd been standing strong, and the next I was flying, backflopping onto the bed like a kid does into a pool. Except that I hadn't jumped. After a half second of how did I get *here*? confusion, I popped back up. I was one of those toys where you press the button, the springs release, and the whole thing collapses. Then you let go and *whoop!* Up she goes! That was me. He threw and released. I collapsed. Once his hands were off, up I went. And down I went again. As soon as I stood up, he did it again. For a second time, I flew through the air. For a second time, I got right back up. Really, he must have been as shocked as he was infuriated. I could practically hear the wheels turning. What now? What now? Bright-blue eyes focused on something beside me. I followed the gaze as, in some sort of strange slow motion, he snatched the small ceramic Minnie Mouse from my bedside table. I loved that little thing. Tiny and sweet and pink and delicate. Who in the world hurts Minnie Mouse? He did. Because he could hurt me. With the swing of one arm, he'd thrown her careening toward me and into the wall, shards of ceramic glass flying everywhere. I heard myself scream—half in fear, half in anguish. Someone shouted in the hall. He looked at me then, so strangely. As if, for one moment, my friend had returned, confused, asking, *How did we get here, Jenny? What did I just do?* And then it was gone.

Darkness flashed over his face, and the innocence fell to fury. He took a step toward me, and in a flash, I slapped him. Right across the face. Just like indignant women did to badly behaved men in movies. Only I wasn't really indignant. I was afraid. And sad. I didn't just haul off. I didn't blow my top. I followed the script and, like a good little girl, did what I'd been taught. Restricted and repetitive behavior is part of our diagnostic profile. Sameness feels known, like a comfortable chair to return to when the world is too chaotic and taxing. And since our reciprocal conversation skills are also less than expected, it's no wonder that so many of us know the entire book of a musical or script of a movie. Characters, nuance, timing, and responses are all delineated—sometimes even with stage directions. Social "scripts" are actually a tried-and-true therapeutic tool to help anticipate dialogue and reactions in real-life circumstances. In other words, scripting is an intrinsic part of how our brains learn to mimic desired behaviors and prepare to meet social expectations more automatically.

During *Class, Dismissed*, the play during my last year of high school, I'd played the female lead—a somewhat cliché cheerleader dating the popular quarterback who also happened to roughhouse her and share more than his fair share in the locker room. Near the end of the show, she finally confronts him with all the humiliation and disrespect and shame and fear he's caused—he takes one step toward her, and she slaps him. That is, I slapped him. The actor. I was told to. I was taught to. I rehearsed it. That, said the script and every bit of affirmation that followed, was what a confident woman does when the bully keeps coming. And the audience had burst into cheers.

There were no cheers now.

Now, the same hand that had defiled my rose—the same one that had obliterated Minnie—that same hand drew back and fell, hard, on my left cheek, sending me toppling into the edge of my bed, then ricocheting in the other direction and onto the floor.

The weight of the explosion hung like a hot fog in the air. For a moment, everything was absolutely still. Then came the noise.

Banging on my door. Maybe four or five voices outside. "Open up right *now*!" someone yelled. I got to my knees, plucked a small shard of broken ceramic from the carpet, and crawled out to the light. A mob of girls engulfed me, but I couldn't find words in the sounds. All I could do was repeat, "He hit me . . . he hit me." In my mind, not until that last strike had I been abused. Fingerprints were blooming on my arms. Soon they would become matching handprints. Masticated rose petals fell off with my tears. The poor flower. I felt so sorry for the poor, beautiful flower. And Minnie, sweet Minnie, was destroyed. What a particularly awful obscenity that something so innocent, so happy—was now so tainted. Diminished. Right in the palm of my hand, kindness had turned jagged. Gentleness had snapped into sharp angles. Tenderness had shattered into fury. I squeezed the glass in my palm. Piercing the flesh. Drawing blood. I wanted the pain. Welcomed its vivid colors. In the absence of passion, this bright feeling was the only clarity. The only way to be sure I was real.

I was, of course. All of it was real. And somehow—somehow—I was safe. Safer than I had been in such a long time. Everyone knew what had happened. There had been six witnesses listening outside the door. Now it would be okay, I reasoned. He *had* to be nice. He *had* to see how mean he'd been. *Had* to remember the time he'd shoved me just a little too hard into a snowbank. Or the time he'd "moved me" on the icy street, and I'd fallen, and somebody saw. *Had* to know he'd gone too far. For one moment, *he would have to see how badly he'd treated me, his "beautiful, brilliant Jenny."* Or at least, that's what I believed would happen.

A half-hour later, the hall had all but emptied. He was still inside, though, a wary-looking friend said. I wasn't surprised, really. His public face mattered too much to emerge and risk being swarmed by a dozen angry women. I turned the handle slowly and found him sitting on the floor right where I had landed, a pen in his hand and paper in his lap. "I was writing you a letter," he began. "I know it was wrong to hit you, but you have to remember that *you* hit *me* first. You can't tell anyone unless *you* want to get in trouble." Suddenly my inner resolve buckled. I hadn't thought of that. Which meant . . . oh no, I'd brought *this* on myself, too. "You have to understand, yes, I'm sorry I hurt you. Very sorry. And . . . ," he paused to look at me, "I still think you're a bitch and a whore. You know that, right?" I nodded. I knew. I knew I always got it wrong. "Good," he exhaled, and put down the pen. "I think it's time for bed." Okay, I nodded, and began to get undressed. My heart and soul were deflating to nothingness. "I'm sorry," I choked. "So sorry for everything. I love you." He smiled and reached out his hand . . . that same hand. "Come to bed now, Jenny."

Finger Paint Bruises

Days later, I was called into a dean's office. The university had received an anonymous call about what had happened that Saturday night, and she needed to follow up. Yes, ma'am, I understood. Jenny always did what school said, even now. Even when she asked me if I had any marks on my arms (clearly, one of my friends had made the call and provided enough specifics to guide the questions), I told the truth. Even when she asked me to please take off my cardigan so that she could see, even though I felt naked and ashamed and stupid and weak, I did it and saw her eyes widen. Purple-blue finger paint palm prints that a child might make in preschool. Only these weren't on construction paper. They were ugly reminders on my arms.

Had he been drinking? No. Did I want to press charges? No, I didn't. It had been my fault anyway. She furrowed her brow. What did I mean by that? I was trapped. I couldn't lie to protect myself—and I didn't want to have to leave. So, very slowly, I told the story—for the first time. I explained about the pledge and the moving. About throwing me down . . . twice. About spitting the rose in my face. About throwing Minnie at me. And finally, my face burning with shame, I explained how, when he'd taken another step toward me, I'd slapped him. And then what? she asked. Then he hit me, and I'd fallen down. So, couldn't she see now how, if someone was going to get in trouble . . . it had to be me? Her expression changed, though I couldn't tell what she was thinking. Probably about whether or not to call the police on *me*. But that wasn't it.

"When someone calls you vicious names, throws you, spits on you, *and* throws objects, all of those actions are assault, Jennifer," she explained. "Taking another step toward you after hurting and frightening you is a threat and intimidation. You didn't attack him, sweetheart. What you did is called self-defense. And when he hit you, that was retaliation. Another assault." This was news to me. All of it. I didn't understand. But he'd said—and I—I believed him, and I had to in order to work things out, because I always started these things, didn't I? The anguished scream was silent but for my pleading eyes: Didn't I? The dean assured me that if I didn't want to press charges, that was my prerogative (that burden is no longer on the victim of domestic assault, by the way). "*Please* consider your options, Jennifer," she entreated. "Don't decide anything because you think you'd get in trouble—you had already been assaulted *five times* before you defended yourself. His actions didn't become a problem when his palm struck your cheek. That wasn't act of abuse number one. *It was act number six.*" She paused. "Of *that* night."

Meanwhile, the school would insist that he go to counseling, a suggestion I jumped at, happy to collect the name and number of the therapist referral. Now he *would* have to get some help—and I wouldn't be the villain making it happen.

Just as I got up to leave, the dean called me back. "Here," she said, scribbling something onto a different slip of paper. "Take this," she offered, handing me the note. "Keep it tucked away . . . for yourself." On the paper was the name of a female counselor. For me. "You deserve help, Jennifer." I needed help, yes. I had no idea what I *deserved.* I couldn't have known it, but that scrap of paper was the silver lining of a very dark April. For the very first time in my life, I began working with a therapist. In our sometimes twice-weekly sessions, she walked me through several more months of horror . . . and along our journey—which ended up lasting a full year—I began to unpack the disempowering absolutes that haunted my thinking and poisoned my self-image. She taught me to consider alternate possibilities in moments when I saw despair and to notice how much certainty I attributed to my perceptions of other people's perspectives and motivations . . . even though, I started to realize, I was wrong about them as often as they were wrong about me. She encouraged me to look backward in time, and she let me know when stories I shared were, in fact, accounts and dismissals of a seemingly endless parade of abuse. And most important, she taught me to observe, examine, and question disparaging opinions about me that, for a lifetime, I had accepted unconditionally as fact. Because of that relationship, I continued a journey of self-awareness that sustained me through the hell to come and continues here, with you, today.

In the short term, life grew into a hell like I never could imagine. Several girlfriends and I were renting a house for the summer, where my room happened to be in the attic. Houses in Providence are often old, as this one was—seasoned and lovely. The ceiling sloped on an elegant diagonal, the walls ached with a warm wooden glow, and when the window swung open, you could escape the lack of air conditioning by climbing out onto the tiny fire escape, book in hand, and disappear in the breezy leaves of the tree that tickled the glass and metal.

The Piss Jar

I'd not been able to get an actual bed up the narrow stairs, but I figured it was only for the summer. A mattress on the floor with fresh sheets and a wide-open window would be fine. And maybe it could have been. But it wasn't. Most nights, my boyfriend stayed at the house, and that started out all right . . . except that now, the girls could really hear what was happening—and, frustrated with me, they simply stopped coming close. He felt the judgment, for sure. Called them terrible names and soon found new, quieter ways of punishing me.

Insomnia still plagued the nights, and despite the oppressive heat, he wouldn't allow me to open the window. Sounds from the street below were too noisy, he said. Damned house. Why the hell did I have to pick this stupid room anyway? Ashamed, I shut the window and bought a box fan instead, hoping that would make us both happy. Instead, we immediately had a new problem. He drank a lot of water because he was a runner. It wasn't uncommon, then, that he'd get up in the middle of the night to use the bathroom. The trouble was that in *this* house, getting there required going out into a creaky hall, down a flight of steep steps (in the dark), down another hall, and then having to do the same to get back to the attic. By the time he returned, he couldn't get back to sleep. Honestly, I didn't see the big deal, but I empathized at the discomfort of not being able to fall back asleep after waking in the middle of the night. I spent every single night in a twilight doze, anticipating whatever would wake him and whatever I would have to do to bear the hostility. It was better to be awake, emotionally prepared, waiting for the unknown than to be woken, startled, by an already angry man. More and more often, the only way to bring back any tenderness—or at least possibility of peace—was for me to roll over on what had become a dank, sweaty floor mattress and look up into the corner far above and across the room. No matter what was happening to my body on the ground, when the first tear would roll, I'd quickly wipe it away so as not to cause trouble and fly away to the farthest, tiniest crevice of the room, shrink into the wood, and feel nothing at all.

Despite all that I endured, nothing could have prepared me for the Piss Jar. As an alternative to the apparently unbearable night trek to the restroom, he arrived, one night, with an oversized, plastic pickle jar.

Without a lid. It was set next to the bed in the sweltering attic, and when he had to go (often twice in the night), he just stood up and started urinating. The Piss Jar, as he'd named it, was a portable latrine. Right there. In my room. Only two feet from where I lay on an increasingly grubby mattress on the increasingly filthy floor.

Early in the morning following its use, he opened the window and poured the Piss Jar contents out over the fire escape—his urine flooding the ground just beyond the front door below. I was completely horrified . . . mortified . . . terrified that I'd lose any last chance of keeping any friends at all if they discovered what he'd done. That was the stuff of medieval cities, I implored. It was disgusting and unhygienic, and no, he could *not* do that—my friends would have to walk through it now whenever they left the house. And if they got a whiff, it wouldn't take much detective work to figure out where it had come from. They'd tell me to leave. They'd make me go. So, please, wasn't there another way?

Sure, he agreed smoothly. "If it's that much of a problem for your bitch friends, then here—" He shoved the still-wet jar at my face, yellow droplets speckling my skin. "It's your job now. Every morning. You take care of it." Out the door he went. (I should mention that a typical control tactic is to disparage friends or relatives so they cannot be trusted. My parents were "rich, condescending snobs," and friends were all "bitches" and "whores." By that logic, any store I placed in them was an insult to his judgment *and* a guarantee that I'd follow "bad" advice and end up doing something else wrong.) Just like that, I became the scullery maid. He was intentionally, passive-aggressively careless, sloshing it around and never wiping up. And every morning, I wanted nothing more than to get that wretched thing out—but that was when he held me to my daily "responsibility." Beneath his sweaty skin, I would disassociate and vanish as often as I could (while still trying to pretend to be happy). Far in my ceiling corner, my mind focused on what would come *after* this. *After* he was done. That was when I would try to hide the jar.

I didn't want any of the other girls to see what he was doing—what I was allowing. But there was no way to carry a giant, uncovered, transparent jar of urine down two hallways and a flight of stairs, past four bedrooms, and back again without someone seeing. My only choice was to push it behind a trunk and leave it in the room until everyone else went out. Unfortunately, that didn't usually happen until after dinner. So all day, every day, the Piss Jar sat open in the oppressive August heat, fumes soaking into the wooden floor and walls and ceiling until just walking in and not choking on the ammonia stench became an accomplishment. I was filth. I was covered in his filth. Filled with his demand. Carrying his filth. And pretending to sleep while he polluted my small, tragic space even more. There was little hope of kindness or love now, I saw. Yet I couldn't imagine how to change plans. How to problem solve. Whom I could tell who would understand when my heart exploded and my already diffuse sense of self shattered over a man who hit me, called me disgusting names, spat on me, sexually abused me, and now humiliated me with a Piss Jar, too. I didn't know how to solve this problem. Besides, I didn't hate him. I hated *me*. I hated myself for a lifetime of "taking it." Of screwing up. Of making people hate me. I could entice and entrance . . . if everything is your fault, you don't get rid of the other person. You wish you could get rid of yourself.

Autism by Gaslight

In 1944, Ingrid Bergmann and Charles Boyer starred in a movie called *Gaslight*. Bergman played a sensitive, trusting wife struggling to preserve her identity in an abusive marriage. In order to maintain control within the relationship and prevent his true character from coming to light, Boyer's character convinces his wife that she is mentally ill. When he "dims the gas lights," he tells her that she's imagining the darkness. The more she loses trust in her thinking, the more dependent she is on his authority. From that film came the term *gaslighting*, a particularly malicious form of mental and emotion abuse meant to weaken the sense of self, breed internal confusion, and instill doubt in one's own perception of reality.

From childhood—recall the stories of the Smurf and the grand sleepover party deception—through adulthood, we are not only primed by omnipresent predators (young and old), we are taught to second-guess *everything* about ourselves and doubt the very ways our brains interact with the world around us—our emotions, conversations, interests, relationships, directions, senses, ideas of fun, manner of speech, the way we joke, wonder, play, and even love. All are subject to the apparent constant course correction required to undermine our natural intuitions and reframe . . . everything.

The truth of it all is that we—I—have not been the cause of all the problems. As circumstances stand, we are set up to fail. We, autistic people—with or without the title—are the perpetual other in a world where neurotypical is never, ever wrong. And autistic is never really right.

Which is why when I told my mom that all the girls in my second-grade class hated me because their "leader" told them to, she was certain that I was exaggerating. Or why she observed that nobody I wanted to be friends with seemed to want to be friends with me. So maybe I could figure out what I was doing wrong. It's also why, during my senior year of college, when I first suggested that I might press charges, family members questioned whether I really needed to push things like that. After all, I was told, "it's not like he put you in the hospital."

With the distance of time, I can now see that, however miserably executed, she was trying to protect me from public courts, from the vulnerability that could come from lots of people knowing some terribly personal details of my life . . . and most of all, from the possibility that the police wouldn't agree that what had happened constituted an illegal act. She didn't say what he'd done was acceptable or even tolerable. But he *hadn't* put me in the hospital. How much worse would I feel if the authorities rejected me, too?

At the time, I was devastated. Those words, as you might imagine, left an indelible scar on my psyche, which is why I can remember them so clearly twenty years later. I also know that there is no certification process for how to parent a child, let alone one whose life seems riddled with strife. That my mother messed up. Big time. Though unintentional, she sent a new round of shame and insecurity flooding right over me. Discovering that something foisted upon us *is* against the law is, inarguably, validating. It *does* help to hear that, after a lifetime of autism by gaslight, we are not crazy or being hyperbolic. That what has happened is so wrong that it's criminal. The truth remains, though, that most of the traumas we endure and accept *aren't* illegal—yet they are *all* immoral and terrible. Regardless of whether our physical selves are injured, that which endures is soul-deep, not skin-deep. My bruises healed decades ago. My heart, too. I hold no bitterness. No anger. Honestly, I'm no longer invested enough to think or care about him one way or another. All of that is long since over. Yet last week, when that man grabbed me and "kissed" (read: assaulted) me, my subconscious mind went into an utter tailspin. Crying, shaking, unable to think straight for two days. I was filled with doubt, questioned my perception of all that had happened, revisited everything I'd said, how I'd sat, and—of course—what I'd worn.

Recall the lengths to which I went just to prove to *myself* I wasn't overreacting. I was a professional domestic violence counselor for two years. I've written articles and chapters about sexual assault. Have spoken about it on several continents. So much time and expertise gained and gathered and shared. And for all of that, one two-hour dinner with a stranger, and my entire frame of reference evaporated. All faith in my own personal and professional authority vanished. I trusted Google and an audience of strangers more than my own mind. *That* is the lasting effect of autism by gaslight. Whether we're known to be autistic or not, our experience of life is, according to other people, oversensitive, overdramatic, drama making, and attention seeking. According to us, it's just life. But we are the "Them" to your "Us." Every "Do it your way, only not *quite* like that" redirect is a snowflake that rolls and collects, gathers and grows, then is a snowball that rolls and collects and gathers and grows, then is an avalanche that rolls right over us, leaving us to question our own memories, perceptions, and, if we will admit it, our sanity. Decades of "training" in living with autism by gaslight logically make us more likely to love by gaslight, too. Counselors who specialize in recognizing the dynamics of bullying and abuse describe three phases of gaslighting. Most people first experience it in all-or-nothing friendships and, later, in romantic relationships, too. First is idealization, during which victims are whisked off their feet by the often-charming and charismatic gaslighters. In turn, they are incredibly dedicated to the business at hand—constructing, inhabiting, and publicly projecting an image of themselves as the perfect mate.

Enter here the sunset walks and winter beach picnics, under-the-window serenading, rings and pins and driving cross-country in a blizzard because he just *had* to see me. Imagine you are the girl who was on the social margins, the butt of jokes and pranks and told to go home and kill herself . . . then seductively took off her clothes—per school approval—in front of eight hundred people for three nights in a row. You've been cruelly tormented, then largely lusted after . . . and now held up like a treasure, made a fuss over by all those who look up to the brilliant, athletic, good-looking man who cannot get enough of you and is, finally, your match in wit, passion, intellect. He is the passage into this new, wonderful life of music and parties and quiet mornings and a brotherhood full of gentlemen to always make you feel safe—a new reality where rejection is unknown and roses and guitar songs celebrate *you*, the love of his life.

Autistic women are particularly vulnerable to this kind of manipulation. The journey is subtle; after all, no one falls in love with a person who hurts, degrades, or insults her on the first date. No one expects to trade her dignity for affection. No one surrenders her sense of self without reasons . . . reasons that seem, in the moment, clear and right and convincing. We misunderstand jealousy and control as proof of how much we're wanted. Shapeless, selfless, we fit our words—our appearance—and our behavior to match others' ideas of love and sex. But we are nowhere to be found. Our inability to spontaneously shift perspectives and limited experiences with healthy friendships make it incredibly difficult to see someone's motivation as anything other than what he or she claims it to be. But there is much to be wary of. Codependency and trauma expert Darlene Lancer writes, "Someone capable of persistent lying and manipulation is also quite capable of being charming and seductive. . . . Expressions of love and flattery are concocted to confuse you . . . and increasingly, you doubt your own senses, ignore your gut, and become more confused." Precisely what we've *already* learned to do.

Then comes devaluation, when we rapidly go from being adored to being incapable of doing anything right. Clandestine manipulation easily escalates into verbal abuse. Just as I was, we're told we are crazy. Manic. Pathetic and depressed. Oversensitive, insecure, ungrateful, stupid, promiscuous, and deceitful. We are not desirable. We are immoral liars. Boiled down to the core of everything else, I've flat out been reminded that I am simply "not a good person." No matter how gently we challenge a twisted version of reality, the challenge itself is regarded as a personal affront, escalating the dynamic to include intimidation and punishments, anger, bullying, and threats of abandonment. Shame erodes any confidence we *do* have in our intelligence, professional and day-to-day capabilities, parenting, or overall value as a partner. Suffering and destabilized, we are reminded over and again that we are responsible for every unkind word. That we never should have argued in the first place. And eventually, we stop questioning. In the self-serving, twisted version of reality that an abuser creates (and believes), we will never be right. And he or she will never, ever be wrong. So we get frantic. Desperate to fix whatever's gone wrong—even if we can't see what that is. Having felt the high of highs, having been "idealized" and, to some degree, "idolized," having *just* gotten comfortable being free of the worry we'd thought was an inescapable fixture of our lives . . . there is nothing—nothing—we won't do to put things right again.

But we *can't* put things right that we haven't put wrong in the first place. That's true in relationships *and* in relationship to the world. Our autistic selves are not inherently bad or worse. Still, the world identifies us by the words "autism spectrum *disorder*." Diagnostic tools assess us in terms of negatives, in terms of measurable deficits and "frequency and severity of problems."

When you to cut to the chase, we are advised to change this and stop doing that—to stop behaving like ourselves, really. And, if we don't, we will be burdens, disliked, undesirable, unemployable, isolated, mistreated, and, generally, rejected. That is to say, everything an abuser tells us is so. There has to be a reason, we figure, for the serious dislike we seem to inspire over and over again . . . *something* that would explain how we could mean well but always end up making everything come out so wrong. After all, what has every disaster—*every* want-to-crawl-in-a-hole-and-die moment—had in common? It's not the other people involved. It's not the places where they happened. Nope. The only common factor we can find in every disaster is ourselves. To my mind, experience had proven over and again that given enough time, I could successfully irritate and tire out any coworker, friend, boyfriend, or family member into not just being done with me, but into seriously disliking me . . . and quite possibly even hating me. "Enthusiastically wanted" for just "being me"? No. That didn't make any sense at all.

By the time we get to the final stage of gaslighting—when we are "dropped" and discarded for all of our "flaws"—we are scratching for any means of psychological survival. Not only is the relationship dying, so is the lovable woman we first saw in our partner's eyes. Now those eyes look elsewhere—to pornography, to the sex industry, to grooming, to a lover—whatever manner of "anyone but you" the abuser knows will be most emotionally obliterating. It's no wonder, really, that we are apt to internalize the criticism, blame, and judgment long after the relationship is over. The path of destruction is already well worn.

For Good.

Two weeks later, I let myself into his apartment to cook a surprise gourmet lunch for the two of us. Water was boiling, olive oil and garlic were popping in a pan. He loved it when I cooked, so I smiled, thinking how happy he'd be to come home after a long run to mouthwatering aromas and a very dolled-up me. The one thing I didn't have was paper towels, and heaven knew he didn't keep kitchen towels handy (to be fair, how many twenty-three-year-old guys do?). Undaunted, I walked into the bedroom. There had to be a not entirely gross facecloth or *something* I could use. Lo and behold, there were some odds and ends that would do, but as I turned back to the kitchen, I saw something out of the corner of my eye that lit my heart. It was just a floppy, worn-out spiral notebook to anyone who looked. To me, though, it was his "deep thoughts" journal (and running log). This was the pad of paper he'd lovingly shown me a year earlier in his childhood bedroom in Chicago. He'd written all about telling his mother that I was "the One." That they'd gone ring shopping together, and that he was madly, madly in love in a way he'd never imagined he could be. I hadn't seen it often, but when I did, I'd always jot a little note for him to discover. So, I ran in to turn down the stovetop, grabbed a pen, and flopped down on the bed with the notebook. Flip, flip, flip. Finally got to the last entry—aww . . . just last week when he'd gone home to visit his mom—scanned to the bottom of his handwriting, lifted my pen to write . . . and stopped cold. "Watched *Playboy* and jerked off." That's what he'd written. He'd been away from me for only a few days—from me, who . . . I began hyperventilating . . . who let him do anything . . . and . . . the room was spinning . . . and he wrote it down. Not only did it happen, *he wrote it down*?! Who *does that*? I cried out loud and ran to the bathroom, seconds before I threw up. About half an hour later, the stove was off. I'd left the dishes where they stood. The front door opened. He was sweaty from the run and smiling to have found me there. "Hi, Beautiful!" he beamed, planting a kiss on my cheek. "Sorry I'm so gross. Great run though. Are you . . . cooking?" I sat on the couch, expressionless. Silent. "What?" he laughed. "What's going on?" I pulled the open notebook from behind me and pointed. He read. Waited.

My voice was calm. Small. Distant. "Is there anything else you need to tell me?" His expression changed. The warmth had vanished. Hostility and bravado possessed him instead. "Yeah," he said cockily. "When I was home, I called Jenny. You know. The *real* Jenny. My first love. The one that got away. I'm going to see her next time." It suddenly occurred to me that he had asked if he could call me "Jenny" when we started dating. I was delighted—Jenny was and is the name I call myself. I didn't like "Jen," and "Jennifer" sounded like a name I'd use for work someday. I'd just never realized that actually, he loved *her* name. He'd named me after *her*.

"Oh, and one more thing," he announced. "I got bored of looking at you, so I went down to the Foxy Lady for Legs-n-Eggs the other morning." That was the local strip joint. The thing I'd always told him I couldn't tolerate. Wouldn't tolerate. He'd gotten bored of looking at me. And gone for breakfast.

Hell no.

We all have our breaking points. Our thresholds. Our limits. This was mine. He had spat in my face. Slapped me. Thrown me. Humiliated and insulted me. And still, I'd tried to be everything—sexy and playful and sweet and tender and gentle and adventurous. If I knew nothing else—*nothing else*—I knew that there was nothing I *hadn't* done or given or had taken from me. I'd accepted everything else and made myself crazy in the constant race to stay ten to fifteen steps ahead of disaster. And—there was *no way* this was on me. No way I would accept those horrible words. No. If I couldn't say it about anything else—*this was not my fault*. I had hollowed out my body and mind for this man's satisfaction. With this one chink, though, the armor had begun to fall. Today was cruelty and lies. Nothing but cruelty and lies.

And finally, I was done. For good.

I wish I could tell you that the road to Next was clear and pretty and, finally, gentle. It was anything but. When anger came, it possessed me, bringing gut-wrenching, animalistic howls of grief and pain and humiliation, then, alternatively, hollowing my voice to an unearthly calm. The raw traumas rioted through my body and mind like a soldier fresh home from war. Which, in nearly every sense, I was.

I wish I could tell you that from that day until last week, I was never demeaned or manipulated. Never mistreated or called names or shamed. Never loved by gaslight. But that would be a lie. I have, however, learned along each step forward and back. Once I learned how to spot "danger signs" in dating partners, I *was* able to end relationships sooner, *before* my heart got so wrapped up. I can still remember telling one very sweet man, "Thanks so much for the time we've spent, but I think we've taken our relationship as far as it's going to go." Yes, he asked to stick around. I declined. And I was alone. And it was okay.

On the other hand, I made some of my most significant life decisions having already seen evidence of things I'd been unwilling to tolerate before—but because other aspects of my life were in such tumult, I convinced myself they'd been handled. I thought I'd come far, knew I had worked incredibly long and hard to find independence and confidence. I should have remembered Oprah's saying: trust people the *first* time they show you who they really are. Everyone makes mistakes. Sometimes terrible ones—and still, I do not believe that those mistakes define us. The trouble comes when we bury ourselves in denial and make too many excuses for those we love, because by then we have long since missed the first evidence of truth. We're long past the second and probably even the third. Certainly, I was. I needed something—someone—to hold onto. To be a fixture. And really, that's never a position for anyone involved.

Nevertheless, I have grown and am still growing. I have come to know myself, and, even in writing this book, I am *still* discovering how little it really takes for me to feel loved . . . and how much less I've accepted. I am blown away that this week was the first time someone close to me—much less a friend who really, truly knows my deepest and darkest corners—said, "Jenny, you are a beautiful person." And meant it. I may have taken forty-two years to get here . . . but here I am. Thanks to autism. Through the refocus and clarity of that lens, I've discovered that no, I wasn't *ever* the common denominator to every disaster. The people who devoured the most unique, most lovely parts of me, recognized my vulnerabilities, and took advantage and control of me to lift themselves by putting me down—*they* are the truly disordered among us.

Being on the spectrum does *not*, in any way, mean that a woman or a girl is destined to be in an abusive relationship. Not at all. On the contrary, being aware that she *is* different and of the *ways* that she is different is the cornerstone to knowing how to empower her. What to teach her to watch for. What to teach her to cherish. To know, above all, that yes, like everyone in the world, there are things she can do and ways she must grow to be the best friend and partner she can be. And before she looks outward, she needs to know herself. Needs to know that without exception, she is believed. That even when her perspective is limited or her reactions feel extreme to others, they are entirely authentic and real for her. That we will honor and love her *for* them, not in spite of them. More than a promise, that's a responsibility.

When you're there, rock bottom can feel like the final, almost inevitable destination. It's not. No matter how hard or how many times we hit, I'm living proof that rock bottom can also be the lonely, terrifying, deep-dark place where we change direction. Where we push off and swim like hell until, finally, we can breathe again.

CHAPTER 9

Hurts So Good: Our Epidemic of Self-Harm

Content Warning: *This chapter contains explicit descriptions of my own experiences with self-harm that some survivors may find triggering. I respectfully offer the power of forewarning and the choice to read or move to page 232. Whichever decision feels best is the right one.*

For *at least* ten minutes, not one of the "idea knots" cluttering my brain had been willing to untangle itself into any semblance of coherent writing. Time for coffee. Not to mention a bunny trail toward distraction. Or direction. You never know which you're actually chasing until you arrive.

Pages clicked shut. Mail bounced open. And my life changed.

The Woman I Almost Knew

April 20, 2017

To: Jennifer O'Toole
From: Rebecca M.
Hi Jennifer,

I read the *Scientific American* interview you did with Maia Szalavitz last year and am fascinated by your work. I wanted to know if you have had anyone contact you about female autism and eating disorders.

In February 2016, our daughter Kathryn, thirty-one, died from complications related to an eating disorder, and we have been trying to make sense of her death for over a year. It wasn't until I heard an interview about Szalavitz's book and then recently read the article with your experiences detailed that I began to put together Kathryn's problems and perhaps piece together some answers.

Kathryn's young son is autistic and until I have recently started digging and researching more about the connection between autistic females and addictive behaviors like eating disorders (EDs), I never really considered that her social awkwardness, her food sensitivities, her endless "causes" that obsessed her—she was a voracious reader all her life, and like you, she seemed to try to mimic behaviors that didn't work at all for her, including *my* behaviors—were signs of autism. Perhaps I wasn't paying attention, but we just accepted that this was who she was. Even in the last years of her life, she read biographies, so she could, as she once told me, "figure out how to be." She never seemed to have body image issues at all, but she did suffer from extreme anxiety and I think used food as a control for that. Still, she could never answer the questions we had about her behaviors and honestly, I don't think she fully understood herself either, although having her son and . . . learning more about him, I think, was beginning to help her too.

I have been invited to speak at an event for the National Eating Disorders Association and am just reaching out, in my grief, to see if you have any knowledge of any other autistic women who have suffered with EDs or other addictions and how they have coped. Kathryn moved in 2007, and so spent nearly ten years outside of our sphere of influence; but the level of ignorance about eating disorders, even in the health-care community was shocking and the negligent treatment she received indirectly led to her death.

—Rebecca

A year after my best friend, Lori, died, I got the chance to go to dinner with her parents in New York. In some ways, they were as they'd always been. She, perpetually poised, eloquent, and caring. He, lovably goofy, reflective, and warm. United, above all things, by their complete and utter devotion to their only child, Lori—beautiful, generous, and, objectively speaking, one of the most brilliant people I'll ever know.

I've been present, thus far, for three births and two deaths. Of course, I am forever grateful to have been the president of my children's "It's Your Birthday!" Welcoming Committees. Birth is a big, booming, screeching song of arrival. Death is quieter. Gentler. A slip. Having been present for life's beginnings and endings, I believe there is an exquisite permission granted to those allowed to share the moment. An honor. An intimacy. I held my grandmother's hand. I sang my father to sleep.

True grief changes you permanently. Especially when that grief is a parent's. That kind of bottomless hell hollows cheeks and souls and tears the living from life. There is something profoundly sacred in being allowed past the masks of polite society, beyond expectation to real. After everyone had gone back to "real life," over hummus and pita bread, Lori's parents allowed me into the stain and confusion and agony and anger of "ever after." And in doing so, they prepared me for Rebecca.

Perhaps that's why Rebecca's email resonated so deeply. She told me, just this week, that when most people learn she's lost a daughter, they offer condolences, of course, quickly followed by platitudes, topic changes, and a scurry toward less "uncomfortable" friends. Spectrum-brand empathy: expose us to humanity's hurt, show us what will help. We *will* lean in, open up, and run *toward* the hurt.

Lori had celebrated my way of turning something broken into something beautiful. I couldn't save her. I couldn't save Kathryn. But because Lori had believed in me, maybe I *could* turn something broken into something beautiful for Rebecca. So, I wrote back. Immediately.

April 20, 2017
To: Rebecca M.
From: Jennifer O'Toole
Oh, Rebecca.

First—let me express my most heartfelt sympathy to you and your family.

Second . . . you couldn't have come to a more "right" place.

I was hospitalized for two months at age twenty-five for anorexia—and, sadly enough, will tell you that eating disorders are absolutely epidemic in the world of women with autism, though because of the disproportionate lack of recognition of "the pink on the spectrum," we don't get appropriate or effective treatment. In fact, this July, I'm actually presenting a talk at the Autism Society of America's National Conference in Milwaukee called, "Salads and Spreadsheets: Women, Girls, and Our (Unspoken) World of Eating Disorders." I would be so very honored if you were able to come—and if not, then to allow me to dedicate the talk to Kathryn. . . .

My goal is to reach out beyond the autism world and to find some way into the eating disorder community, where I might be able to educate professionals, change common "vernacular" concepts, and, hopefully, get people to understand the big, terrible "misses" that are killing girls and women daily. I am most undeserving, but still very much hope that, even now, Kathryn can be in my camp.

With all of the love in my heart,
—Jennifer

April 20, 2017

To: Jennifer O'Toole
From: Rebecca M.

Thank you so much, Jennifer, for this heartfelt response. I am overwhelmed at your willingness to reach out to us.

I cannot believe that I found you and that you, too, have struggled with an eating disorder, enough to be hospitalized. Like you, our daughter was beautiful and vivacious, a show-tune-belter-outer-in-the-car young woman who absolutely loved life. But she confessed on more than one occasion to me that she always felt like a scared little girl inside, and the effort it took to function at a "normal" level each day was exhausting. So it is not surprising that no one really "got it." She hid it so well behind a veil of bravado and tallyho-forward-to-the-next-day spirit.

Your sweet email reduced me to tears, tears of joy that FINALLY someone gets it. I knew instantly that you would when I read about your love of Disney characters and your love of books, although Kathryn often read books as an avoidance to social interactions. Did you do that too? She came in second in the National Youth Storytelling Championship and loved the stage too, traveled to Kenya and Belize to do volunteer work and yet struggled to find a career, hold a job, make close friends anyplace besides Facebook, or maintain a relationship. She was a walking contradiction and at times maddeningly frustrating to deal with.

Thank you Jennifer for the warmest reply. You do not know what you have done for me today.

—Rebecca

Keep as many options open as possible. That's what Lori used to tell me about pretty much everything. I have to admit, the girl knew what she was talking about. She couldn't decide whether she wanted to be an attorney or a doctor after Brown, so she completed all necessary pre-course work for and applied to Harvard Law *and* Harvard Med. And got into both. The point wasn't lost on me: unhindered, unencumbered choice *is* power. It's being able to set your own course rather than have it dictated or restricted. It is, on a practical level, the real-life freedom gained through financial success, professional connections, individual talents, and personal endeavors. More friends to choose from on a Saturday night. More tuition available making more educational opportunities possible. More job prospects. More self-determination in healthcare, travel, food, brand of toothpaste. In that sense, I was a young woman with every advantage: financial freedom, a great education, parents who loved me, a fierce intellect, and, apparently, I didn't look too shabby, either. Choices were mine for the making.

Why, then, did I lose my way so entirely after college? Simple. I had no idea where to go.

Again and Again And Again

Life, they say, is about the journey, not the destination. Well, whoever *they* are, they are very clearly neurotypical. For spectrum minds, too much choice will halt you in your steps. Waypoints and destinations are the only indications of trajectory. The only dependable kind of feedback. The *only way* we have of knowing we're making progress toward almost anything.

Very early on, typical kids learn to gauge their successes by social cues. Smiles and laughter are sought-after prizes that don't take long to learn how to elicit. But for differently wired minds, facial expressions are unreliable and hard to read. Mind-blindness makes steering toward positive social feedback as difficult as aiming for a moving target. While wearing a blindfold. If you literally *can't* be sure what is pleasing or displeasing another person, how on Earth can their approval be a valid marker of your success?

A few years back, researchers at King's College London set about to discern whether autistic individuals were as motivated by "social rewards" as their neurotypical peers. They weren't. Instead, the ventral striatum (reward center) in autistic brains lit up when engaging in repetitive behaviors or gathering data on our "restricted" (a.k.a. special) interests. Plainly put, we rely on more quantifiable barometers than smiles to assess achievement and social approval: grades, points, degrees, titles, Instagram followers . . . and, as I'll come to explain, less innocuous, body-focused standards, too.

Whether we're judging our jeans size or our GPA, it's easy to understand why we come off as perfectionists. During the 1980s, my Saturday nights were filled with babysitters and television I don't think I was actually allowed to watch. And most definitely, that included *The Golden Girls*, a show about four not-so-young-but-way-too-lively-to-be-over-the-hill gals who become housemates . . . and then typical comedy hijinks ensue. Blanche, a former Southern belle, was the vamp of the bunch. She was used to men's attention and unapologetically enjoyed their affections as much as they enjoyed hers, delightedly continuing that Scarlett O'Hara role into her "golden" years.

In one episode (which obviously must've affected me, as I can still remember it), an unexpected snafu upset Blanche's typical finesse. She'd met and fallen quite hard for a devastatingly handsome man who was equally taken with her. What, then, her friends wondered, was wrong? Why did she seem so very nervous and agitated? The problem was this: her beau was blind, and Blanche could not imagine how on Earth she would keep the attention of a man who couldn't see her. Her looks, her body language, her come-hither charm were what she was "good at." Without those, what did she have to offer?

Like many of us, Blanche valued herself based upon what had, in the past, brought her acceptance, approval, and a sense of worth. Everyone wants to feel like a success. And we, on the spectrum, have often had more than our fair share of unexpected "mess ups," leading to more than our fair share of teasing, rejection, and insults. It's not really too surprising that, if we are told we "are" something special—smart, talented, creative—then maintaining that identity holds a great sway over our self-esteem.

And so, in trying to keep up appearances, we feel perpetually anxious that we'll make a mistake and lose whatever it is about ourselves that has *finally* garnered approval. Like Blanche, take away our "something special," and we're sure that we are suddenly nothing at all. We beat ourselves up for being imperfect when, in fact, trying to be perfect is the most imperfect goal imaginable. It's not achievable. It doesn't even exist. So we end up utterly terrified that we'll "look stupid"—be laughed at—be called out as "posers," or frauds, not really as good as the world had thought. We feel we have to be better or more special than everyone else around us. Basically, we have to be better than human.

Like Blanche, we attach our value to our performance rather than to our personhood. We become bullies—of ourselves. But perfectionism isn't about being precise or meticulous. It's a measure of great insecurity. Of fear. Of "what ifs" gone haywire. What if I make a mistake . . . what if I let everyone down . . . what if they all laugh at me . . . what if I ruin everything . . . what if I'm not good enough? Yeah. Really. What if? The world will not end, and nobody actually dies of embarrassment. I know. I'm the lab rat.

Social scientists could not be more wrong in assuming that social rewards aren't important to autistic people. Nor is our proven preference for nonsocial rewards evidence that we are less interested in relationships. We *absolutely* want to be liked . . . we *do* want to feel loved. The issue isn't apathy toward other people. The issue is that people are malleable and affected and, often, false. So, what delights one individual on one particular day in one particular circumstance can cause utter mayhem, outrage, or rejection in the same person in the same circumstance on a different day. It takes *thousands and thousands* of experiences to even begin to assemble a pattern that *may* lead us toward inclusion. And that's just too many maybes and maybe nots—too many subjectives by which to live your life (which would be the *entire* reason I wrote my second book about "secret social rules").

Einstein determined the theory of relativity, arguably one of the most abstract concepts divined by mankind, by considering an *actual* bus as it traveled past an *actual* clock tower. Concrete avenues measured by fixed points. Controlled barometers in a chaotic existence. That is how we understand whether or not we are succeeding. Smiles are just too fleeting and too easy to fake. And perfectionism isn't a condition—it's a description of how it *looks* when a person is bound by rigid, external, artificial criteria and compelled to seek solutions, not in change, but in repetition.

A choose-your-own-adventure "journey" may be paradise for neurotypicals—but it's deer-in-the-headlights, anxiety-producing chaos for us. To spectrum minds, too much choice is paralyzing. Part of the pediatric diagnostic process, in fact, is allowing a child access to lots of toys, then watching what she does. Typical children flit around and explore. Spectrum kids choose one, maybe two, that they can master—then repeat it. Why? They know what to do. They can do it well. And they feel safe in that. As of 2015, "restricted and repetitive behaviors" are two of the criteria *required* to achieve an autism identification. Before then, our social "deficits" (read: differences) were the main thrust of diagnosis, but as far back as a century ago, Hans Asperger observed his patients exhibiting a strong "insistence on sameness." This is *not* new stuff. And, what's more, I'd venture to bet that the sameness Asperger's boys preferred could also be empirically measured, so as to leave no room for hedging bets.

Repetition within known parameters *is* a comfort to everyone on the human spectrum—the rhythm of our mother's heartbeats, the soothingly familiar words of nursery rhymes and lullabies, the feeling of being rocked when we were small and afraid and upset. Redundancy is a fundamentally human way of achieving physical and emotional calm, of imposing a sense of control upon a random, subjective world—especially when we feel overwhelmed. Reciting decades of prayers over rosary beads. Bowing at the Wailing Wall. Coloring books. Long runs. Busying the body releases perseverating minds and calms anxious spirits.

All of which is healthy and good and the thrust of pretty much every stress-management technique under the sun—techniques that work for typical minds. But our brains are not typical. Our stressors. Our fight-flight response. Our need for the objective affirmation and the security of rules and routine. Our sensory reactions. Our mind-blindness. Our executive functioning: problem-solving, impulse control, emotional regulation, predilection for compulsivity. It makes perfect sense that, unrecognized and misunderstood by most everyone—including ourselves—we try to protect ourselves by imposing a facade of order on everything and everyone around us. And when that doesn't work, which it never does, we turn inward . . . and, through all sorts of body-focused repetitive behaviors, try to control ourselves.

The terrifying truth is that certain deadly, dangerous, disfiguring specters haunt girls on the spectrum more than any other population: eating disorders, cutting, burning, hair pulling (trichotillomania), skin picking (dermatillomania). It makes sense if you just think about it; genetically, we are prime candidates. We're socially programmed to judge ourselves harshly. We're neurologically wired to be rigid and exacting. To be perfectionists with obsessive and depressive tendencies. To have minds that get stuck on something and replay the idea endlessly all day and night. And we don't like to feel out of control. We are, literally, the textbook illustration of the kind of girl/woman most vulnerable to self-destructive chemical and process addictions.

As years pass, brilliant, capable, undiagnosed girls grow to be undiagnosed women who have had to endure bullying, violence, and systematic professional failures. Not surprisingly, for many of us, rejecting compliments and believing insults is just more comfortable—we're not sure whom to trust, and we probably hear a lot more of the rough stuff. You could say the volume on the negative dial is louder as a result. And more than that, accepting even honest compliments means confronting how very little we actually believe in ourselves. So we skip that part. We may become promiscuous, abuse drugs or alcohol. Or we try to fix ourselves by creating wombs of artificial control. And worst of all, most obscenely true is this secret: when we "succeed" in being "perfect"—via maladaptive behaviors like obsessive-compulsive disorder, isolation, perfectionism, unbalanced relationships, eating disorders, and self-harm—we feel elated. Even superior. The reality, though, is the complete opposite. Our coping mechanisms are nothing but self-sabotage because we are responding to unknown selves. So instead of introspection and healing, the fruits of self-awareness and assertiveness, we become increasingly mentally fragile, emotionally vulnerable, and physically unhealthy.

This is the pattern of life for girls and women on the spectrum. We expect love to be mixed with anger, seeking out relationships and situations that match the way we already see ourselves . . . even if that means reinforcing our insecurities by choosing "mean girl" friends or insulting romantic partners. If you believe you're unattractive, hearing even the sincerest compliment about your appearance is scary—it feels like a trick. If you believe you're not very smart and someone honestly praises your thinking, you're apt to feel that you're being teased. If you believe you're very hard to love, you may just figure that no matter how hard you try, everyone will end up hating you. Believing someone's kind words, then, only feels like a giant setup for heartbreak.

The Wandering Years

My sorority sisters had arrived at Brown clear that they would continue on to law school or med school, or, for some, graduate study toward professorships. But me? I'd had no further plan. My parents had thought that was a good thing—a world full of possibilities. The fruit of a liberal arts education. Except open-ended had turned out to be confounding. Like a toy sailboat whipped to and fro in a maelstrom, I had no sense of where I was going, where I *should* go, or even what worthwhile skills I might possibly have for which anyone would pay. Of course, I'd have much rather stuck with academia than gone into the workforce, but I was scared. As seniors, my friends had gotten perfect LSAT and MCAT scores, heading on to Harvard, Yale, and the like. And though I was graduating from our Ivy League school with all *A*s and with honors . . . I couldn't face the possibility of embarrassing myself on an entrance exam or being rejected. Not less than a year after ridding myself of the boyfriend who'd told me, whispered right in my ear, that I was a stupid bitch. I couldn't face the fear. So, I didn't try.

Instead, I found strength and purpose by channeling experience into a job as a domestic violence counselor in far-off North Carolina. It was emotional, round-the-clock work in a strange city where I had no friends or family. Still, I was determined to do something good with the pain I'd suffered. What was more, I was determined to prove to myself how very capable I actually was. But, only six weeks after I'd moved into my first apartment—eleven hours from home—my mother was diagnosed with stage III breast cancer. Though I went back to New Jersey for her mastectomy, she insisted that I continue with my plans in Charlotte. I didn't want to leave her. Not at all. It was, however, *her* cancer, she explained. I would be the most help by letting her write the narrative. And that was that. I was back to work in two weeks, trying to make friends, figure out how to negotiate a work environment where I was surrounded by—literally—thousands of men, and continuing to heal.

Over the next year, numerous personnel changes meant I had to learn and relearn an already foreign professional *and* regional environment . . . only it seemed that however much I tried, I was succeeding with my clients and bombing with my new boss. I was lonely. Flailing. And I'd managed to put on about fifteen pounds. There wasn't much I could figure out how to fix at work. And there weren't a whole lot of opportunities (not safe ones, anyway) for a single girl without any friends to go out and *make* them. So, I found a way to fill the long, empty hours . . . to make and achieve goals . . . and to lose myself in repetition—I became the star pupil at Weight Watchers, budgeting and journaling every food value "point" I took in. The "smoking-hot" redhead out for two-hour-long runs, knocking out increasingly ritualized minutes on the elliptical machine, calories burned, and flights of steps climbed.

Research has shown there are similarities in the way people with autism and addictions use repetitive behaviors to manage emotions, as well as in the tendencies toward impulsivity and compulsion. Indeed, for me, over the course of just one summer, fitness became an all-consuming obsession . . . a process addiction that hijacked my brain's reward center and got me caught in a loop of self-destruction. My skin turned orange from eating too many carrots, my body bruised from lack of vitamins—doctors even performed a bone marrow test, afraid that I had leukemia. Unable to handle the uncertainties of restaurant menus, I began collecting as many as possible—planning what I would eat before lunch dates or book clubs. Or, if I didn't know what I'd encounter, I'd either avoid eating all day—or decide not to go at all. Social situations became more and more frightening. I began to leave work early to exercise and soon even snuck out to the gym when I was meant to be on duty. The risks and consequences were amping up—and still, I didn't stop. I didn't even let up. I honestly wouldn't even have known how.

If *Anyone* Had Known

April 27, 2017

To: Jennifer O'Toole
From: Rebecca M.

Am reading your books and I feel like I am reading Kathryn's diaries, only she was in the belly of the beast, and you are looking back over the ruins of your tortured thought processes at a desperate time in your life with the kind of clarity that only hindsight and recovery can offer. . . .

One of the things that my husband and I find very valuable that you are suggesting is that the "vernacular" of EDs change. I am neither doctor nor clinician nor therapist, but I am a university-trained researcher by profession, and I have spent the last year since Kathryn died searching for answers to what seems like a cosmic misunderstanding, which happened to her, and to us who loved her so much.

I always rejected the notion that Kathryn had body image issues, and she would agree with me. She didn't suffer from a perfectionist mindset or a fear of fatness. What she did have was a desire for ritual and pattern, an intense need to please and be accepted by others but the social awkwardness to not quite ever succeed. Constant feelings of inadequacy and a failure to fully understand how to navigate ("to everyone else, I know I seem confident, Mommy, but I am so defective . . . I'm always just a scared little girl inside") the world around her each day ultimately led to near-stratospheric levels of stress. . . . In food and the rituals that surround its creation and consumption, she found a way to control the stress, what she called her "nervy-b's" and thus be praised and socially accepted.

> It all boils down to the fact that if anyone had connected the dots between autism and eating disorders, if I had found your work earlier, if the professionals who were supposed to be experts in the field had known what autism even looks like in girls or women . . . we might have saved Kathryn's life.
>
> —Rebecca

Salads and Spreadsheets

Despite education or intelligence, despite unmatched levels of creativity, of soul-piercing sincerity, or analytical genius, women on the spectrum are the most likely to find themselves under- or unemployed, financially dependent, and without guidance. Looking back at my own faltering steps and seeing the pattern repeat in so many young women, I've called these the "wandering years." A time when opportunities are missed, decisions become dangerous, and hope is lost . . . not because of a lack of talent or passion or effort, but because of social gaffes, communication gaps, self-doubt, and plain old mind-blindness.

For the first time in my life, I had no map. And I most definitely was wandering.

Unsure of where to go or how to shine in the great, big world, I turned to the one thing over which I *could* exercise dominion—my own body. I could feel confident and deliberate, see direct cause and effect between my choices and the results. That inertia translated into a sense of confidence I'd forgotten I could feel. You might say I got my groove back. In a matter of weeks, I decided to go to graduate school, rocked the GRE, won an alumnae scholarship from my sorority, had letters of recommendation from two judges and a member of the Governor's Task Force, and got into every single master's program to which I applied. Even better, once I'd matriculated to Columbia University, I was asked to consider a dual program whereby I could get a law degree along with my master of social work (MSW) while interning at the United Nation's Council for Women and Children. The dean of the School of Social

Work even invited me to switch from the MSW program to a PhD if I might please consider joining the university faculty. The possibilities were sky-high again.

But my personal life had gotten complicated. My dog, who hated the noise of the city, was staying with my parents in nearby New Jersey, and darn it if I wasn't losing his loyalty, as he became more and more attached to my (treat-bearing) mother than to me. Home felt . . . different. My mom was still tired and recovering. My dad was either busy with work or spending time on his boat. My best friend from high school was local, but she was getting divorced, and truly, I had no idea how to handle an unexpected change in our life plans. I didn't know what to say, so I just stopped calling her. My course grades were stellar (I'd accept nothing less), but I was having panic attacks during the commute to my field work assignments, found myself inexplicably scared and overwhelmed once there, and had no friends to spend time with on the weekends. (The other students didn't invite me to hang out because, as I've since learned, they thought, surely, I *had* to have an absolutely *packed* calendar. Nope.) True to form . . . I reverted to known patterns and tried-and-true rituals. A certain number of laps around the track. A certain grocery allotment from the bodega. Up early to prepare the day's meals. Waiting until as late as possible for dinner so that I could go to bed full.

And always, I was on edge. Intimidated by the confusion and enormity of simultaneously trying to make friends, handle a long-distance relationship, navigate my field work, and get a grip on trying to learn to counsel others while feeling perpetually, profoundly alone in the busiest city on the planet. Then, after only a semester, I did the unthinkable. I dropped out of school and ran from what should have been the adventure of a lifetime. Plainly put, I was not all right. I had no plan B. I'd never needed a plan B. I had no other idea. No siren song calling to me. I just knew I had to get away.

Now what? What to do? Where to go? I had a boyfriend in Charlotte, and not much feeling of belonging anywhere. So back I went to North Carolina and got a job in advertising on my first day job hunting, which seemed a good sign. They thought I was witty and I knew I could, at least, write well. By summer, I'd gotten engaged . . . stability was paramount. True to my experience, though, calm never lasted for long. I'd gotten gently "transferred" from the first ad agency (where the boss was really just too nice to let me go) to another. There, without any prior warning, I was called into the conference room one morning, told that my clients were feeling "unheard"—and sent home, permanently, with a warm, condescending smile.

Typically spectrum-minded, it was all or nothing. Black or white. Every seed of doubt ever planted in my heart that I was a fraud and a pretender proved true, as I'd always known it would. Every accolade and accomplishment was just part of the charade. The girl who didn't mess up her performances—who got *A*s and standing ovations and had set out to change the world for the better—had failed. And if I wasn't that girl anymore, who was I? Without an answer or even an idea how to find an answer, I did some freelance writing and found something new at which I could excel: the gym. I busied my mind by busying my body—step classes, spinning, cross-training. I spent hours in the grocery store comparing labels, whipping through mental tallies, then went home and made spreadsheets (talk about quantifiable rewards) of every calorie, every gram of fat, protein, and carbohydrate I ate that day. There were "safe foods" whose caloric impact I could guarantee. Safe times to weigh myself. I was light and numbed to hurt and confusion I'd otherwise not escaped. No longer a "failure," I was constantly buzzed, chemically addicted to starvation—and, terrifyingly, I loved it.

The wedding was two months later. Two months after that came the hospital.

As babies, when we get overwhelmed, we seek the comfort of repetitive movement (rocking) and sucking (nursing, a bottle, and so on). That is, we find relief from our big, scary feelings through sensory input. Adults fill our unhappy mouths with sweet, rich tastes . . . we calm down, and everyone's happy. It makes perfect scientific sense, then, that even though we may not realize it consciously, our brains (smart as they are) haven't forgotten how to switch on the self-soothing mode. Maybe we're feeling left out or defective, ashamed or insecure. The feelings get too big and . . . for many of us, the fix is to binge on treasure troves of sugar and fat: pizza, ice cream, cookies, cheese, chocolate. For a little while, the chemical relief numbs out the hurt. Hurt? Worry? It's all shoved deep down beneath layers of chips or donuts. Hidden. Out of sight and out of mind. Until the chemical buzz begins to wear off . . . and it turns out that the feelings never went away. They're still here. And worse, now there's self-loathing and shame to add to the mix. So we punish ourselves . . . until the hurt gets too big, and the cycle starts again.

For those of us who starve ourselves, the story isn't much different. We're still trying to escape overwhelming feelings—of being a fraud, not good enough, unworthy, a failure. Instead of indulging in cover-up chaos, undereaters (like I was) discover relief—even a sense of power—in artificial control. As I got hungrier and hungrier—and then suddenly, somehow . . . numb (my brain literally shutting down)—there was a kind of euphoria. Even arrogant achievement. I didn't feel the hurt. I didn't feel much of anything.

It's the same out-of-body, dissociative effect I've felt from picking at what are, I know, my own distorted perceptions of imagined imperfections in my skin. The initial physical pain is a distraction—a repetitive action with sensory-seeking intensity sufficient to override the emotional. Then the brain's pain response system kicks in—reacting to emotional *or* physical injury in the *same* way: a rush of endorphins, endogenous opioids, to deaden the hurt and induce a flood of calm. It's a self-sabotaging relief that epidemic numbers of autistic women seek through substance use, high-risk, repetitive processes (gambling, gaming, sex or porn addictions), by pulling their hair, cutting the skin, or, very often, an amalgamation of more than one. Hours lost to hyperfocus in a particular private place, using particular tools, often in response to a particular theme—generally, for me, transitions when I'm filled with the dread of being insufficient, inadequate, uncertain as to how to move forward. And I'm left . . . wounded. Embarrassed. With more problems than when I began.

Cutting. Starving. Compulsive exercising. Drinking. Drugs. Hair pulling. Skin picking. These are *not* attention-grabbing strategies, or else why would we, who employ them, work so very hard to keep our behaviors secret? They are evidence of poor coping skills. Of terrible anxiety. Of invalidation and loneliness—and shame. Manifestations of anxiety and cognitive rigidity to the point of epidemic levels. Why? It's all about relief. About trying to escape from your own feelings and experiences of the world that those of us on the spectrum are constantly told are *wrong*. And for a while, it may feel like it works. Being left out is what many of us have come to expect—what we *should* expect without spectrum-tailored anxiety management, sensory controls, goal planning, and social skills work. We aren't just hungry to be wanted. We're starving. And bleeding. And dying. And though we'd never say as much out loud, it's not a far stretch to say that broken hearts will *do* anything—*believe* anything—to be loved.

I had no desire to "recover" from my best friend—my success—my best-ever coping mechanism. In fact, on some deeply troubled level, I was actually proud of the "achievement." Proud of getting so good at losing weight, at being so skinny—(in reality, so malnourished)—that I had to be admitted to a hospital for a month. When I was admitted, I was 106 pounds. At five feet eight inches tall, that put me at a dangerously low body fat percentage with a checklist of consequences (besides the steadily declining numbers that still felt like victory to me). I'd stopped getting my period, was cold all the time, and dreamed about food nightly (a physical marker of starvation).

It all seems surreal to me now, but you can't really argue with the facts. Things were pretty serious. I was an inpatient for a month—and goodness, how I wish the psychiatrist had known about Asperger's in women back then. Having personally met thousands upon thousands of women and girls around the world—I can attest that eating disorders are practically par for our course, something now backed by quantitative studies, as well. But he didn't know. The nutritionist didn't know, nor the psychologists. No one at the health center and, to be fair, barely anyone in the field knew (or know now) that pharmacologically, psychologically, bulimia, compulsive exercising, anorexia, and binge eating should *always* be evaluated in terms of a possible larger spectrum diagnosis. So they guessed at how to help me. Guessed at what might be underlying the behavior that was endangering my life. And for the most part, they didn't guess very well, including characterizing what I *now* realize was a preschool-aged social anxiety meltdown as a "repressed memory" (very similarly to what Kathryn's team also did).

Had the staff been able to help me discover that I was not a catastrophic burden or some intrinsically defective fake . . . had anyone named the autism they were all witness to, they might have saved me—and my family—ten more years of disordered thinking, of self-sabotage, of chaos, danger, and pain. Had they paid closer attention to the social dynamics on the ward, they might even have noticed that I was crying into my pillow not because I was sick, but mostly because I was being teased by a group of inpatient teenagers, too embarrassed to tell the therapist, and too scared to keep it together without my coping mechanism. A lethal coping mechanism that, for an autistic person, would *have* to be replaced by something equally repetitive and sensory-based *but* that had built-in limits, was bolstered by social and life skills training, and supported me with my own emotional regulation. Instead, they doped me up on antipsychotics that made me ill, taught me to binge eat as compensation for my starvation, and fed me lies about my own life story. I left that program filled with even faultier coping skills than I'd brought with me on admission and with zero plans for what would come next. Nothing had been solved. All I could do was keep guessing and misunderstanding. Keep trying to figure out and follow the rules. Perfectly. To do what I was told. Always.

Because really, I had *no* idea what to do.

Kathryn's Birthday Present

Late March, 2018. At the end of April, I would be heading out to the Midwest to speak at a fundraiser for the National Eating Disorder Association—thanks to Rebecca and the herculean efforts of Kathryn's best friend, Paige. Each day, the three of us touched base, sharing odds and ends, creating a running dialogue, becoming more and more like family with every text.

I am of the firm belief that there is no such thing as coincidence. We all push new moments into this shared world and collide with the castoffs of others. We all breathe in one another's exhalations before we speak. And what happened next only made me that more certain. Rebecca had been scrolling through Kathryn's old Facebook page and noticed something striking in a photo her daughter had posted. Taken on Kathryn's final birthday, the image showed a charm necklace and two books, along with the delighted caption: "My birthday gifts!" Bold as can be was the marbled black-and-white cover of my second book. "There are more things in heaven and earth, Horatio, than are dreamt of in your philosophy," Rebecca texted. "She has steered our paths to cross. . . ."

For a moment, I sat breathless, wondering how to share what I was thinking. Kathryn's son was on the spectrum, and, logically, Rebecca would be assuming the book was to benefit him. But even now, three years later, he was still in grade school. When this photo was taken, he'd have been in kindergarten or even preschool. The title of this book includes the words *for tweens and teens*—and an easy one-quarter to one-third of the twenty-thousand-plus readers are undiagnosed *adults* who are "aut-curious." That is, people who are wondering whether the profile fits—this is a big part of how they figure it out. There was just no way, I wrote, that this book had been for a small child.

Within minutes, Kathryn's father confirmed my inkling. He'd asked his daughter what she'd like for that last birthday. She'd told him. And he'd placed the order. My book. For her. Eight months before she died . . . a year *before* the *Scientific American* article featuring me was written and the follow-up National Public Radio interview recorded . . . two years before Rebecca reached out to me, then told a National Eating Disorder Association crowd that "O'Toole believes firmly enough in this goal that she thinks everyone who suffers with an eating disorder of any kind should always be evaluated in terms of a possible larger spectrum diagnosis, not to discover what's wrong, but to assure them of what's okay about their thoughts and feelings and to help move them toward recovery."

Now, more than ever, I hold to that truth. Which is precisely why I texted Rebecca the following:

> To me, this is about the strongest sign I can imagine to let you know, Rebecca, how truly you know your daughter. You recognized her. What's more, you recognized her in ME. Someone of whom you'd never heard, but someone of whom, very clearly, *she* had. You may think that you missed it—her autism . . . but Rebecca, you didn't. You didn't know a word. You knew—and you know—a woman. You know her so well that you recognized the most authentic, private version of Kathryn in a printed article about someone else . . . because she had, too. You found her. And she found you.

And *we* owe it to *both* of them to find each other.

CHAPTER 10

Semicolon: The Story of a Sisterhood

"When you first meet another woman," I turned, voice lowered, "be sure of this: she's sizing you up. Who are you to her? Friend? Foe? Threat? Asset? It shouldn't be that way, of course. And I'd love to say otherwise, but in my experience, anyway, it's been the truth. The trick is turning the culture of mean-girls-gone-wild ridiculosity into a game change. You *both* get to be mighty and beautiful . . . and yes, you pretty much have to communicate that in about five to ten seconds."

She looked stricken. "Really?"

"Tops," I nodded. "Not easy, but possible. And necessary. Because, look, Anne-Louise, girls like us. Well, we're not exactly likely to stumble into social ease, are we?" She huffed and shook her head. "You've got to study this. Learn the dance. The moves, the expressions, the costumes—practice until it looks effortless. Like Ginger Rogers. She used to say that she did everything Fred did, only backwards, in heels. It takes a lot of hard work to make this 'girl' thing look easy. Especially for us."

My eyes cast casually about the mulling crowd, lingering and smiling whenever gazes unintentionally tangled. I tilted my head and shifted the pose, knowing—from a thousand hours before a thousand studio mirrors—precisely the way the movement would make my hair fall, exactly the swivel my hips would take.

A bit more red wine? Yes, I nodded to the server, yes, indeed, thank you very much.

Only a few hours ago, I'd been eating lunch with an actual princess. Potato croquettes, Bellini, and champagne, in case you're curious.

Our conversation had been genuine and important. An authentic moment between two mothers—two women who wanted to empower girls on the autism spectrum—and not just "girls" in the abstract, mind you. Real, actual, flesh-and-blood people. Like someone she knew and cared about. Like Anne-Louise. Like my daughter.

The Yank Meets the Princess

I clenched my teeth and blinked hard at the next luncheon memory. Out of nowhere had come a woman—a good deal older, yet otherwise similar to me. Copper-haired. Slender. As she'd cut in, I realized I'd not met her, which meant that I had no frame of reference to use as calibration. No explanation for why this stranger was suddenly humiliating me. At least . . . I thought she was.

"How very American," the woman had smiled wryly and turned to Her Highness. "Here we all are just falling over ourselves, and *she* has no concern about striking up a chat and showing all of her *things*." The cut of the last word rang in my ear. I'd looked, bewildered, at the countess. How had this happened? Another lifetime highlight smudged by another social blunder? I blinked. Hot, dry eyes. Thick, pulsing air. Daylight pouring weakly into the VIP suite. Get a hold, I thought. Breathe, I thought. Wait.

I'd read up on royal protocol and every site said to bring a gift. This had been mine. And "mine" had been wrong, it seemed.

What now? My hands hovered above the crinkled tissue paper, the emptied bag, the inscribed book I'd just presented. Perhaps it was a bit "Little Drummer Boy" of me, but in tossing and turning over what present to offer, something I'd made seemed like the very best choice. The book was one I'd written, you see, with great love and at great emotional expense. That it was an award-winner and bestseller gave it legitimacy, I suppose, but the fact that I'd created it . . . well, that's what gave it value. To me, anyway.

What had happened next? I honestly couldn't remember, I realized, cheeks burning hot so many hours later. The princess had seemed very much to appreciate the book I'd given her. She'd thanked me. Would give it to the daughter of a dear friend who was struggling. Would very much like to receive my upcoming book for girls so that she might send it on. Yes, please, would I give my card to her assistant.

And then the other woman had ushered her away, murmuring apologies for me. Someone had said to be seated for lunch . . . I'd found my chair and folded the paper bearing my name . . . fold once, twice, three times, and again. Sit. Blink away the tears. Smile.

All the planning imaginable still doesn't make the world figure-out-able when you are a girl—a woman—like Anne-Louise . . . or like my daughter . . . or . . . well . . . like me.

Which is how I came to be in England in the first place. On my own. Across an ocean from my family. I'd delivered a keynote address in an auditorium the size of Carnegie Hall that morning, spotlights targeted and body mic on. I'd winked and laughed, implored, and explained. I'd painted word pictures full of ruby slippers and authentic beauty, of passions, and talents, and real people and real dignity. Of what it is to live thirty-four years without understanding the "why" of who you are and how you are. Of the greatest lesson autism has taught me—not how to be autistic, but how to be human.

And then the room burst open with cheers. "Mind-blowing," they'd told me. "Life changing," they'd said. Two hours of book signing and a rush-to-it on-camera interview with just enough time to fix my lipstick before . . . lunch happened. The inevitable, keep-you-humble pitfall that seems to await even the most celebrated women on the spectrum.

Now, darkness full upon us, a cocktail reception purred with life. Hearty bursts of gentlemen's laughter. The toss and turn of ladies' conversations. Servers choreographed themselves through the crowd, and every few seconds, a flash burst as someone took a picture . . . less to remember the evening, I guessed, than as an essential post or tag or tweet. But I would remember this night, and so would Anne-Louise.

I looked to the clock on the wall. Ten minutes remained before she'd have to leave, headed back to a life that made her nervous and unhappy. I'd walk into the awards dinner . . . and soon afterward, travel back to America. I'd go on supporting her, guiding her, employing her, of course, just as I had for the past two years . . . but for a few more minutes, I could stand beside her.

Thelma and Anne-Louise

Our "Thelma and *Anne*-Louise" story had begun two years before, and close as we'd become, this visit was the very first time we'd ever actually met in person. In 2013, I was scouring the web for spectrum artists whose work I might feature in my upcoming *Not-Your-Average Coloring Book*. Almost immediately, I stumbled upon a sketch of a ball gown inspired by the geek culture favorite, Doctor Who. My first thought? This thing was nothing short of breathtaking. Second thought? Bingo. This person *has* to be one of us. An hour or so later, I'd tracked down the artist who, much to my surprise, was only seventeen—a young lady by the name of Anne-Louise Richards, living in England. Via Facebook, I introduced myself, congratulated her on her work, described the coloring book project, and referred her to my website for validation. She replied almost instantly, thrilled by the prospect of having some of her drawings published.

Yet, right away, even through Messenger, something about her tone struck me as . . . fragile. We continued to chat, and before long she confided, "I can't tell you how much it means that you like my work so much. Usually, I just feel like a mistake."

There it was. Typed out in black and white. In thirty minutes' time, I'd already learned that Anne-Louise was incredibly talented. Self-taught. Intensely creative. Highly articulate. Deeply connected to several common fandoms (Doctor Who, Disney, Harry Potter, mermaids, and *Sherlock*). And, more often than not, felt as if she, herself, were a mistake.

My counseling background took over. Instead of reassuring her or arguing how clearly ridiculous that idea might be, I asked one question. "Why, Anne-Louise? Tell me why you feel that way." In a torrent of words, she shared that she had left home because of deep disconnects with her family and lived with a boyfriend whose treatment of her sounded a bit dubious. She wasn't continuing to university (even though she was clearly brilliant). She self-harmed. Had suicidal thoughts. And so much more.

Finally, I told her to take a breath, that her world was about to change. "You're not a mistake, sweetheart," I wrote, smiling. "You're an Aspie." Over the next year, across an ocean, I had the honor of helping her to find knowledgeable clinicians and to explain her story in terms they would recognize. And in the end, the conclusion was just as I'd said. Anne-Louise had Asperger's. With that declaration came relief and hope and faith. With the diagnosis, appropriate local medical and therapeutic support . . . and opportunity.

It seemed to me, someone who'd felt so many of the same feelings and known so many of the same fears, that if I could patiently, insightfully teach a younger spectrum woman how to develop her potential and learn to notice pitfalls in real time without punishment, then I had damned well better do it. No one else would. And really, besides someone *like* Anne-Louise, no one else would really know how.

So I hired her. At first, for small Asperkids projects and then, in 2014, to illustrate my upcoming book, *Sisterhood of the Spectrum: An Asperger Chick's Guide to Life*, which, even before I'd finished writing, had hit number one on Amazon's wish lists. Not only did she draw every image in the book (and there are lots), Anne-Louise's artistic voice synced with my words, an authentic testimony of love from two real-live autistic women. At nineteen, Anne-Louise Richards was the illustrator of an international bestseller.

"Jennifer," she wrote in yet another Facebook chat, "I have to thank you. I used to think I was a mistake. Now I know that I'm a miracle."

Within the month, I was headed to England to keynote for the National Autistic Society's largest annual professional conference. Would it be possible, I asked my hosts, to downgrade my room and use the money to surprise Anne-Louise with a round trip to the conference? We could room together, and perhaps they would allow her to sit up front in the enormous auditorium, the place from which Her Royal Highness, the Countess of Wessex, would take in the day. With wonderful enthusiasm, they agreed. And Anne-Louise and I finally got to share a hug, two years in the making.

The morning of the keynote, Anne-Louise caught a glimpse of what life could hold for her. While I'd set up for my talk—aligning my computer with the jumbo screens, threading the body mic through my dress, requesting particular stage lights, laying my trademark red shoes in a centered spotlight—she'd stretched out on the hardwood stage, drinking in the hugeness of the room.

Barefooted, I walked silently across the warm wood, bathed in swirls of red and blue lights. "What do you think?" I'd asked her, smiling.

This would be breathtaking, heady stuff for anyone. I hoped it was a thousand times more so for her. Not just the scope of spectacle, but this public commitment of confidence in her as an artist and human being. An assurance that I believed her barely-dared-hope-for dreams were absolutely hers for the taking.

"It feels . . ." She searched for the word, exhaling her answer with relief: "free."

That was exactly it. What I wanted for her. For me. For all of us whom the world doesn't recognize as we truly are, shackling us in its mistake.

Soon afterward, I took the stage alone, for real, addressing an audience of about seven hundred. And entirely to Anne-Louise's surprise, I began by telling this enormous gathering full of Europe's most esteemed professionals the story of our journey. Of her heart. I flashed one of her pieces on the jumbotrons, smiled at that girl in the front row, and said, "Will the miracle of a person who made this please stand?" Shaking a bit, Anne-Louise rose from her seat and turned toward the room . . . to a standing ovation.

Of all the things I've seen—and will see, I'm sure—life just doesn't get better than that.

Now, this particular adventure was coming to a close. She cleared her throat, black eyes darting through the crowd then back to me for a moment. She was listening. Well, she was trying. A cool gust of air rushed over my cheek; that's what had distracted Anne-Louise. Ushers were opening doors to the golden inner hall where the evening's gala would begin—without her. Damn. There wasn't time enough. I recognized the bitten-lip expression she wore. Goodness knows, I'd worn it too many times myself, wondering what hid just beyond "now"—a happy afternoon? An easy night? Tears? Insults? Tenderness? Whispers? Unpredictability. A never-ending, utterly exhausting improvisation that gobbled up time and talent and confidence. And dreams. And possibility.

She shifted anxiously. She looked terrified. "Remember," I stared hard. "There's very little you can actually control in this world, or that you should. So your own decisions? Yeah, you'd better take hold of those. If you don't want to go tonight, don't go. You know you can be my roomie again, if you'd rather. You can't control what someone else does or says, or how he behaves," I insisted. "But tonight, you have a choice. And you have me. Which means you have power. You *can* control whether or not you choose to leave this evening. That said, be very sure that neither option is wrong and neither is right. No one's judging. The important thing here is to simply realize that you *have* an option. And that *because* you have an option, you have the responsibility to *yourself* to make a conscious, active choice. Life doesn't happen to you, girlie," I smiled gently. "You happen to it. And no matter what anyone says, you, young lady, are a miracle. Remember that. Forever." It is a message for us all to hear and learn by heart.

Recently, a mother named "Sara" wrote me this note on the Asperkids Facebook page:

> A few months back I commented on one of your posts, saying that our doctor told me our daughter was just "tired." And I was like, pretty sure tired kids don't pace the house in a set pattern and swing all the time. I will never forget leaving that doctor's office in tears.
>
> You encouraged me and told me why it IS important to diagnose. Well, we went back and the doctor finally said "Yes. She's on the spectrum, I just don't like to diagnose it because it's a hard label to remove." Even now, she said she is only doing it for us because she thinks it will get us more services at school. I pushed thanks to your encouragement, and she is finally willing to "say it"! Now my girl can understand why the world is so frustrating AND we can work on the positive in this. She is crazy-smart and will do AWESOME!

Sadly, this one clinician's attitude is not only professionally irresponsible, it's extremely common, dripping with ignorance, covered in bias, and wrapped up in shame. It is the very opposite effect of what spectrum identification can and should be: a "label" that saved me and, when allowed to communicate great hope and provide actual tools, reclaims life for thousands the world over, from girls in preschool to ladies in their golden years. Insight that remains unknown to most "experts," kindness and self-awareness kept from the women and girls who need it most.

Lola

Watching Anne-Louise draped across the stage and feeling free had sent my mind back twenty years to another stage where my life, too, had turned on a sharp pivot point. Not every girl can say that one of her life's most revealing moments involves a pink feather boa and a dangling microphone. Then again, I'm not every girl. But the feathers and microphone thing? Yep. That's all me.

All right. Let me try to set the scene for you. Imagine a dark high school auditorium, every one of those flip-up seats filled. The air is humid—maybe a little dank. The school orchestra is playing a show tune at full volume. And through colored films, a single, white spotlight directs all eight hundred pairs of eyes to one person: me. Years of academic perfection hadn't gotten me the one thing I most wanted: friends. My best friend from middle school had recently done a bit of a social hierarchy about-face. She had managed to reinvent herself—with some minor adjustments to her appearance and dress, she'd first caught the boys' attention. Once they wanted her around, the "popular" girls did, too. The truth is, though, that her goal wasn't really popularity for popularity's sake. It was freedom and agency over her own public persona. Not a breakthrough into any particular social echelon, but social fluidity—the power to being welcome wherever *she* chose to be.

Hindsight is much more than twenty-twenty. At the time, I didn't see her evolution as a young woman as anything other than a departure from *me*. Suddenly, I was left behind, ill-fitting and outgrown. Too stuck in my loneliness to appreciate her autonomy. Too mired in my mind-blindness to emulate more than the obvious.

For the previous ten years, I'd been playing the same pigeon-holed role in my (still beloved) small town. And truth be told, it never occurred to me that what was about to happen in March of my sophomore year of high school would change any of that. I didn't realize what power I, too, could gain by directly challenging the archetype to which I'd been reduced.

Center stage. All alone. I was fifteen, with flowing red hair, black satin slip dress, black fishnets and heels—someone completely opposite from the girl my classmates (thought they) knew. That night, I was starring as Lola in *Damn Yankees*—and quite quickly, I'd be showing the four-hundred-person audience that, indeed, "Whatever Lola Wants, Lola Gets," by means of "A Little Brains, a Little Talent" with the emphasis on the "talent." And Lola's talent was winning men. She was—and therefore I had to be—"hot." The heartbreaker. Singing about how "you gotta stack your deck with a couple o' extra aces . . . and this queen has her aces in all the right places." "Dictionary Brain" had shaken up the scene, indeed. And although I was in costume, singing someone else's lyrics, speaking someone else's dialogue, and dancing someone else's choreography, I somehow made that character my own. Gave her life and vulnerability. Acting, after all, is a way of trying on personas and leaving some of yourself on every stage. Perhaps that's why, in many ways, I'd never felt more *me*.

The music was electric, and every move was right. Until the railing.

Often, life's biggest events happen without any warning. They just . . . happen. Suddenly, in the blink of an eye, the whole world seems to shift. Gravity loses hold on you. And everything turns upside down. Other times, well, you can pretty much guarantee that the day will be special. Graduations. A big game. Special trips. Birthdays. Sometimes things turn out as expected—sometimes not. Either way, you know from the get-go that the day isn't going to be run of the mill.

But. The most game-changing events—the ones where you really find out who you are . . . what you're made of . . . how much you'll take . . . whom you'll defend . . . what you'll (actually) try, even if you never knew you had the courage to do it . . . well, those events are a mix. You know something is ahead . . . you just can't say how you'll act in the moment or how life will change after the fact.

That March evening in the spotlight was one of *those* defining moments. That night was, without exaggeration, a proving ground. In front of a sold-out crowd, I was either going to break out of the social branding I'd been assigned in kindergarten—or be such a poor excuse for "the most beautiful woman on the planet" that escaping from a New Jersey suburb to the Australian outback might seem like a completely rational move.

You know, looking back, I'm not really sure if I was unbelievably brave or just incredibly naive. Probably, it was a mix of the two. What I do know for sure is that as I crossed that stage, every step was perfect, every note true—and every person in the crowd was hypnotized. I'd danced since I was two. I'd read countless poems and stories to school audiences. I'd done this performing thing before. But never like this—never in a way that was entirely out of the pigeonhole I'd been assigned. That night, I was singing my lungs out, wholeheartedly declaring to the entire student body (and anybody else who happened to waltz through those doors) that I was much more than a Dictionary Brain. That I could be fun and funny and jaw-dropping, too. That I deserved to be wanted, not just endured. And they were listening.

Then I got to the railing.

During the next sequence of the dance, I was going to have to continue to sing while bending waaaaay back over the banister at the top of the stairs that led down from the stage. The choreography had me doing the dip and wiggling the boa, then slinking down the steps and into the crowd, where I would have to continue to sing and interact with audience members. But suddenly, while blinded by the spotlight in the dark auditorium in front of eight hundred people, there was a problem. I straightened up from the rail and felt an odd pop in the small of my back. Then a sudden catch—something was yanking off my dress!

Just one covert glance, and I knew what had happened. Before showtime, the battery portion of my wireless microphone was hooked onto the waistband at the top of those oh-so-glamorous fishnet stockings. Somehow, in the process of leaning backward, the handrail had managed to knock the battery pack loose, and now the entire (really heavy) thing was dangling between my legs while pulling down the front of the dress where the mic was actually clipped. Oh yes, and I was still singing and—in a quick mental check—realized that I had only a few measures left to twirl that boa before I was supposed to be shimmying down the steps.

There was no time to think. There was only time to act. And that, probably, was what saved me.

Many things that seem perfectly clear to typical girls couldn't be more confusing for us. Friendships. Fashion. Flirting. We don't just "pick those things up" without effort. Instead, we study scripts—stage directions, novels, movies, social media posts—and mimic better than any neurotypical I've ever seen. We anxiously overthink some things and impulsively underthink others. What we almost never do, though, is to listen to our instincts (let alone trust them). That is, with one exception: when life comes at you really, *really* fast, it doesn't always leave time to think. Or overthink. There's just time to do. You may think that you can't go on. You go on. Straight from the gut.

What did I do? I bent at the knees, did a sly, winky peek-a-boo through the bars of the railing, and snatched the battery pack without anyone seeing. There was a hitch in my voice, yes, but video playbacks barely recorded a hiccup. I spun those feathers. I sang my song. And I kept going.

That weekend was a seventy-two-hour coming of age in front of twelve hundred people. It left quite an impression on them. It also made quite an impression on *me*. In the span of three days, I literally went from having almost no social life to becoming some sort of honeypot surrounded by awfully hungry bees. It felt like I was Alice through the looking glass, and I did *not* want to leave—because for the first time in my life, I'd proved to myself that I *wasn't* the one-dimensional, disposable caricature of my classmates' creation, that I needn't be permanently defined by a caricature based on years of misunderstanding.

Years later, when my school guidance counselor wrote a college recommendation letter for me, he didn't write about my grades. He didn't write about my extracurricular activities or my civic leadership. Instead, he wrote, "For many years now, I've put forth candidates for admission to your school. Each one was brilliant. Each one was a standout. So I never understood why each one was, in turn, rejected. That is, I didn't understand until I met Jenny." He then went on to tell the story of the fishnets and the microphone. Everything in that moment had spelled disaster, he said. Every insecurity and fear should've been triggered. Instead, I'd taken one (secret) breath to steady myself and never stopped moving. It was, he wrote, remarkable—part of some edge, some depth to everything I felt and said and did. Survival. Resilience. Inner beauty.

The magic came, he said, from some unnamed, extraordinary combination of complexities, of distractions and focus. But I *can* name it. Now. It's a difference, all right, but not one unique to *me*. It's a difference unique to *us*. And it's called autism.

The neurological hardwiring that makes me blind to social self-sabotage is the same one that tells me that actions speak louder than words. That resilience trumps precision. That bravery isn't something you plan for. That wonder and possibility and wild imagination are truer and more beautiful than anything I know. Quirks, misunderstandings, hurts, and blunders—courage, tenacity, fidelity, and joy—they are all part of being the kind of different we are. Keep calm and carry on? No thanks. I'd rather stir it up and change the world.

On the inside of my left wrist, I have a small tattoo. A semicolon. And while it's only been there for a few years, it is very much the anthem in my heart. Of course, most people logically assume the squiggle is a reference to being an author. Or maybe to my geektastic love of grammar. And sure, both of those explanations are convenient extra layers of fun; they are not, however, the real message of the semicolon. This is: at the end of a sentence—a completed idea—comes a period, or full stop if you live outside of the United States. With one small dot, we say, "I'm done." But, if you complete one sentence and still have more to say, you join them with a semicolon. My tattoo, tiny as can be, is a constant reminder that no matter what—no matter how wonderful or lousy or crazy or confusing today is, there is more to say. More to come.

My story isn't over yet. Really, it's only just begun.

This kind of resilience is as permanent as tattoo ink. It cannot be stolen from us. It cannot be wiped away. It is the gift of self-knowledge, precisely what everyone deserves.

Of the personal triumphs I've seen, none are quite as powerful as watching what happens when a spectrum girl discovers how on purpose she is. How much she matters. How powerful and joyful she can be. What an honor to witness the strides made by these women—the toxic relationships they've come to question, and then end. The resources and *real* friends they've made. The personal and professional one-step-at-a-time evolution of women who are learning to trust their voices, to believe in themselves. The self-harm that they acknowledge and fight back against.

These are real people. In their stories—and in mine—we offer a chorus of testimony to what can happen when identification is proactively gifted. To many more decades of authenticity and insightful encouragement.

It is my life's celebration to watch every wonderful thing that comes after a diagnosis, understanding flourishing, questions asked and answered, solutions abounding. To hear hope come alive. To say, "You are your own wondrous occasion. More than a one-in-a-million kind of girl, you're a once-in-a-lifetime kind of *person*." And to hear in reply, as one precious nineteen-year-old put it as she lay on a half-lit stage, "Jennifer . . . now I make sense. And I feel like anything, anything is possible."

Because it is. With love, knowledge, visibility, patience, and courage, anything *is* possible—for every single woman on the human spectrum.

Our story isn't over yet.

;

Works Cited

"Absent-minded professor." Wikipedia. January 1, 2018. Accessed January 2, 2018. https://en.wikipedia.org/wiki/Absent-minded_professor.

Angelo, Megan. "16 Unforgettable Things Maya Angelou Wrote and Said." Glamour. January 12, 2016. Accessed January 3, 2018. https://www.glamour.com/story/maya-angelou-quotes.

Baron-Cohen, Simon, Donielle Johnson, Julian Asher, Sally Wheelwright, Simon E. Fisher, Peter K. Gregersen, and Carrie Allison. "Is Synaesthesia More Common in Autism?" *Molecular Autism* 4, no. 1 (November 20, 2013): 40. doi:10.1186/2040-2392-4-40.

Baron-Cohen, Simon, Sally Wheelwright, Jacqueline Hill, Yogini Raste, and Ian Plumb. "The 'Reading the Mind in the Eyes' Test Revised Version: A Study with Normal Adults, and Adults with Asperger Syndrome or High-Functioning Autism." *Journal of Child Psychology and Psychiatry* 42, no. 2 (February 2001): 241–51. doi:10.1017/s0021963001006643.

Bermond, Bob. Review of *Disorders of Affect Regulation: Alexithymia in Medical and Psychiatric Illness*, by G. J. Taylor, R. M. Bagby, and J. D. A. Parker. *Clinical Psychology & Psychotherapy* 7, no. 3 (1997): 240. doi:10.1002/1099–0879(200007)7:3<240::aid-cpp245>3.0.co;2–7.

Briggs, Helen. "Study Links Synaesthesia to Autism." BBC News. November 20, 2013. Accessed December 20, 2017. http://www.bbc.com/news/health-24995232.

British Psychological Society. "Autism and Friendship: It's Different for Girls." ScienceDaily. January 5, 2016. Accessed December 20, 2017. http://www.sciencedaily.com/releases/2016/01/160105223948.htm.

Carpenter, Siri. "Everyday Fantasia: The World of Synesthesia." Monitor on Psychology. March 2001. Accessed December 20, 2017. http://www.apa.org/monitor/mar01/synesthesia.aspx.

"Charles Addams > Quotes." Goodreads. Accessed January 11, 2018. https://www.goodreads.com/author/quotes/52274.Charles_Addams.

Dean, M., G. F. Adams, and C. Kasari. "How Narrative Difficulties Build Peer Rejection: A Discourse Analysis of a Girl with Autism and Her Female Peers." *Discourse Studies* 15, no. 2 (2013): 147–66. doi:10.1177/1461445612471472.

Dean, Michelle, Connie Kasari, Wendy Shih, Fred Frankel, Rondalyn Whitney, Rebecca Landa, Catherine Lord, Felice Orlich, Bryan King, and Robin Harwood. "The Peer Relationships of Girls with ASD at School: Comparison to Boys and Girls with and without ASD." *Journal of Child Psychology and Psychiatry* 55, no. 11 (2014): 1218–225. Accessed December 20, 2017. doi:10.1111/jcpp.12242.

Diagnostic and Statistical Manual of Mental Disorders: DSM-5. 5th ed. Washington DC: American Psychiatric Association, 2013.

Jeopardy! Sony Pictures, Jeopardy Productions Inc. December 18, 2017.

Laertius, Diogenes, and Robert Drew Hicks. *Lives of the Eminent Philosophers*. Cambridge, MA: Harvard University Press, 1979.

Lancer, Darlene. "How to Know If You're a Victim of Gaslighting." *Psychology Today*, January 13, 2018. Accessed January 13, 2018. https://www.psychologytoday.com/blog/toxic-relationships/201801/how-know-if-youre-victim-gaslighting.

Maccoby, Eleanor E. "Gender and Group Process: A Developmental Perspective." *Current Directions in Psychological Science* 11, no. 2 (2002): 54–58. doi:10.1111/1467–8721.00167.

Markram, Kamila, and Henry Markram. "The Intense World Theory—A Unifying Theory of the Neurobiology of Autism." *Frontiers in Human Neuroscience* 4, no. 224 (December 21, 2010). Accessed December 20, 2017. doi:10.3389/fnhum.2010.00224.

O'Toole, Jennifer Cook. *Asperkids: An Insider's Guide to Loving, Understanding and Teaching Children with Asperger Syndrome.* London: Jessica Kingsley Publishers, 2012.

________. *Sisterhood of the Spectrum: An Asperger Chick's Guide to Life.* London: Jessica Kingsley Publishers, 2015.

Rogers, Kimberley, Isabel Dziobek, Jason Hassenstab, Oliver T. Wolf, and Antonio Convit. "Who Cares? Revisiting Empathy in Asperger Syndrome." *Journal of Autism and Developmental Disorders* 37, no. 4 (2006): 709–15. Accessed January 8, 2018. doi:10.1007/s10803-006-0197-8.

Rose, Amanda J., and Karen D. Rudolph. "A Review of Sex Differences in Peer Relationship Processes: Potential Trade-Offs for the Emotional and Behavioral Development of Girls and Boys." *Psychological Bulletin* 132, no. 1 (January 2006): 98–131. doi:10.1037/0033–2909.132.1.98.

Rowling, J. K. *Harry Potter and the Philosopher's Stone.* London: Bloomsbury Publishers, 1997.

Salters-Pedneault, Kristalyn, PhD. "BPD and Identity Problems." Verywell. October 30, 2017. Accessed January 8, 2018. https://www.verywellmind.com/borderline-personality-disorder-identity-issues-425488.

Schwartz, Allan, PhD. "The Loneliness of Alexithymia" (comments section). MentalHelp.net. December 11, 2012. Accessed January 6, 2018. https://www.mentalhelp.net/blogs/the-loneliness-of-alexithymia/.

Serani, Deborah. "The Emotional Blindness of Alexithymia." Scientific American MIND Guest Blog. April 3, 2014. Accessed December 30, 2017. https://blogs.scientificamerican.com/mind-guest-blog/the-emotional-blindness-of-alexithymia/.

Spectrum, Rebecca Brewer, and Jennifer Murphy. "People with Autism Can Read Emotions, Feel Empathy." *Scientific American*, July 13, 2016. Accessed January 6, 2018. https://www.scientificamerican.com/article/people-with-autism-can-read-emotions-feel-empathy1/.

Star Trek: Into Darkness. Directed by J. J. Abrams. Performed by Zachary Quinto. Roma: Universal Pictures, 2013. Transcript.

Szalavitz, Maia. "Autism—It's Different in Girls." *Scientific American*, March 1, 2016. Accessed December 20, 2017. https://www.scientificamerican.com/article/autism-it-s-different-in-girls/.

Tick, B., P. Bolton, F. Happé, M. Rutter, and F. Rijsdijk. "Heritability of Autism Spectrum Disorders: A Meta-Analysis of Twin Studies." *Journal of Child Psychology and Psychiatry, and Allied Disciplines* 57, no. 5 (May 2016): 585–95. Accessed December 20, 2017. https://www.ncbi.nlm.nih.gov/pmc/articles/PMC4996332/.

University of Miami. "Sex Differences Aren't Specific to Autism." ScienceDaily. June 8, 2015. Accessed December 20, 2017. https://www.sciencedaily.com/releases/2015/06/150608213117.htm.

Vagianos, Alanna. "Reminder: 'Groping' And 'Unwanted Kissing' Is Definitely Sexual Assault." *Huffington Post*. October 17, 2016. Accessed January 14, 2018. https://www.huffingtonpost.com/entry/reminder-groping-and-unwanted-kissing-is-definitely-sexual-assault_us_57ff9f7be4b0e8c198a6642f.

White, Emily I., Gregory L. Wallace, Julia Bascom, Anna C. Armour, Kelly Register-Brown, Haroon S. Popal, Allison B. Ratto, Alex Martin, and Lauren Kenworthy. "Sex Differences in Parent-Reported Executive Functioning and Adaptive Behavior in Children and Young Adults with Autism Spectrum Disorder." *Autism Research* 10, no. 10 (2017): 1653–662. doi:10.1002/aur.181.